Medieval Military Monuments
in Lincolnshire

Mark Downing

BAR British Series 515
2010

Published in 2016 by
BAR Publishing, Oxford

BAR British Series 515

Medieval Military Monuments in Lincolnshire

ISBN 978 1 4073 0644 5

BAR Publishing is the trading name of British Archaeological Reports (Oxford) Ltd.
British Archaeological Reports was first incorporated in 1974 to publish the BAR
Series, International and British. In 1992 Hadrian Books Ltd became part of the BAR
group. This volume was originally published by Archaeopress in conjunction with
British Archaeological Reports (Oxford) Ltd / Hadrian Books Ltd, the Series principal
publisher, in 2010. This present volume is published by BAR Publishing, 2016.

Printed in England

BAR
PUBLISHING

BAR titles are available from:

         BAR Publishing
         122 Banbury Rd, Oxford, OX2 7BP, UK
EMAIL   info@barpublishing.com
PHONE   +44 (0)1865 310431
  FAX   +44 (0)1865 316916
         www.barpublishing.com

CONTENTS

LIST OF MAPS

LIST OF FIGURES

Unless otherwise stated all photographs are the copyright of the author

ACKNOWLEDGEMENTS

The author wishes to acknowledge the help and advice of Sally Badham and Phillip Lindley who read through the manuscript and made a large number of helpful comments and Sally's assistance with publication. Also to Philip Lankester, Richard Knowles, John Lord, Brian Kemp and Brian and Moira Gittos, who provided relevant information. A huge gratitude is owed to Anne Norman for allowing me the use of the library of my dear friend, the late A. V. B. Norman (Nick).

Upon the completion of my catalogue of military effigies in Worcestershire during 2002, Claude Blair suggested that Lincolnshire would be a very worthwhile county to do next, with some very fine effigies, with most never been published before, and a series, which he and his son John considered publishing themselves in the 1970s. However with 62 effigies in the county, it has taken me seven years to bring this work into print, with many weekends spent travelling Lincolnshire and collecting information at my local library. From the start, Claude has commented on the manuscript and given me advice on armour. Therefore this book is dedicated to Claude Blair.

Finally, I would like to thank Tony Carr for kindly indexing this volume.

1.1 Background and context

Military monuments in Lincolnshire have hitherto received little attention, with only four being the subject of published studies. No attempt has previously been made to produce a corpus of surviving examples. Indeed, the monuments of only half of the English counties have been recorded in print. With the exception of volumes I have published on the military monuments of Shropshire and Worcestershire, most were published in the first half of the twentieth century. Much of this early work requires revision, in part because of the significant advances in our knowledge of the dating of armour and the consequent revision of dates given to early military monuments in particular. Account also has to be taken of new work on the attribution of some effigies. Moreover, some monuments were previously unrecorded and others have been newly discovered, for example in excavations of monastic churches.

I should begin by clarifying what we mean by military effigies or monuments. A monumental effigy is an image of a person carved in three dimensions and set up as a memorial to the deceased. However, few effigies are true portraits and these are mostly restricted to high-status monuments, for example to royalty, particularly when copied from death masks. The fourteenth century effigies of Edward III, Philippa of Hainault, Richard II and Anne of Bohemia in Westminster Abbey are almost certainly true portraits. In contrast, most effigies were essentially stereotypes. The faces of ladies conventionally show a delicate serenity; those of priests portray spirituality and knights the determined warrior. The people commemorated are always shown in attire appropriate to their status in life. With few exceptions, until the end of the seventeenth century the nobility and gentry appear on their monuments in armour. Whether or not they had seen active services was irrelevant to this image; the point was that being clad in armour identified them as forming part of the dominant landed and politically active element of society. These armour-clad effigies are known as military monuments.

I have personally viewed every complete or fragmentary example of three dimensional military effigies in England and Wales (totalling 978) including those removed from the churches in which they were originally set up to museums or archaeological stores, apart from two, which at the time of writing are inaccessible.[1] This volume is the third county survey of military monuments I have published and my aim is to continue with a chronological catalogue of England and Wales, published in parts, of which the first will include the counties from Bedfordshire-Cumberland. The reason for concentrating solely on military monuments is my keen interest in medieval armour, chivalry, genealogy, heraldry and history. For the purpose of this study the pre-1974 county boundaries have been used. Lincolnshire, being the second largest county, has the largest collection of pre-1500 military effigies in any one county, if one excepts Yorkshire, which is divided into three Ridings.

There are 62 military effigies in Lincolnshire, including some of national importance as well as many others of great interest. In the former category are the effigies at Careby, Halton-Holegate, Holbeach, Kirkstead Abbey, Stoke Rochford and Surfleet, not necessarily due to their condition, as some are damaged, but because of their artistic excellence or because they show armour of a type rarely seen. At Kirkstead Abbey for instance, is a rare example of an effigy wearing a flat-topped cylindrical helm. The mid-fourteenth century figure at Surfleet is very unusual for showing the coat-of-plates in its entirety; on most contemporary effigies it is covered by coat armour. Effigies at Halton-Holegate and Holbeach are fine examples showing armour from the transitional period; the sculptors have portrayed them as wearing highly decorative military equipment. At Careby and Stoke Rochford are unusual double effigies to men in armour and their wives, shown with their bodies covered by a blanket from which only their upper bodies and feet protrude.

The main object of the critical catalogue which follows this introduction is to provide an accurate analytical description of these figures as they appear today; a project that has been long overdue, for what is some of England's finest extant medieval monumental sculpture. The catalogue is arranged chronologically, with the monuments being divided into four main groups, as explained on pages 14-18. Every effigy is illustrated and the accompanying catalogue entry gives a description of the effigy and the armour shown and an account as to the person thought to be commemorated by the figure.

1.2 Methodology

In compiling a list of the 62 effigies I have consulted Sir Nicholas Pevsner's series *The Buildings of England, Lincolnshire*,[2] *Lincolnshire Church Notes* compiled by G. Holles,[3] *Bonney's Church Notes*,[4] and the personal catalogues of two of my friends, P. J. Lankester and the late A. V. B. Norman. Research into whom might be commemorated by the effigies presents more of a challenge than in the case of those in most other counties. The sole volume published of Lincolnshire *Victoria County History* deals only religious houses. There are no other histories of the county, although some towns, notably Lincoln and Boston have been the subject of several monographs.

---

[1] Those at Chester (formerly Holy Trinity, now walled up), Toppesfield (underneath the organ).

[2] Pevsner and Harris.
[3] Holles.
[4] Bonney.

Antiquarian evidence, chiefly in the form of church notes and heraldic manuscripts, is a valuable source for the study of tomb monuments. Such evidence can contain information about lost or damaged parts of monuments, including inscriptions and heraldry, which may help pinpoint the name of the person commemorated. Monuments have frequently been moved over the centuries, and parts of different monuments have sometimes been muddled up. Exceptionally, some monuments that no longer survive are recorded in church notes. For example, the church at Market Deeping contained a cross-legged wooden effigy, thought to have represented Sir Baldwin Wake (died 1282), which disappeared before 1782.[5] The early documentary evidence for the monuments in the county is limited, with two seventeenth-century manuscripts preserved in the British Library forming our main source. They are church notes by Gervase Holles (British Library, Harleian MS 6829), who appears to have copied the manuscript of F. Thynne, Lancaster Herald, church notes taken *c*. 1603-5 (British Library, Additional MS 36295). Holles is the most valuable antiquarian source for students studying stained glass and church monuments of the county of Lincolnshire. Fortunately his manuscript has been edited by R. E. G. Cole, and published by the Lincoln Record Society in 1911; therefore references are given for this accessible publication.[6] It should be noted, however, that these antiquarians did not visit every Lincolnshire church.

Some monuments have only recently been discovered, buried in the churchyard or once used as part of the structure of the church. More changes will inevitably happen. In 1974 the church at Panton was also sold, and then used as a store. It once contained built into the north wall of the chancel, the upper half of a military effigy *c*.1345 (figure 1), but was removed from the building before 1989 and nothing more is known of its whereabouts.[7] At the time of writing, the church at Maltby-le-Marsh was also being sold and the future of the effigy there is uncertain.

---

[5] Fryer 1924, p. 89.
[6] Fryer 1924, p. 89.
[7] Holles.

Fig. 1. Effigy formerly at Panton church. Removed before 1989. ©Crown copyright NMR. Photo taken 1972

We know very little about where and by whom English sculptured effigies were made, in contrast to the situation in various parts of the continent, where far more documentary evidence survives to show how sculptors such as Andrè Beauneveu, Jean de Liège and Claus Sluter worked.[8] Prior and Gardner, whose *Medieval Figure Sculpture in England*, published in 1912, was the most influential book on sculptured monuments written in the 20th century, saw tomb production in the medieval period as overwhelmingly urban-based, being essentially the work of schools centred in towns, particularly towns with large churches, where there would be a ready market for the workshop's products.[9] This view has recently come under challenge, particularly as a result of expert geological identification of the stone types used for monuments, which has revealed that some apparently coherent stylistic groups of effigies have been made from different stone types.[10] Other stylistic groups of effigies, however, have been shown to be carved from a single stone type.[11]

Rivers would have played an important part during the Middle Ages for the transportation of effigies from their production centres or raw stone from the quarries, landing to the nearest place for the church or the religious building. The freestone examples are very heavy, making transportation across land difficult, however there is evidence of stone being transported by carts and sleds, as for example between 1433-1435, when four cartloads of Egglestone marble was transported to Durham Cathedral.[12] In some cases sculptors may have moved around the country, like modern builders, as there is some evidence to suggest that some effigies were carved in the vicinity of their respective churches, as suggested by an unfinished military effigy at Grosmont, Monmouthshire.

Effigies in Lincolnshire are made of three different materials: Purbeck marble, alabaster and limestone; each is discussed in turn below.

2.1 Purbeck marble effigies
Purbeck marble is one of a group of so-called sedimentary 'marbles', in which natural calcite cement has filled the original pore-spaces to such an extent that the stone is capable of receiving a high polish. Purbeck is characterised by a distinctive pattern of massed, tiny round fossil shells of the freshwater snail *viviparous carniferus*. This stone comes in a variety of hues, including green, greyish-blue, reddish-brown and faun.

Purbeck marble is found only in the Upper Purbeck beds of Dorset, which run from Peveril Point westwards to Worbarrow Tout, approximately halfway down the northern slope of the southern Purbeck Hills. The most extensive evidence for quarrying is around Wilkeswood and Downsay near the village of Corfe. Raw stone and worked products were transported by sea to London marblers workshops and throughout much of England.[13]

Only three effigies carved from Purbeck marble are recorded in Lincolnshire, Gedney,[14] Hougham and Kirkstead Abbey. The effigy at Kirkstead Abbey shows similar characteristics to other effigies made from the same material, especially one at Walkern, Hertfordshire (figure 3).[15]

Military effigies made of this material (43 in total) are mainly found in the southern half of the country, with only a small number in the north. The material was used in the twelfth-century for some the earliest effigies in the country, those of abbots and bishops, but not for military effigies until *c*. 1250. Use seems to have continued until the early fourteenth century, when effigies in freestone or wood became more popular. It was formerly thought that London was the major centre for effigy production in Purbeck marble, but this is questionable, as one would assume a larger concentration around London.[16] Effigies were more probably carved and finished at the quarry workshops in Dorset, but unfortunately there is no evidence for this. The two effigies at St Mary's Wareham must have been carved in the vicinity; also there is a possibility that in 1252-3 the effigy (now lost) sent to Tarrant Monkton Priory was carved in Dorset.[17] Unlike the use for three-dimensional effigies, the material was used constantly from 1350 for monumental brass production, with the material being imported from the Isle of Purbeck to London, which his where the major production centre was.[18] A medieval contract states that John Bourde of Corfe carved the elaborate Purbeck marble tomb-chest of the monument of Richard Beauchamp at Warwick, whereas the cover slab with brass inscription came for the workshop of John Essex of London (figure 4).[19]

2.3 Alabaster effigies
There are eight alabaster effigies of knights in Lincolnshire. Alabaster is a form of sulphate of lime,

---

[8] Nash, pp. 144-177.
[9] Prior and Gardner, pp. 616-620.
[10] Church Monuments Society Conference York, 25th October 2008. Badham S., and Oosterwijk S., (eds.), *Monumental Industry: carved tomb production in Fourteenth century England* (forthcoming).
[11] Gittos 2002, p. 15.
[12] Badham and Blacker, p. 32.

[13] Blair J. 1991, "Purbeck Marble", p. 44.
[14] I am grateful to Sally Badham for this reference (email correspondence 1/6/2009).
[15] Tummers, Plate 20.
[16] Blair J. 1991, "Purbeck Marble", p. 52.
[17] Blair J. 1991, "Purbeck Marble", p. 52.
[18] Blair J. 1991, "Purbeck Marble", p. 53.
[19] Blair J. 1991, "Purbeck Marble", p. 54.

otherwise known as gypsum. Today, the Fauld mine in Staffordshire is the only commercial mine extracting the material. When the material is first quarried it is very soft and easily carved. Once it is dry it then can be polished easily, to a finish resembling marble, also it is very translucent. However, it is the second most soluble mineral known in the United Kingdom, the first being rock salt.[20] If an effigy is exposed to damp or water the alabaster will eventually dissolve, as can be seen where a number of effigies have been damaged by water dripping through leaking church roofs, most notably the effigy at Scropton, Derbyshire, where the right side of the waist has been eroded by dripping water (figure 2).

Fig. 2. Alabaster effigy at Scropton, Derbyshire eroded by dripping water.

The renowned alabaster geologist, the late Ron Firmin, believed that the material was first discovered at Tutbury Castle Hill, Staffordshire, when the castle and the nearby priory church were being built.[21] Parts of the castle and the priory have foundations made of slabs of alabaster, and it is at the priory, on the second order of the Norman west doorway, that we find the earliest known use of the material (c.1160-1170). Firmin believed that the material was exposed when excavations for the castle began during the first decade of the fourteenth century, although the material was not in abundance, as is recorded in a document from John of Gaunt's register.[22] John of Gaunt held the land at Tutbury Castle, and it is recorded in 1374 that he ordered six cartloads of alabaster from Tutbury, for his and his wife's lavish tomb[23] in St Paul's Cathedral London.[24] If the alabaster was not pure it was to be sought elsewhere. It is not known whether Tutbury alabaster was ever used for his tomb, as John of Gaunt was aware of the depleting stocks of pure alabaster at Tutbury. He also owned land at Castle Hayes-Fauld, Staffordshire, a short distance from Tutbury, where the largest quarry of alabaster was during the Middle Ages;[25] it was very likely that Tutbury and not Chellaston

supplied the pure white alabaster for the early effigies of Edward II at Gloucester Cathedral and John of Eltham, in Westminster Abbey.

Alabaster was quarried in pillars, approximately 12 feet in diameter and from 8-9 feet thick, divided from each other by a soft material called 'foulstone'.[26] From surviving material the average yearly amount of white alabaster required for monuments and other artefacts such as religious images in the Middle Ages would have been around 70 tons, 20 tons from Chellaston and 50 tons from the Castle Hayes-Fauld areas, where white alabaster occupies the top third of a pillar.[27] Some alabaster was quarried at Ripon Parks, Yorkshire; Burton-on-the-Wolds, Leicestershire and Red Hill, Nottinghamshire, which may have been suitable for effigies and tombs, but it is more likely that all the alabaster required for monuments came from either Chellaston, Derbyshire, or Castle-Hayes, Staffordshire; Tutbury only produced a small quantity.[28] Most workshops probably acquired alabaster from the region and then carved effigies in their respective workshops. There is documented evidence for carvers working near or on the quarry site of Chellaston[29].

John Leland, writing in the first half of the sixteenth century, recorded alabaster quarries in the Isle of Axholm, Lincolnshire: 'The upper part of the isle hath plentiful quarres of alabaster, communely there caullid plaster: but such stones as I saw of it were of no great thiknes and sold for xijd. the lode. They ly yn the ground lyke a smothe table: and be beddid one flake under another: and at the bottom of the beddes of them be roughe stones to build withal'.[30] He also recorded at Burton-on-Trent: 'Many marbelers working in alabaster'.[31] Firmin believed that the quarries in the Isle of Axholm did not produce large enough blocks for effigies, perhaps only producing thin slabs for reredoses or altar images. The term 'plaster' which Leland comments may be building grade gypsum. It is, consequently, unlikely that any of the alabaster effigies in Lincolnshire were carved from this source.

The earliest alabaster effigies probably date from the 1340s, and up to c.1380, workshops were experimenting with this lustrous stone. C. Blair's re-dating of the Hanbury effigy[32] from c.1300 to c.1340 brings its date close to the two other early alabasters; those of John of Eltham, Earl of Cornwall, and his father Edward II. John

[20] Firmin 1993, p. 7.
[21] Firmin 1993, pp. 7-11.
[22] Armitage-Smith, pp. 212-213.
[23] Armitage-Smith, pp. 212-213. I am grateful to Professor Brian Kemp for this translation from French.
[24] The tomb was destroyed in the Great Fire of London. A drawing of the tomb by W. Hollar is reproduced in Harvey, J., 1944, Plate 51.
[25] Ramsay, N., 1991, "Alabaster", P. 31

[26] Firmin 1984, p. 171.
[27] Firmin 1984, p. 174.
[28] Firmin 1984, p. 171.
[29] Bilson, pp. 32-37.
[30] Smith 1, p.38.
[31] Smith 5, p.19.
[32] Blair, Claude 1992, pp. 3-18.

Fig. 3. Purbeck marble effigy at Walkern, Hertfordshire c.1260/70

Fig. 4. Effigy of Sir Richard Beauchamp at Warwick, Warwickshire c.1450/60

of Eltham died in October 1336,[33] and was buried in Westminster Abbey on 15 January 1337; his tomb in Westminster Abbey was ready by *c*.1340 (figure 5).[34] A survey of lion footrests by the author[35] confirms that the lion below his feet and that at his father's feet are so alike they must have been carved by the same hand. It seems very likely, therefore that they were both carved at the same time, *c*.1340. The Hanbury effigy appears stylistically to be slightly earlier than John of Eltham, and therefore remains the earliest alabaster effigy in the country.

The Hanbury effigy is made of red mottled alabaster, which is more normally associated with effigies from the end of the fifteenth century onwards. Rather interestingly the face is carved from a separate piece of pure white alabaster, which C. Blair believes was chosen specially for the features.[36] As the effigy is located near an alabaster quarry, it is very likely that the origin of the alabaster would be either Castle Hayes-Fauld, Tutbury, or Hanbury, it was quite possibly carved *in-situ* at the church, by a local sculptor. An early record of an alabaster tomb is that of Queen Isabella *ob*.1358, formerly in Friars Minor, Newgate, London.[37] It was started before her death in 1358 by Agnes, daughter of William Ramsey III, and was completed between 1358 and 1364. Whether Agnes was responsible for carving the effigy, we do not know. She may have continued her father's business; he was most probably the craftsman responsible for the effigies of John of Eltham and Edward II as he was the Royal Mason until his death in 1349.[38]

In 1362 Queen Philippa of Hainault ordered six cartloads of alabaster from Tutbury,[39] probably for her tomb in Westminster Abbey. The tomb was contracted in 1367, two years before her death, to, Jean de Liège at a cost of £133 6s. 8d.[40] The use of a continental sculptor for the effigy is perhaps rather surprising since there were some leading English sculptors working in London at this time. But particularly as documentary evidence is so lacking, it is possible that there may have been more continental sculptors working on tombs in the country about whom we know nothing.

As we have seen above, on 14 June 1374 John of Gaunt ordered six cartloads of alabaster from his land at Tutbury[41] for the elaborate double tomb of himself and his wife Blanche, who died in 1369. The tomb was contracted to Henry Yevele, and Thomas Wrek at a cost of £486 and was to be completed by 1378 (though John

of Gaunt himself did not die until 1399). The tomb once stood in St Paul's Cathedral[42] until the Great Fire destroyed it in 1666.[43] Henry Yevele is known to have been involved in the production of a number of tombs, but what of Thomas Wrek? He, like Yevele also worked on secular and church buildings, but nothing much is known of him, whereas Yevele must have been a huge driving force in London until his death in 1400.[44]

Thomas Prentys is also named in two important contracts, the first for a tomb that still survives in Lowick, Northamptonshire (figure 6).[45] The contract, written in medieval French and dated February 14th, 6 Henry V (1418-19), was made between Katharine who was the widow of Ralph Greene, esquire, William Aldwyncle and William Marshall, clerks; and Thomas Prentys and Robert Sutton, carvers of Chellaston. The tomb was to be completed by Easter 1420 at a cost of £40. The contract stipulates that it was to be carved well and honestly in alabaster, Ralph's effigy was to be fine and pure. The effigy was to be seven feet in length, armed at all points and holding the lady's hand, a relatively unusual feature. The tomb-chest to be decorated with angels bearing armorial shields of the deceased, together with an arch over the tomb and gablette over each of the effigies heads. Under Ralph Green's head was to be a helm, and a bear at his feet. Although the canopy is missing, the tomb remains in a good state of preservation. Exactly when the canopy was removed has not been documented. It was perhaps taken down due to having become unstable. Interesting the contract stipulates that only pure alabaster was to be used, veined alabaster was presumably regarded as inferior and only used when the pure white variety was exhausted. Veined was not favoured by all, as in a case of 1443 when Sir Thomas Cumberworth sued Robert Sutton, Thomas Sutton and John Chaloner for not using pure and clean alabaster, as specified in their contract.[46]

The second document was made in 1421 between Robert Broun, dweller of the Savoy for one part and Thomas Prentys and Robert Sutton of the county of Derby carvers of the other part. The latter were contracted by Richard Hertcombe to construct a tomb, and images of an Earl and Countess of Salisbury at Bisham Priory, Burghfield, Berkshire.[47] The contract specifies that the effigies and canopies were to be made of alabaster, whereas the tomb-chest was to be made of marble. The tomb appears to have been destroyed, but a number of monuments were transferred from Bisham to Burgfield, but this effigy is not one of those that were transferred. It is not unusual

---

[33] Southwick, p. 8, note. 2.

[34] Binski 1995, p. 177.

[35] Downing 1998, p. 22.

[36] Blair, Claude 1992, p. 5.

[37] Blackley, pp. 161-164.

[38] Harvey, J. 1987, pp. 242-245.

[39] *Cal. Patent Rolls Edw. III* 12, p. 232.

[40] Binski 1995, p. 180.

[41] Armitage-Smith, pp. 212-213.

---

[42] Drawings of the tomb by William Sedwick are reproduced in Lindley 2007, pls. 4, 5.

[43] Harvey, J. 1987, p. 360.

[44] Harvey, J. 1987, p. 364.

[45] Quoted in translation by Hope 1904, pp.230-231 and Crossley, 1921 p. 30.

[46] Lindley 1995, p. 26.

[47] Bayliss, pp. 22-29.

Fig. 5. Effigy of John of Eltham at Westminster Abbey c.1340

Fig. 6. Tomb-chest and effigy of Ralph Green at Lowick. c.1420

for effigies to be made of alabaster, but the combination of alabaster effigy with a tomb-chest made of Purbeck marble is very rare from this period.

Stylistically four out of the eight alabaster effigies in Lincolnshire appear to be from the Prentys and Sutton workshop: those at Stamford, Spilsby (3), Broughton and Wellingore. The effigies at North Cockerington, Saxilby and Spilsby (1) are possibly from the Prentys/Sutton workshop but this is questionable. Transportation of alabaster from Chellaston to the county would have been very easy by means of the river Trent.

2.4 Limestone effigies

Far less is known about the different varieties of Lincolnshire limestone used locally both as a building material and to produce tomb monuments. It has been less extensively studied and little documentary evidence is known, none of it relating to effigy production. Limestone was the most common material used for carving effigies in the county up to *c*.1380, when alabaster became popular for high-status tombs. The limestones in this belt are not uniform in character and some are more suitable than others for carving detail such as chain mail. In parts of the Lincolnshire Wolds the limestone is soft and chalky, which makes it of borderline suitability for carving effigies, as exemplified by those in this stone at Ewerby and Friskney. The surface is powdery and mail had to be fabricated with applied gesso rather than being carved.

In contrast, the limestones around Ancaster and Stamford are both hard and fine-grained, making it ideal for monumental sculpture. Quarries from the medieval period were situated around Ancaster, Castle Bytham, Kesteven, and Stamford, also at Lincoln, which supplied the cathedral.[48] Some of the quarries were under royal control and stone from them was used for many building projects, including Windsor Castle.[49] As I have noted, it is not known where limestone for effigy production came from, although in 1364 there is a record of a mason, Hugh Kympton (*fl*.1343-1388), extracting stone from the quarries at Careby and Holywell.[50] Also Thomas Mason II, (*fl*.1498-) a mason probably from Boston, worked stone from nearby Swineshead.[51] On the whole it seems that stone would have been easily accessible for sculptors. Most quarries were situated near watercourses and transporting stone or effigies to their destinations would have been straightforward using the rivers Witham, Kyme Ferry, Welland, Nene, Car Dyke and roadways.[52]

2.5 Surface finishes on medieval effigies

Colour was a very important part of medieval church decoration with surfaces being splendidly painted with oil-based pigments and applied gilding to achieve a bright and eye-catching effect. The appearance of effigies today is dull and lifeless, compared with what they looked like when they were first produced. The conservation and analysis of the wooden effigy at Abergavenny Priory church of John, second Baron Hastings, *ob*.1325, by Carol Galvin is one of several cases, which give an insight into how an effigy was painted and gilded.[53] Although the effigy is made of wood rather than stone the technique of decoration remains principally the same on both. First a number of gesso base-coats, consisting of a mixture of chalk and animal glue, were applied to the surface and then painted with realistic lead-based colours; pink, red, black and greens etc, also with an heraldic charge: the mail would have been applied using strips of tin-foil, fabricated in moulds, which was then laid down onto wet underpaint.[54] The whole surface was then finished with a number of coats of glaze. The base beneath this particular effigy appears to have been painted to resemble Purbeck marble.[55] The Abergavenny effigy and those at Belleau and Spilsby (1) are from the "Westminster Workshop", whether they were carved and painted by the same person is purely speculative, as workshops sub-contracted colouring out to painters.[56]

Effigies carved from freestone and wood probably had the entire surface covered with polychromy and other applied decoration. By contrast, the translucent finish of polished alabaster was highly prized. In consequence only certain parts of the figure and armour were painted and gilded, mainly the borders, hinges, crests, lion's mane, dagger, sword and coat-armour etc. The breastplates and leg-defences on the other hand were left uncoloured.

Considering the large number of effigies that survive in England from the period covered by this catalogue, there is only a small number surviving that have any notable decoration remaining on them. To gain a good idea of this original decoration, therefore we need to look outside the county. The effigies of Edmund Crouchback *c*.1300 and Aymer de Valence *c*.1325/1330 at Westminster Abbey, while dark and discoloured,[57] have large amounts of gesso mail and paint decoration on their surfaces.[58] The effigy of John de la Pole, Duke of Suffolk, *ob*.1491 at Wingfield (Suffolk) has its decoration very well preserved.[59] Some items of the knight's equipment were

---

[48] Alexander, p. 111.
[49] Alexander, p. 110.
[50] Harvey, J. 1987, p. 169.
[51] Harvey, J. 1987, pp. 198-199.
[52] Alexander, pp. 124-129.

[53] Lindley and Galvin, pp. 86-93, at p. 90.
[54] *Victoria and Albert Museum Conservation Journal*, pp. 4-7.
[55] Lindley and Galvin, p. 90.
[56] Brodrick and Darrah, p. 69.
[57] The monument were painted with Japan gold size to preserve their surfaces but has turned very dark . Scott, p. 160.
[58] Stothard pp. 40, 46.
[59] Stothard p. 100.

decorated with coloured glass or paste to resemble precious stones or jewels as can be seen on the effigy at Aston, *c.*1370 (Warwickshire), which has dark blue inserted into the hip-belt and the bacinet's mount.[60] On the lion footrest of a military effigy at Meriden (Warwickshire), *c.*1400/5, the eyes have deep hollows, once containing glass, a rare occurrence.[61] Another fine example is the bacinet on the military effigy at Ingham (Norfolk) to Sir Robert de Boys (*ob.* after 1394) commissioned in his own lifetime. This is a unique survival on the armour of effigies of applied decoration in moulded gesso and fictive jewels to replicate the jewelled precious metal borders of high quality armour.[62]

In many cases the loss of original polychromy is due to Victorian and later refurbishments of effigies. In some cases, monuments with patchily remaining colour were scrubbed clean or whitewashed over to present a tidier appearance, which can be cited at Spilsby (2). In other instances an entirely new paint finish was provided, too often one, which did not respect the original colour scheme. We are fortunate that the nineteenth-century antiquarians Charles Stothard (1786-1821) and father and son combination George (1793-1842) and Thomas Hollis (1818-1843), produced some exquisite drawings of effigies, in which they recorded colour decoration that they discovered on the effigies at the time; in most cases the decoration has since disappeared. Stothard drew three effigies in the county, Gosberton, Holbeach and Surfleet, but unfortunately did not record any paint on their surfaces[63].

---

[60] T. and G. Hollis, pt. 4, no. 8.
[61] Chatwin, Plate 8, fig. 2.
[62] Badham 2007, p. 29.
[63] Stothard pp. 34, 59. Lankester 2004, p. 8.

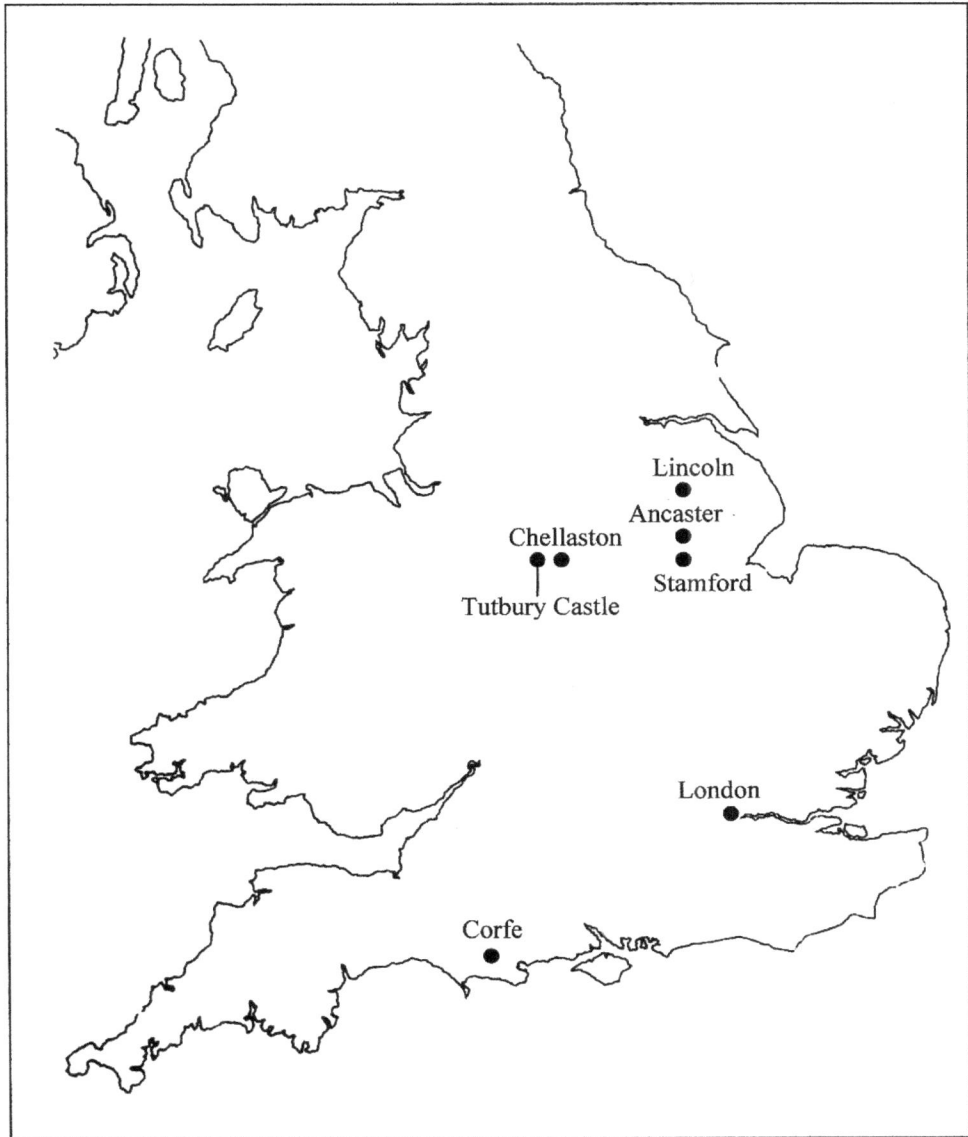

Map 1. Showing main sources of stone used for effigies in Lincolnshire in relation to possible workshop sites in Corfe, London and Lincoln

3.1 Post-medieval losses of monuments

A cocktail of political and religious causes led to the destruction of church monuments during the regime of Henry VIII, Edward VI and Oliver Cromwell. The dissolution of the monasteries between 1534 and 1540 saw the virtual destruction of religious buildings in the country. An example of this destruction is cited by Stow in 1547, where in the London Grey Friars church nine tombs of alabaster and marble were pulled down and sold for fifty pounds.[64] The dissolution of the chantries in 1547 and the destruction of religious imagery also in the reign of Edward VI caused many thousand monuments to be destroyed in parish churches. We have records of military effigies in England that have been destroyed over the past three hundred years, but we do not know the full extent of losses since the Reformation. An analysis of 195 noble wills, covering two centuries in the late Middle Ages, has revealed that more specified burial in a religious house than a parish church; in consequence few of their tombs survive.[65] Destruction was not necessarily confined to the sixteenth century, as many tombs were destroyed during re-building and re-modelling of churches during the eighteenth and nineteenth centuries. Although much destruction occurred during the reign of Elizabeth I, she issued a proclamation in 1560 demanding that the destruction of monuments was to stop and if any person was found defacing a monument they were ordered to pay for its repair.[66] At Kingerby, Holles recorded two cross-legged effigies, of which there is one now remaining,[67] also an alabaster effigy at Gosberton, which has since been destroyed.[68] John Leland recorded effigies destroyed from Lincoln Cathedral and Gainsborough parish church.[69] It is likely that other losses in the modern period went unrecorded. In counties with fuller antiquarian notes, higher numbers of monuments are known to have been lost in the past 300 years, for instance Yorkshire. At Escrick (Yorkshire, East Riding) alabaster effigies of a knight and lady have been destroyed.[70] A fine wooden monument at Brancepeth (Durham) commemorating Ralph Neville, 2nd earl of Westmorland and his wife Margaret, was destroyed during a huge fire of the church in 1998. During the early part of the nineteenth-century, a wooden effigy formerly at Radcliffe-on-Trent, Nottinghamshire, was dressed up by the local people as Napoleon and then burnt on a bonfire to celebrate a victory over the French.[71] Even in the present day monuments are not treated with respect they deserve, which is mainly due to lack of funding for their conservation, damp conditions and inadequate protection from church clutter, including water damage from flower arrangements thoughtlessly by placed upon them.

3.2 Dating of tomb monuments

Dating of sculptured effigies is extremely difficult because, particularly before the second half of the fourteenth century, relatively few of those commemorated by them can be certainly identified.[72] Lawrence Stone summed up the problem, as follows: 'All too often, the current system of dating effigies depends on the tautological process of fixing a date as a result of stylistic analysis, finding a personage whose date of death approximately coincides and then using the latter to demonstrate the reliability of the former'.[73]

Even when a certain identification is possible and the date of death known, there is the ever present problem of the possibility that the monument was erected some years before or after death, as is known to have happened in quite a number of documented cases. Clerics were particularly likely to order their own tomb monuments, as they had no direct descendant to whom they could entrust the task. The two-tier effigial monument to Archbishop Henry Chichele in Canterbury Cathedral was complete by 1426, yet Chichele did not die until 1443.[74] There were other reasons why monuments were commissioned in the lifetime of the person commemorated. From the late fourteenth century, in particular, it was quite common for the aristocracy and gentry classes to establish a family chantry chapel in their parish church. Often the person establishing the chantry would order his or her own monument as part of the fitting out of the chapel. This can be cited at Threekingham, when in 1325 Sir Walter de Trikingham obtained a licence for a chantry for the souls of himself, his father and mother.[75] Double tombs for husband and wife could be erected by a widow or widower after the death of the spouse, as happened in the double effigial alabaster tomb to Ralph and Katherine Green at Lowick (Northamptonshire). Ralph died in 1418 and his widow commissioned the tomb the following February: the contract stipulated it was to be completed by Easter 1420.[76] But, here again, there could be some delay, as in the case of another alabaster tomb to John of Gaunt and his first wife Blanche. Blanche died in 1369, but alabaster for their double tomb in Old St Paul's Cathedral, now lost, was not ordered until 1374. It was to

---

[64] Lindley 2007, p. 22.

[65] Lindley 2007, p. 12.

[66] Weever, pp. 52-53.

[67] Holles, p. 68.

[68] Holles, p. 172.

[69] Smith 1, p. 33 and 5, pp. 121-122.

[70] Lankester 1993, pp. 25-44.

[71] Fryer 1910, p. 490.

[72] Lankester 1987, pp. 145, 150.

[73] Stone, p. 114.

[74] Wilson, p. 476.

[75] Moor 5, p. 49.

[76] Northants Record Office, No.55 42 39: Published in, Hartshorne 1876, p. 117: translated in Crossley 1921, p. 30.

be completed by 1378 though John of Gaunt himself did not die until 1399.[77]

Monuments could also be erected some years after the death of the person commemorated. In 1408, Joan of Navarre, wife of Henry IV, exported an alabaster tomb, now lost, to Nantes in Brittany for her first husband, John, Duke of Brittany, who had died in 1399.[78] In the case of Richard Beauchamp, Earl of Warwick, who died in 1439, work on his exceptionally lavish tomb in St Mary's Warwick, with its cast copper-alloy effigy, did not begin until 1447-8 and continued well into the 1450s.[79] An example of a monument being set up many years after death can be seen, for instance, at Hatfield Broad Oak (Essex).[80] The effigy commemorates Sir Henry de Vere, 3rd Earl of Oxford, who died in 1221. The Lombardic inscription to the Earl is still visible, although less clear than when it was recorded by John Weever in 1631, (Sir Robert de Vere the first, 3rd Earl of Oxford, lies here. God, if it please him, have mercy on his soul. Whoever shall pray for his soul shall have forty days pardon. Our Father). Stylistically the date of the effigy points to the early part of the fourteenth century.[81] H. A. Tummers has pointed out that the presence of double cushions with attendant angels should be dated after *c*.1300.[82]

Nevertheless, as others have concluded, such delays in erecting a monument were probably the exception rather than the rule. In the case of the lost tomb of Sir Nicholas de Louveyne at the Cistercian Abbey of St Mary Graces, near the Tower of London, the contract for the tomb is dated May 1376, only eight months after Sir Nicholas's death, and the tomb was to be completed 19 weeks later.[83] Ralph Green's tomb at Lowick was to be completed two years after he died. In his study of the sequence of the early London brasses in the period from the late thirteenth century, Paul Binski relied on dates of death. He acknowledged that there were some exceptions but felt that such an approach was 'vindicated by the fact that the sequence of death-dates yields a coherent stylistic sequence [which] would not happen if death - and engraving - dates were usually significantly different'.[84] The late Roger Greenwood's study of Norfolk wills from the 1490s to 1550s showed that the vast majority of those who requested a tomb stone be provided within a certain time, stipulated one year or less: while others asked for burial under the already existing stones of their spouses.[85] The one year period may not always have been adhered to but it probably gives an idea of what was considered a reasonable period for the provision of a brass. For a sculptured tomb, which may have taken a little longer, a two-year period is probably a reasonable estimate.

Dating effigies by arms and armour is a good starting point; however it should be realised that sculptors might be a number of years behind the most up-to-date armour styles, possibly carving similar effigies for a number of years after the armour was outdated.

[77] Harvey, J. 1987, p. 360.

[78] Crossley, pp. 26-7 . Harvey, J. 1987, p. 68.

[79] Lindley 1990, pp. 120-123, pls. XXIc, XXId.

[80] Blair, Claude 1993, pp. 3-11.

[81] Blair, Claude 1993, p. 9.

[82] Tummers, pp. 44, 51.

[83] Blair, J. 1980, pp. 66-74.

[84] Binski 1987, p. 70.

[85] Greenwood, J. R., pp. 92-96.

4.1 Lincolnshire military monuments

Out of the 62 effigies within the catalogue, 36 appear stylistically to be have been carved in Lincolnshire, with a number of others less certain. Styles can vary; those at Caistor (1) and South Kelsey are represented with straight and ridged features and are in low relief compared to those at Harrington, Rippingale (2) and Threekingham, which are carved more in the round with undercut legs, flowing drapery, and with a much more relaxed posture. They are very likely from the same workshop, but Caistor (1) and South Kelsey are earlier in date; however 15 years later the workshop was producing higher quality effigies. I have observed, that the effigy at West Tanfield (North Yorkshire) is from the same workshop as Harrington and Rippingale (2); the effigy at Threekingham is related to Flintham, Gonalston (2) (both Nottinghamshire), Hornsea (East Yorkshire) and Womersley (West Yorkshire). This underlines the need for caution to be exercised in any county-based survey of monuments.

Some effigies carved between 1330 and 1350, are portrayed with fine amour detail and well undercut, for instance at Buslingthorpe, Spilsby (1) and Surfleet, whereas the effigy at Edenham is not undercut and is in lower relief; the last may be a cheaper and lower quality monument. The limestone effigies carved later, between 1350 and 1410 are very likely from local workshops, patronised by people who could not afford the most prestigious material, which was alabaster. While alabaster was fashionable, effigies carved from limestone show little difference from their lustrous counterparts. For example the effigy at Uffington of *c.*1400 is imitative of large numbers of alabaster effigies from the same date, such as at Acton and Barthomley (both Cheshire).

The effigies at Belleau and Spilsby (1) are from the so-called "Westminster Workshop" as perhaps is that at Holbeach. These effigies are related to those of Edmund Crouchback *c.*1300, Aymer de Valence *c.*1325/1330 and John of Eltham, Earl of Cornwall, *c.*1340, at Westminster Abbey, and were thus probably carved by sculptors patronised by royalty. It is not known which master mason was responsible for carving the effigies in Westminster Abbey, but the surname Canterbury appears to have been associated with building work at Westminster Abbey from the late thirteenth century until the 1330's.[86] The first mason of that name appears to have been Michael, actively employed as a royal mason between 1275 and 1321.[87] He could well have been the designer of the tombs of Edmund Crouchback (*ob.*1296) and his wife Aveline of Lancaster (*ob.*1269). Michael of Canterbury's successor was Walter of Canterbury (*fl.*1319-1327).[88] Supporting Walter was Thomas of Canterbury (*fl.*1323-1335), who worked with him on the chapel of St Stephen's and the Painted Chamber.[89] William de Ramsey III (*fl.*1323-*ob.*1349) appears to have succeeded either Walter or Thomas as royal mason and was very likely the designer of the tomb of Aymer de Valence (*ob.*1324).[90] Henry Yevele (*fl.*1353-*ob.*1400) was yet another royal master mason known from documentary evidence to have supplied tombs.[91] While these master masons may have been contracted to oversee the work at Westminster Abbey, they may not have been personally directly involved in carving these effigies.

The semi-effigial monuments at Careby and Stoke Rochford may be alleged as Lincolnshire products, but in the opinion of the author they are East Midlands products, the workshop possibly based either at Leicester or Nottingham, which is where other related examples are to be found, for instance, a knight at Staunton-in-the-Vale (figure 7), Nottinghamshire and a female at Thurlaston, Leicestershire.[92]

Fig. 7. Effigy of Sir William Staunton c.1326, Staunton-in-the-Vale, Nottinghamshire

---

[86] Harvey, J. 1987, pp. 46-47.
[87] Harvey, J. 1987, p. 45.

[88] Harvey, J. 1987, p. 47.
[89] Harvey, J. 1987, pp. 46-47.
[90] Harvey, J. 1987, pp. 242-245.
[91] Harvey, J. 1987, pp. 358-366.
[92] Others can be seen for instance at Kedleston (Derbyshire), Headon, Mansfield Woodhouse, North Collingham (Nottinghamshire) and Washingborough.

In this section the military monuments of Lincolnshire are listed chronologically within four main groups. Each group is defined by a distinctive type of armour.

4.2 Chronological development of armour
Group A
The first group consists of twenty nine effigies of mail-clad 'knights' with their legs crossed or straight, wearing a long open surcoat; a mail hauberk with long sleeves, a coif, mail hose, poleyns; and, when shown, a long shield on the left shoulder. The earliest surviving effigy in Lincolnshire *c.*1250, that in Kirkstead Abbey, is straight-legged. Only about twenty straight-legged examples from this period survive in England, compared to the large number of cross-legged effigies.

The guidebooks of churches that have cross-legged effigies often call them crusaders or Knight-Templars and state that if an effigy has his legs crossed he was a crusader and had visited the Holy Land. This is very misleading as there is no positive evidence to support this theory.[93] The crossing of the legs was first introduced about *c.*1250 and continued until *c.*1350, with only isolated instances thereafter, for instance, Dorchester (Dorset) *c.*1380/1400, Tutbury Castle (Staffordshire) *c.*1500/20 and Exeter Cathedral (Devon), (monument to Sir Peter Carew *c.*1589). The cross-legged attitude is purely a phenomenon of England, Scotland and Wales, with the exception of one French effigy from Le Merleault, now in Philadelphia.[94] One question, which is very puzzling, why did the cross-legged attitude end as fast as it arrived? Presumably sculptors reverted to a relaxed and quiet posture, with represented in prayer. Writers have argued that crossing of the legs is a 'psychological change from the standing statue set horizontally to the recumbent effigy, and partly by technical need to give support at the knees if the effigy was to be carved fully in the round'.[95] P. Lindley believes that crossing of the legs is a stylistic way to enliven the figure and infuse energy.[96] Sculptors working in the West Country are believed to have first adopted the cross-legged attitude.[97] This is where some of the earliest effigies in the country are to be found: for example, at Salisbury Cathedral (1) (Wiltshire) *c.*1240, Seaborough (Dorset) *c.*1250, two examples at Shepton Mallet (Somerset), both *c.*1250, and the earlier of the two effigies at Tickenham (Somerset) *c.*1250.[98] The attitude of these effigies is very similar to the statues of 'knights' on the west front at Wells Cathedral, and it is very likely that sculptors working on the west front were responsible

for carving some at least of these fine effigies. The relaxed posture of the body and the smooth refinement of the drapery, an idyllic posture, typifies this early period.

Military effigies from *c.*1250 and 1350 are regularly represented handling their swords, and in some cases the technique is different. If the right hand is holding the grip it is often said that this represents the sword being drawn from its scabbard, and occasionally that it represents the sword being returned to the scabbard. In fact there is no way of telling which is represented because the hands would be in the exactly the same position in either case. It is only when the right hand is on top of the pommel and the sword blade partly out of the scabbard, as for example, at Danbury (1) (Essex) (figures 8, 9) and Englefield (Berkshire), that one can be sure that the sword is being returned and not being drawn.

1. Kirkstead Abbey, *c.*1250.[99]
2. Scopwick, *c.*1250/1340.
3. Gedney, *c.*1270/1290.
4. Swineshead, *c.*1280/1300.
5. Burton Coggles (1), *c.*1280/1300.
6. Goxhill, *c.*1280/1300.
7. Swinstead, *c.*1300.
8. Ashby-cum-Fenby, *c.*1300/25.
9. Stoke Rochford, *c.*1300/25.
10. Careby (1), *c.*1300/25.
11. Burton Coggles (2), *c.*1300/25.
12. Hougham, *c.*1306.
13. Gosberton, *c.*1310/20.
14. Caistor (1), *c.*1315.
15. South Kelsey, *c.*1315.
16. Scotton, *c.*1320.
17. Belleau, *c.*1320/25.
18. Fulstow, *c.*1320/25.
19. Londonthorpe, *c.*1320/25.
20. Old Somerby, *c.*1320/25.
21. Rippingale (1), *c.*1320/25.
22. Saleby, *c.*1320/25.
23. Scrivelsby, *c.*1320/25.
24. Kingerby (1), *c.*1325.
25. Kirton-in-Lindsey, *c.*1325.
26. Rippingale (2), *c.*1325.
27. Harrington, *c.*1325/30.
28. Careby (2), *c.*1327.
29. Threekingham, *c.*1330.

Group B
Twelve effigies in Lincolnshire remain from a period of great interest for the study of armour with highly decorative details. It belongs to a transitional period between *c.*1340 and 1360, when many people appear to have continued to wear mostly mail externally, while others reinforced it with plate or leather to a lesser or greater extent. The coif is replaced with a bacinet fitted with a visor and an attached aventail. From about *c.*1345/50 short coat-armour with kilted skirt replaces the

---

[93] For a detailed discussion on cross-legged effigies see Tummers, pp. 117-126.

[94] Hurting, fig. 13.

[95] Stone, p. 115.

[96] Lindley and Galvin, p. 67.

[97] Tummers, p. 111.

[98] Tummers, pls. 3, 4, 5, 8, 12.

---

[99] All the dates given for the effigies are those by the author.

Fig. 8. Danbury (1), Essex, c.1280/1300. Effigy depicted with the sword being returned into the scabbard

Fig. 9. Detail of Danbury (1)

long surcoat of the preceding period: it is laced at the sides and tight to the upper body. The torso is protected by a coat-of-plates, worn underneath the coat armour.

The splendid mid-fourteenth century effigy at Ash (Kent) (figure 139) is laced along the right side of the body, revealing the coat-of-plates worn beneath the coat armour.[100] Whilst lacing is represented on a number of effigies the lames of the coat-of-plates are sometimes omitted. When omitted, they were presumably represented by paint. Examples of coats-of-plate, excavated on the site of the battle of Wisby (1361) in Sweden clearly show the construction method.[101] An early representation of the coat-of-plates is illustrated on the statue of St Maurice, at Magdeburg Cathedral[102] *c*.1250, where he wears a "poncho" type garment over a mail haubergeon, which reaches to the hips at the front, whereas the back is shorter. Clearly represented on the chest and back are rows of rivets, which indicate the iron plates, riveted to the inside of the textile covering on a real coat-of-plates. They are presumably, vertical plates running around the body. The garment is joined in the middle of the back by three straps with buckles. An effigy at Coberley (2) (Gloucestershire) *c*.1345, wears a coat-of-plates underneath a long surcoat, where the plates are indicated attached to the inside of the textile by flower-headed rivets. A beautiful effigy at Horley (Surrey) *c*.1345, wears a similar coat-of-plates underneath a short-fronted surcoat.[103] The coat-of-plates continued to be worn until the solid breastplate and backplate became fashionable in the last quarter of the fourteenth century. The arms in some instances are represented in vambraces with closed cannons and the legs in closed greaves. Gauntlets have cuffs of plates fitting the forearm closely and strapped round the wrist. The fingers covered by straight or curved plates, attached to a leather or cloth lining. The feet are protected by sabatons made of overlapping lames, again attached to a cloth or leather lining.

30. Maltby-le-Marsh, *c*.1330.
31. Somerby, *c*.1330
32. Halton Holegate, *c*.1335/40.
33. Winteringham, *c*.1335/40.
34. Burton-upon-Stather, *c*.1340.
35. Buslingthorpe, *c*.1340/45.
36. Lea, *c*.1350.
37. Surfleet, *c*.1346/7.
38. Spilsby (1), *c*.1348.
39. Wilsthorpe, *c*.1350.
40. Edenham, *c*.1350/60.
41. Norton Disney, *c*.1350.

Group C
Seventeen military effigies in Lincolnshire fall within the third period of armour development. Effigies have now become straight-legged and rigid, with the hands in the

act of prayer. The bacinet is pointed with a mail aventail, attached to its lower edge. In most cases tilt-helms with crests have replaced the cushions under the heads. The body and limbs are represented wearing a mixture of mail, textile, leather and plate metal, with the coat-armour tight-fitting, and has its hem cut short below the hips; on the feet are sabatons.

42. Holbeach, *c*.1350/60.
43. Great Grimsby, *c*.1360/70.
44. Ewerby, *c*.1370.
45. Friskney, *c*.1370/80.
46. Saxilby, *c*.1370/80.
47. Spilsby (2), *c*.1375.
48. Lincoln Cathedral (1), *c*.1375.
49. Caistor (2), *c*.1380.
50. Kingerby (2), *c*.1380.
51. North Cockerington, *c*.1380/90.
52. Stamford, *c*.1400.
53. Kirkby-cum-Osgodby, *c*.1400.
54. Uffington, *c*.1400.
55. Spilsby (3), *c*.1400.
56. Lincoln (City & County Museum), *c*.1400/10.
57. Broughton, *c*.1410.
58. Deeping St. James, *c*.1410.

Group D
Only four Lincolnshire effigies belong to this final phase in development of armour from *c*.1420 to *c*.1500. Armour from this period is known as white armour with the whole body encased in metal plate without any textile covering, and is arguably the finest period for the armourer.[104] Mail remained in use to supplement plate. Pieces of mail were attached to an arming-doublet to protect the gaps in the plate. They consisted of gussets covering the armpits, elbow-joints and also a skirt covering the tops of the thighs. Pieces of armour were also attached to the arming-doublet by laces, for instance the pauldron and couter. Armour was attached to the body and limbs by straps and buckles and also to the arming-doublet by the method stated above. Movement was achieved by sliding rivets and leathers. The bacinet with attached aventail is now replaced by the great bacinet as represented at Wellingore, which in turn is superseded by the sallet, positioned under the head at Rippingale. In most cases what we see on an effigy can be related to actual pieces of armour and carved with exquisite detail, but how did the sculptor know what actual piece of arms or armour looked like? It is possible that they used pattern books, but more likely they had actual pieces if armour in the workshop, perhaps armour of the deceased. The armour represented on the cast copper-alloy effigy of Richard Beauchamp, Earl of Warwick who died in 1439, replicates actual armour. In this instance a wooden pattern effigy was made by John III Massingham of London *fl*.1409-1450,[105] and the casting by William Austen, also London.[106] While patrons would have

---

[100] Stothard, p. 54.
[101] Thordeman, pls. 28, 30.
[102] Thordeman, figs. 288, 289.
[103] Waller, Plate to face p. 187.

[104] Blair, 1972, p. 77.
[105] Harvey, J. 1987, p. 200.
[106] Chatwin, p. 62.

ordered a monument, setting down details as to how they wished to be represented, I believe that the Prentys/Sutton workshop would have had a stock of effigies, similar to a modern day builder's merchant, as it would have been false economy to have sculptors waiting for the next commission.[107] Many of what survives from this workshop, nationally, are probably from the same-hand, with designs being changed in accordance with the advancement of armour and the patron's wishes.

59. Boston, *c.*1430/50.
60. Wellingore, *c.*1430/40.
61. Rippingale (3), *c.*1470/75.
62. Lincoln Cathedral (2), *c.*1470.

---

[107] Apart from identical similarities the effigies at Bakewell (2) (Derbyshire), Darfield (Yorkshire, West Riding), Nuthall (Nottinghamshire) and Swine (3) (Yorkshire, East Riding), from this workshop measure 6ft 2in, while others from this group are only an inch longer or shorter.

Goxhill
Winteringham
Burton-upon-Stather
River Humber
Broughton Somerby Great Grimsby
Caistor Ashby-cum-Fenby
Scotton South Kelsey Fulstow
River Trent Kingerby North Cockerington
Kirton-in-Lindsey Kirkby-cum-Osgodby
Lea Maltby-le-Marsh
Buslingthorpe Belleau
Saxilby Saleby
River Witham Harrington
Lincoln
Scrivelsby Spilsby
Norton Disney Kirkstead Halton Holegate
Scopwick Friskney
Wellingore
Ewerby Boston
Hougham
Londonthorpe Swineshead
Threekingham
Old Somerby Gosberton
Burton Coggles Rippingale Holbeach
South Stoke Surfleet Gedney
Swinestead Edenham
Careby Wilsthorpe
Deeping St James
Stamford
Uffington

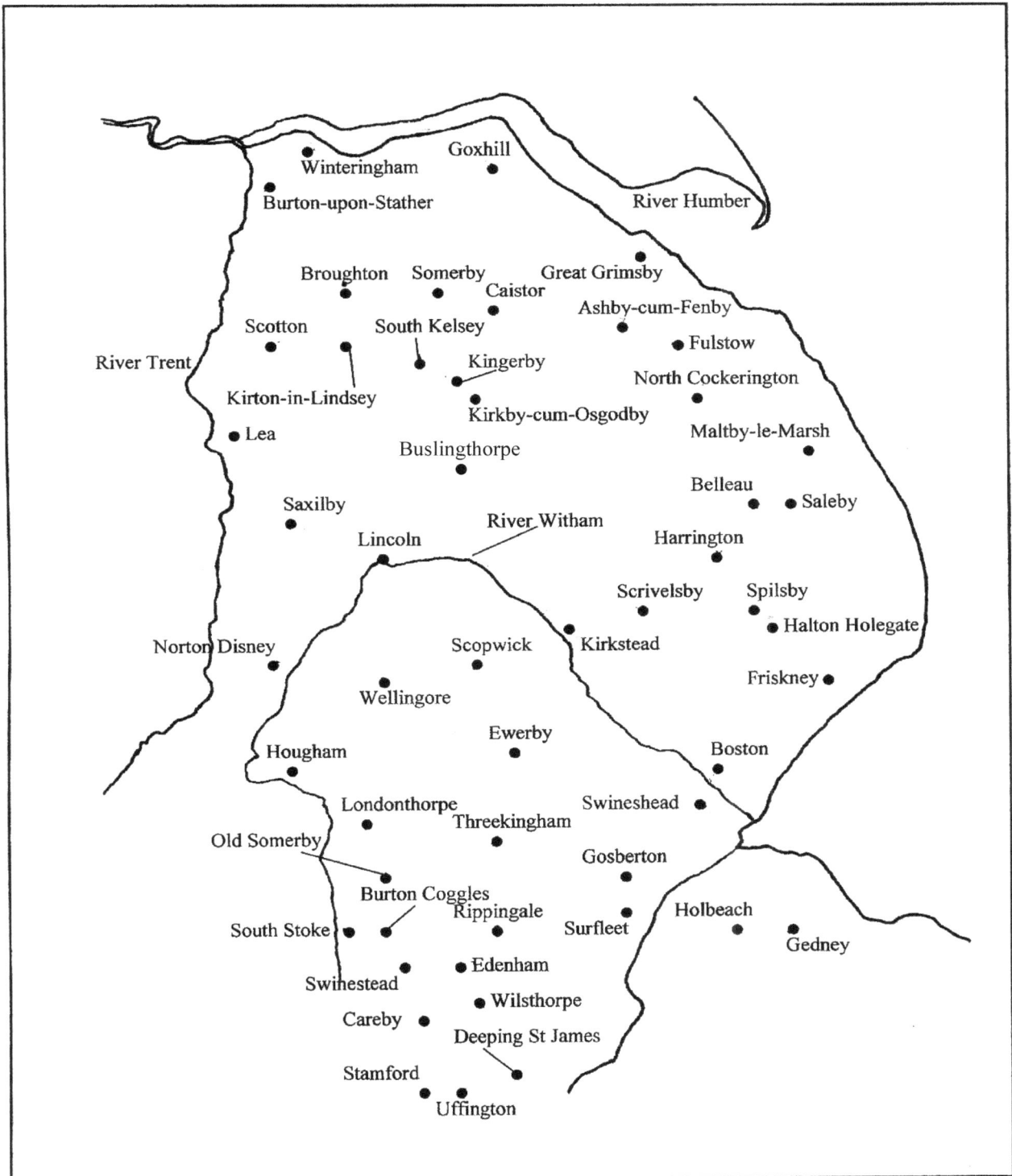

Map 2. Showing the locations of military effigies in Lincolnshire

It can be assumed, unless stated otherwise, that all shields are on the left of the figure, heater-shaped, and when described as suspended from a guige, the latter passes across the chest of the effigy from over the right shoulder, and the arms on the shield are associated with the effigy. There are two methods of representing chain mail, which are either by parallel rows of C's, alternate rows having the curves lying in the opposite directions, or realistically linked. Where no mail is represented, it was presumably rendered in applied gesso. The lengths of the figures have been taken from top of the head to the sole of the foot, or when fragments are concerned the length of the object.

No.1: KIRKSTEAD ABBEY c.1250

Current position: On the floor in the chapel of St. Leonard.

Condition: Badly preserved (including the loss of the legs below the knees and the top half of the shield).

Heraldry: None.

Posture: Straight-legged and sword-handling.

Description: Purbeck marble.[108] The head, slightly facing the right, is supported by a rectangular cushion, flanked by stiff-leaf foliage, which also occurs on the right side of the slab. The flat-topped cylindrical helm has a face-guard, represented with applied reinforcing strips in the form of a cross, of which the horizontal arms contain the vision-slits. The effigy wears a mail hauberk (parallel rows of C's, divided from the line below by a narrow band, so called "banded mail") with mitten gauntlets all made in one with the sleeves, and although the lower legs are missing, enough remains of the thigh to indicate that mail hose protected them. The shield is long; its point extends to the knee. The surcoat is open in the front with a short V-shape fork, held around the waist by a wide belt. The sword, partly drawn from its scabbard by the right-hand exposing the top of the blade, has a globular pommel, and short arched quillons. Since there are no traces of a sword-belt (which may have been painted on) it appears to be simply laid diagonally across the thighs, from left to right, with its lower part under the shield.

Length: 5ft 1in.

Identification: Unknown. The effigy almost certainly represents a benefactor of the Cistercian abbey, but as with the ever present problem of identifying benefactors, it is virtually impossible to make any conclusive attribution, particularly as the person may have been from outside the county. Albert Hartshorne comments that the effigy most likely represents "Robert de Tattershall who died 1212, a local lord who was thought to have built the Kirkstead chapel".[109] Robert de Tateshale's inquisition post mortem in 1249 records that he held various in manors in Lincolnshire, and was succeeded by his son Robert died 1273, also a powerful landowner in the

county and constable of the nearby castle of Tattershall. His son Baron Robert (died 1298) succeeded him.[110] Sir William Dugdale's, *Monasticon Anglicanum*,[111] records a number of Lincolnshire benefactors to the abbey who gave certain lands but to attribute this effigy to any of them would be pure speculation.

Commentary: This is the earliest military effigy in the county. It can be dated on the evidence of the stiff-leaf foliage carved on it, which is similar to that in the Chapter House of Lincoln Cathedral, dateable to c.1245-50,[112] as also to that on one of the capitals in St. Leonard's Chapel. The figure also has the very square shoulders that are found on some other effigies of the first half of the thirteenth century, for instance at Margam,[113] (Glamorgan) and Shepton Mallet[114] (1, 2), (Somerset).

The figure is one of the few that is shown wearing a flat-topped helm. Harry Tummers claims in his survey of thirteenth century effigies in England that it is closely related to products of the London workshops, seemingly justified on stylistic grounds:[115] for example, two comparable helm-wearing effigies at Twyford,[116] (Buckinghamshire) and Walkern,[117] (Hertfordshire), however this remains questionable. Much has been

Fig. 10. Kirkstead Abbey

---

[108] Firman, p. 31. The author is grateful to P. J. Lankester for this reference.

[109] Hartshorne 1883, p. 299.

---

[110] Moor 5, pp. 10-12.

[111] Dugdale, 1846, Vol. 5, p. 416.

[112] Tummers, p. 36.

[113] Preserved by Cadw in the stone museum adjacent to Margam Abbey.

[114] Fryer 1923-4, Plate LXXXIV, figs. 3-5.

[115] Tummers, p. 82.

[116] Tummers, Plate 37.

[117] Tummers, Plate 20.

Fig. 11. Kirkstead Abbey

Fig. 12. Scopwick

written about the so-called "banded-mail" represented on the effigy,[118] but there is no evidence to suggest that this is anything more than the carver's method of representing ordinary mail.[119]

No.2: Scopwick (Holy Cross) *c.*1250/1340

Fig. 13. Scopwick

Current position: In the southwest corner of the chancel.

Condition: Very worn and very difficult to determine details.

Heraldry: None.

Posture: Cross-legged (right over left; the left leg is straight), and appears that the right arm crosses the chest to the left shoulder.

Description: Limestone. The effigy is in sunken relief, in a tapering slab. Above the shoulders are deep sunken-spaces with two holes, which pass through the slab. These are for draining water and it is very likely that this effigy was used for exterior use, covering a stone coffin in the churchyard. A gable-shaped canopy appears to be over the head. No mail is present. It appears there is a long surcoat, worn to the calves.

Length: 5ft 1in.

Identification: Unknown.

Commentary: Because of the poor condition very little can be said, but it is very unusual. Firstly the legs are crossed very low and secondly the drainage holes above the shoulders seem to be a very rare occurrence. I have

not seen this feature on any other military effigy. However it does occur on male semi-effigial civilian monuments at Rothwell (Northamptonshire), Silchester church (Hampshire),[120] Tetbury (Gloucestershire), Garton-on-the Wolds (Yorkshire, East Riding)[121] and a female effigy, portrayed within a quatrefoil at Welby (Lincolnshire).

No.3: Gedney (St. Mary Magdalen) *c.*1270/1290

Fig. 14. Gedney

Current position: On a high tomb-chest at the east end of the south aisle

Condition: Very worn and mutilated (including the loss of the head, left leg, and right arm).

Heraldry: None.

Posture: Cross-legged (right over left). Due to the effigy's condition it is not possible to determine whether the right hand originally rested on the sword. The left arm appears to have been represented on the outside of the long shield, only the hand of which remains.

Description: Purbeck marble. The slab tapers from head to foot and is decorated around its concave edge with stiff-leaf foliage. Enough remains of the head to indicate that the coif was made all in one with the hauberk (no mail represented). Over the hauberk is a long surcoat, with the front of the skirt open, held around the waist by a narrow belt. On the neck is a circular brooch, a feature also found on effigies in the Temple Church (1) *c.*1250 (London) and at Merevale (1) *c.*1260/70

---

[118] Hartshorne 1883, p. 299.
[119] Blair 1972, pp. 35-36.

[120] Lankester 1995, pp. 8-11.
[121] I am grateful to Sally Badham for this reference.

Fig. 15. Gedney

Fig. 16. Swineshead

(Warwickshire). The plain sword-belt is of medium width, with its buckle lying to the right of the wearer.

Length: 3ft 7in.

Identification: Unknown. Holles recorded an effigy on a tomb-chest in the north aisle, underneath a window, which he identified as Fulko de Oyry.[122] It is very likely that the effigy, which he recorded is that under discussion, but why he attributes it to Fulko de Oyry is problematic. The only logical answer is that he observed heraldry, which is no longer visible. In 1212[123] Fulko de Oyry is recorded as tenant of Gedney, who in 1227 had a grant for a weekly market.[124] He died *c*.1282,[125] with his son John, dying in 1329.[126] Other individuals worth considering are Sir Giles de Gousel who in 1258 held land in Gedney, which upon his death in 1286 was passed to his son Peter.[127] Peter's son, Ralph who died in 1294, held the manor of Gedney.[128] The effigy at Goxhill may also represent a Gousel. Simon de Constable had a grant of free warren at Gedney in 1285,[129] also Robert Ros in 1297.[130]

Commentary: If we assume that the left arm was on the outside of the shield it is the second known occurrence in the country, as the effigy at Goxhill was traditionally thought to have this feature (see p. 25). The uniform stiff-leaf foliage on the edge is very unusual, given that in most cases it is represented in isolated areas, for example by the cushion or feet.

No.4: Swineshead *c*.1280/1300

Current position: Affixed upright against the north-east return of the exterior wall of a seventeenth-century house, built on the site of the former Swineshead Abbey.

Condition: Damaged (including the loss of the right arm and legs).

Heraldry: None.

Posture: Although the legs are missing the way the right leg is inclined would suggest that the figure was represented cross-legged (right over left), and the hands raised in prayer.

Description: Limestone. A rectangular cushion supports the head. Entirely in mail (realistically represented), wearing a separate coif with a plain circle, long-sleeved hauberk. On the left temple is a ventail tie. Underneath the hauberk, at the knee, appears to be the lower hem of the aketon. Over the hauberk is a long sleeveless surcoat, with the front of the skirt open, held around the waist by a narrow buckled-belt. The sword, in its scabbard, lies at an angle across the waist. It appears that the pommel is wheel-shaped and the quillons short, with their ends arched towards the blade. The sword-belt is plain and narrow, and hangs low across the waist.

Length: 4ft 3in.

Fig. 17. Swineshead

Identification: Unknown. Richard Gough remarks that traditionally the effigy represents the monk who poisoned King John and then states it more likely represents the founder of the Cistercian abbey, Robert de Grelley or Gresleb who held the manor in the time of Henry III.[131] The widow of Robert de Gresley held the advowson of the church at Swineshead in 1284.[132]

Commentary: As with the effigy at Kirkstead the shoulders are very square and the drapery straight and ridged, indicating a date within the thirteenth century and comparable to the statues on the Wells Cathedral West Front, which are, however, earlier in date than the effigy under discussion.[133] Harry Tummers remarks that the single cushion is mainly featured on thirteenth century effigies;[134] also *The Buildings of England, Lincolnshire*, dates the effigy to the late thirteenth century,[135] which on stylistic appearance seems very probable. Stylistically the effigy cannot be grouped with any other in the county or elsewhere.

---

[122] Holles, p. 179.
[123] *Book of Fees* 1, p. 193.
[124] *Cal. Charter Rolls* 1, p. 28.
[125] Moor 3, pp. 289-290. Brault 2, p. 327.
[126] Moor 3, pp. 289-290. Brault 2, p. 327.
[127] *Cal. Charter Rolls* 2, p. 12.
[128] Moor 2, p. 132.
[129] *Cal. Charter Rolls* 2, p. 308.
[130] *Cal. Charter Rolls* 2, p. 469.

---

[131] Gough 1, p. 190.
[132] Moor 2, p. 145.
[133] Illustrated in Hope and Lethaby 1905, plate L, facing p. 205, figs. N.66 & 64.
[134] Tummers, pp. 45-49.
[135] N. Pevsner and J. Harris, p. 738.

No.5: Burton Coggles (1) (St. Thomas Becket)
***c*.1280/1300**

Fig. 18. Burton Coggles (1)

Current position: Underneath an arched recess in the east wall of the porch.

Condition: Damaged, including the pommel (the feet and right spur are missing).

Heraldry: None.

Posture: Cross-legged (right over left) and handling his sword, his right hand on the hilt and the left on the scabbard.

Description: Limestone. The head is turned slightly to the left and is supported by a single rectangular pillow. Entirely in mail (parallel rows of C's), wearing a coif, long-sleeved hauberk with mitten gauntlets, mail hose, and gamboised cuisses (only the right is visible). A narrow plain circle originally encircled the brow, and is now only visible at the side of the temples. Over the hauberk is a long surcoat, with the front of the skirt open. The sword-belt is plain and of medium width, and has a rectangular D-shape buckle lying to the right of the wearer, the long loose end of the belt falling near the edge of the slab. It is attached to the scabbard by two laces joined by a sennet-knot that is partially concealed by the left hand. The quillons are straight. Above the knee is the lower hem of a longitudinally quilted aketon. The arm of the left spur is curved.

Length: 6ft 1in.

Identification: Unknown. Holles recorded two cross-legged effigies in the south wall of the south aisle,[136] however he did not record any inscription, or mention

whom they were thought to represent. The manor of Burton Coggles has infrequently been documented, but the problem of trying to identify the person commemorated by the effigy is complicated by the fact that there is another Burton near Lincoln, which is also mentioned in the records. The manor of Birton (*sic*) was held in 1242/3 jointly by Richard Torpel and Guy Wake for a quarter of a knight's fee,[137] with the overlord being Oliver de Eyncurt. In 1280, Master Ralph de Witham, received a charter for himself and his heirs for a weekly market and a yearly fair, at his manor at Birton.[138] In 1280 Sir John de d'Aubeny held 1½ knight's fee at Broughton and Little Stapleford.[139] In 1327 Robert de Byrton gave six selions of land in Birton.[140] Holles record heraldic glass in the church, consisting of the arms of Corville *Or, 3 chevrons, Vert*, and Wake *Or, 3 bars Gules, in chief 3 torteaux*.[141] I have not been able to identify the arms of Corville, but those of Wake can be identified with Baldwin, died 1282, and his son and heir, Baron John, died 1300.[142] It is possible that this effigy may represent one of the above mentioned.

Commentary: A boldly carved effigy, with heavy drapery folds and deep-cut mail; one of only four effigies in the county with parallel rows of C's mail. The others are at Kirkstead, Hougham, Holbeach and are probably from a workshop outside the county. As stated above, the rows of mail run around the coif and along the arms in the so-called 'Bristol Workshop' style,[143] a characteristic once considered being evidence that effigies with this feature are products of the 'Bristol workshop' or under their influence. This theory however is no longer tenable, but purely the sculptor's technique of depicting mail.

No.6: Goxhill (All Saints) *c*.1280/1300

Current position: Against the north wall of the chancel.

Condition: Damaged (including the loss of the base of the shield, right foot and foot-support).

Heraldry: None.

Posture: Cross-legged (right over left) and handling his sword.

Description: Limestone. The head supported by a rectangular pillow. The slab tapers from head to foot. Entirely in mail (realistically represented), wearing a coif with a circle set with small shields, long-sleeved hauberk with mitten gauntlets and hose. Over the hauberk is a long sleeveless surcoat, with the front of the skirt open, held around the waist by a belt of medium width with a square buckle lying in the centre of the wearer. Slung loosely around the waist is a plain narrow sword-belt with its buckle placed centrally. The method of attachment to the scabbard is concealed by the left hand. The sword is drawn by the right hand, exposing the blade

---

[136] Holles, p. 248.

[137] *Book of Fees* 2, p. 1048.
[138] *Cal. Charter Rolls* 2, p. 233.
[139] Moor 1, p. 8.
[140] *Cal. Charter Rolls* 4, p. 39.
[141] Holles, p. 248.
[142] Moor 5, pp. 131-133. Brault 2, pp. 440-441.
[143] Fryer 1923-4, p. 3.

Fig. 19. Burton Coggles (1)

Fig. 20. Goxhill

Fig. 21. Goxhill

while the left-hand holds the scabbard. The left quillon (only one remaining) is down-turned towards the blade. A small star-shaped rowel spur is on the left foot (only one remaining). On the left side of the slab, near the feet, are the remains of a cloaked figure.

Length: 6ft ¼in.

Identification: Unknown. The effigy is locally known as Lord Vere who held land in the parish.[144] Sir Simon de Vere held ½ knight's fee at Goushull (*sic*), died before 1 March 1294, and also another Simon Vere (unknown how they are related) held capital messuage in Gosehill (*sic*) died before 1316.[145] Also Sir Peter de Gousel, Inq. 1286 held a manor in Goxhill, which was then passed to his son and heir Ralph Goushill died 1294[146] aged 20, leaving a daughter and heir aged 6 months. Given the above information the effigy may represent one of them.

Commentary: A fine effigy in the way the sculptor has represented the folds of the surcoat, draping on the slab, being slightly underneath the legs, and the mail representation. It is one of a small number not to have the feet resting on an animal, but in all probability it has been destroyed. In the *Archaeological Journal* (1850) the Reverend John Byron published an article on the effigy commenting that the left arm originally hung over the shield, (as the village tradition stated) and the scabbard is made of mail. It is quite possible that the left arm did hang over the shield, similar to Gedney, but no traces of

the arms remain on the shield, and secondly the mail he remarked on the scabbard, is the left hand gripping it. However a woodcut published in 1825 illustrates the effigy in its present condition.[147] Claude Blair informs me that this is one of the earliest English effigies to depict rowel spurs.

No.7: Swinstead (St. Mary) *c*.1300

Fig. 22. Swinstead

Current position: Northwest corner of the nave.

Condition: Damaged (functional parts of the spurs missing).

Heraldry: None.

Posture: Cross-legged (left over right) and handling the sword; the right arm is bent across the chest so that hand can grip the dexter edge of the shield. The feet, which have the toes turned inwards, supported by a lion (mutilated).

Description: Limestone. The head, supported by a rectangular pillow, is flanked on the slab by two octofoils. The large shield covers the left side of the trunk and arm. Entirely in mail (realistically represented), wearing a separate coif with a plain circle, long sleeved hauberk with mitten gauntlets and hose. Over the hauberk is a long sleeveless surcoat, with the front of the skirt open, held around the waist by a narrow buckled belt, with the long end falling to the left of the wearer. The sword-belt is plain and narrow, with the shield concealing

---

[144] Byron, p. 387.
[145] Moor 5, p. 115. Brault 2, p. 437.
[146] Moor 2, p. 132.

[147] Greenwood, p. 33.

Fig. 23. Swinstead

Fig. 24. Ashby-cum-Fenby

the method of attaching the scabbard to the sword-belt. Only the lower part of the scabbard is visible: it ends in a D-shaped chape. Some red paint remains on the base of the slab.

Length: 5ft 8in.

Identification: Unknown. In 1288/89[1] William de Coleville (died 1300[2]) held a knight's fee at Swinstead, and in a charter dated 1311 the church of Swinstead was given to Drax Abbey for the soul of himself and his family.[3] In 1303 John de Coleville held a knight's fee, formerly held by William.[4] Given his patronage of the church and the date of death in relation to the stylistic appearance of the effigy, William seems to be a probable candidate for the effigy.

Commentary: A poor quality effigy, with clumsily carved mail. The effigy does however show a very rare feature that is the right hand grips the edge of the shield. The effigy in the county at Wilsthorpe *c.*1350 has this feature, also nationally at Iddesleigh[5] (Devon) *c.*1250 and Hungerford (Berkshire) *c.*1300. Holles between 1634-1642 recorded the effigy in the chancel[6] and H. K. Bonney, in 1845, said it was positioned upright.[7]

No.8: Ashby-cum-Fenby (St. Peter) *c.*1300/25

Fig. 25. Ashby-cum-Fenby

Current position: Behind iron railings against the south wall of the tower.

Condition: Damaged (including the shield which has lost its point, part of the top, dexter edges and the loss of the pommel, grip and right quillon).

Heraldry: None.

Posture: Cross-legged (right over left) with the hands raised in prayer and the feet resting on a lion looking to the effigy's right.

Description: Limestone. Supporting the head is a square pillow. Clad entirely in mail (realistically represented), wearing a separate coif with a plain circle, and ventail tie on the left of the temples, long sleeved hauberk with mitten gauntlets, the wrist encircled by narrow ties and hose. Over the hauberk is a long surcoat, with the front of the skirt open, held around the waist by a narrow buckled belt with a long loose end, and is decorated with bar-shape plaques. The plain sword-belt is of medium width, and has its buckle placed centrally, the loose end of the belt hanging below. The attachment of the belt to the scabbard is by two bands placed below the scabbard's mouth. A rather unusual feature is the tip of the scabbard being supported on the back of a crouched man. The left quillon is straight. On the right knee is a poleyn with a central keel. The prick spur on the left (only visible one) is slender and down-bent.

Length: 6ft 1in.

Identification: Unknown. Various people held land at Ashby-cum-Fenby; therefore identification of the effigy is uncertain. Thomas de Wydehaye was overlord in 1295,[8] who was last recorded in 1311.[9] Sir Adam de Welles who died 1311 held land, which was passed to his son Robert who in died 1320.[10] Also John de Saunton held land, who was last recorded in 1315.[11] William Garlond also in 1311.[12]

Commentary: The effigy is not of high quality when compared with other examples in the county, with very little undercutting. The folds of the surcoat are shallow and straight, which is uncommon on effigies in the county from this period, as most have deep-cut flowing folds. The most interesting feature is the small male figure supporting the scabbard. It is not purely a support for the scabbard, but a decorative feature, as the end of the surcoat could quite easily have been extended. Why it is there remains open to question. Another effigy with a scabbard support is at Somerby, which has a dog licking its hindquarters. The two effigies are not similar, Somerby being thirty years later and carved much more competently. The figure under discussion however, may be an earlier workshop product, which is also related to an effigy at Wymondham, (Leicestershire) (scabbard support broken) and Pickhill (North Yorkshire), both dated *c.*1300.

---

[1] *Cal. Inq. Edw. I* 2, p. 421.
[2] Moor 1, pp. 225-226 . Brault, 2, p. 115.
[3] Moor1, p. 226.
[4] *Feudal Aids* 3, p. 153.
[5] Tummers, Plate 7.
[6] Holles, p. 205.
[7] Bonney, p. 286.

[8] *Cal. Inq. Edw. I* 3, p. 154.
[9] *Cal. Patent Rolls Edw. II* 1, p. 352.
[10] Moor 5, pp. 174-175.
[11] Moor 4, p. 215.
[12] *Cal. Patent Rolls Edw. II* 1, p. 352.

No.9: Stoke Rochford (St. Mary & St. Andrew) *c*.1300/25

Fig. 26. Stoke Rochford

Current position: At the east end of the north chapel. The church guidebook mentions the monument came from the old demolished church of North Stoke.

Condition: Damaged and worn (including the shield which has lost its point and part of the top and dexter edges).

Heraldry: Effigy, shield: *three leopards, faces jessant-de-lis* [for Nevill] carved in relief.

Posture: Lying underneath a quilt with his wife within a sunken rectangle, only the upper body, and feet (resting on a lion towards the figure) are shown; the hands are raised in prayer.

Description: Limestone. Clad entirely in mail (realistically represented), wearing a separate coif, hauberk with mitten gauntlets and hose. On the left side of the coif are the remains of a circle, decorated with flower heads and with narrow straps around the wrists. Over the hauberk is a sleeveless surcoat.

Length: 6ft 2in.

Identification: There can be little doubt that the arms on the shield are those of the local branch of the Nevill family, *crusuly, three leopards faces jessant-de-lis*, though the crosses of the field are no longer visible, probably because they were painted on.[13] The effigy can be identified with relative certainty from the heraldry on

the shield as Sir John de Nevill. During the first quarter of the fourteenth century there are many references to Sir John de Nevill, however there was more than one family using that name, including the branch of Nevill from Hornby (Yorkshire). The John concerning us is recorded "of Stokes" therefore we can at least discover something about his military/political importance. John was the son of Stephen de Nevill (died 1303 a knight of Leicestershire and Rutland) who was recorded aged 40 in 1303[14] and was pardoned for homicide in the same year.[15] In 1304[16] he was granted free warren in his demesne land in Stokes (*sic*). He was Sheriff for Lincoln,[17] Justice of the Peace[18] and a Commissioner of Oyer.[19] In 1319[20] he was overseas on behalf of the king. His date of death is not known, but he probably died shortly after 1326,[21] when he was last recorded.

Commentary: A second related example from the same workshop can be seen at Careby (1). The symbolism of the husband and wife positioned underneath a quilt perhaps represents conjugal happiness.

No.10: Careby (1) (St. Stephen) *c*.1300/25

Fig. 27. Careby (1)

Current position: In the south aisle.

Condition: Very well preserved.

Heraldry: Effigy, surcoat: *two bars, in chief three scallops* [for Bayous] carved in relief.

Posture: Lying underneath a quilt, with his wife within a sunken cusped rectangle, and presumably is intended to represent a canopy of a tester of a bed, only the upper body and feet are showing; the hands are raised in prayer.

Description: Limestone. Two small human heads are on the top of the coping near the elbow of the knight and lady. Two rectangular pillows support the head; the upper positioned diagonally. Clad entirely in mail (realistically represented), wearing a separate coif, hauberk with mitten gauntlets. Around the brow is a circle, decorated with

---

[13] Lawrence 1946, p. 33.

[14] *Cal. Inq. Edw. I* 4, p. 97.
[15] *Cal. Patent Rolls Edw. I* 4, p. 172.
[16] *Cal. Charter Rolls* 3, p. 40.
[17] *Cal. Patent Rolls Edw. II* 2, p. 243.
[18] *Cal. Patent Rolls Edward I* 4, p. 524.
[19] *Cal. Patent Rolls Edw. II* 1, p. 426.
[20] *Cal. Patent Rolls Edw. II* 3, p. 416.
[21] *Cal. Close Rolls Edw. II* 4, p. 632.

Fig. 28. Stoke Rochford

Fig. 29. Careby (1)

flower heads, and with narrow straps around the wrists. Worn over the hauberk is a sleeveless surcoat. The shield is positioned at a 45° angle.

Length: life-size.

Identification: Suspirius de Bayous. The effigy is traditionally thought to represent Sir William Bayous who died *c*.1327,[22] but as will be mentioned below he did not die until after 1351. In 1282 Suspirius de Bayuse, who died 7 April 1292, held two knight's fee at Careby, formerly held by Baldwin Wake,[23] who died in 1282.[24] Suspirius's son and heir Sir William bore the arms; *gules, three bars argent, and in chief three escallops argent*, (Parliamentary Roll 1312) also; *gules, two bars and in chief three escallops argent* (First Dunstable Tournament 1308). He had a grant of free warren at Careby in 1303, was knighted in 1306 and was summoned as a knight of Lincolnshire to the Great Council of Westminster in 1324.[25] From 1341 until the last record of him in 1351,[26] he is recorded in the *Patent Rolls* as a collector of wool tax in Lincolnshire; therefore the effigy is much too late to be attributed to Sir William. The arms mentioned above are a derivative of the Wake family,[27] but this family does not appear to have held any land here after the death of Baldwin. Baldwin's effigy was formerly on the south side of the chancel at Market Deeping, and was destroyed before 1782.[28] The effigy is more likely to represent Suspirius de Bayuse, the monument being set up in the first decade of the fourteenth century.

Commentary: It is from the same workshop as Stoke Rochford but with cusped decoration framing the figures and vertical quilt folds. The monument was conserved prior to being displayed at the "Image and Idol: Medieval Sculpture"[29] exhibition at Tate Britain between 19th September-3rd March 2002. In 1845 H. K. Bonney recorded the effigy in the chancel.[30] At Welby (Lincolnshire) there is a semi-effigial monument of a lady in a quatrefoil, with a chrysom on top of a quilt, with the top folded down, and very likely from the same workshop.[31]

No.11: Burton Coggles (2) (St. Thomas Becket) *c*.1300/25

Current position: Underneath an arched recess in the west wall of the porch.

Condition: Damaged (the sword's pommel, grip, quillons and lower legs are missing).

Heraldry: None.

Posture: Cross-legged (right over left) with the hands raised in prayer.

Fig. 30. Burton Coggles (2)

Description: Limestone. Two rectangular pillows, the upper positioned diagonally, support the head. Above the head is a gablette decorated with three flying angels. Clad entirely in mail (realistically represented), wearing a separate coif, hauberk with mitten gauntlets, hose and gamboised cuisses. Around the brow is a circle decorated with flower heads and circular studs, and with narrow straps around the wrists. Over the hauberk is a long sleeveless surcoat, held around the waist by a narrow belt, with a long loose end decorated by bar-shape plaques, the front of the skirt is open. The sword-belt is of medium width, with the loose end passing behind the scabbard on the left, where it terminates in a riveted D-shape chape, and is attached to the scabbard by the diagonal thong method.

Length: 5ft 11in.

Identification: Unknown. Holles recorded the effigy in the south wall of the south aisle.[32] See Burton Coggles (1 p. 25) for references to the manor and who held it.

Commentary: The surcoat of this effigy has straight and shallow folds, and not the characteristic flowing drapery associated with Lincolnshire effigies. No shield or guige has been represented, which is very unusual.

---

[22] Lawrence 1946, p. 3.

[23] Moor 1, p. 62.

[24] Moor 5, p. 132.

[25] Moor 1, p. 63.

[26] Cal. Patent Rolls Edw. III 9, p. 180.

[27] For a discussion of arms related to those of Wake see, Blair and Goodall, pp. 47-48.

[28] Fryer 1924, p. 89.

[29] Deacon and Lindley, p. 45, illus. on pp. 62, 63, 66-7.

[30] Bonney, p. 281.

[31] I am grateful to Sally Badham for informing me of this monument.

[32] Holles, p. 248.

Fig. 31. Burton Coggles (2)

Fig. 32. Hougham

No.12: Hougham (All Saints) *c*.1306

Fig. 33. Hougham

Current position: West end of the north aisle.

Condition: Damaged and defaced (lower scabbard missing).

Heraldry: Effigy, surcoat & shield: *three bars* [for Bussy] carved in relief.

Posture: Cross-legged (right over left), handling the sword and the feet rest on a defaced dog.

Description: Purbeck marble. Two rectangular pillows support the head, with the upper positioned diagonally. The slab tapers from head to heel. Clad entirely in mail (parallel rows of C's, the curves arranged contrariwise in alternate rows, which, on the arms here, run longitudinally), wearing a separate coif, hauberk with mitten gauntlets and hose. Worn over the hauberk is a long surcoat, with the front of the skirt open. The pommel is disc-shaped and the quillons down-turned, towards the blade. The spurs are slender; their functional parts not shown.

Length: 5ft 11in.

Identification: Sir Hugh Bussy. He was the son and heir of Sir Lambert de Bussy (died 1293) and his wife, Elizabeth, inheriting her lands in Yorkshire, Hertfordshire, Leicestershire, Nottinghamshire and Lincolnshire in 1293.[33] He was summoned to serve against Scots in 1300 and 1301[34] and died in 1306 holding the manor of Hougham, leaving John (aged 24), son and heir.[35]

Commentary: This effigy, unusually for a Lincolnshire one, is not carved fully in the round. This is one of only four effigies in Lincolnshire, all from workshops outside the county, with the mail represented by the parallel rows of C's, the others being at Kirkstead Abbey, Burton Coggles (1) and Holbeach. Unusually, it has neither sword-belt or waist belt.

No.13: Gosberton (St Peter and St Paul) *c*.1310/20

Current position: Underneath a cusped ogee arch on a tomb-chest with the sides decorated with square flower heads, in the south wall of the south transept.

Condition: Well preserved (lower part of the scabbard is a replacement). The functional parts of the spurs are missing.

Heraldry: Effigy, shield: *St. George's cross*, rendered in paint (modern addition).

Posture: Cross-legged (right over left) with the hands raised in prayer and the feet supported by a lion looking towards the figure's left.

Description: Limestone. The head supported by two rectangular pillows, with the upper positioned diagonally. The figure is clad entirely in mail (realistically represented), wearing a separate coif, hauberk with mitten gauntlets, hose and poleyns with a central keel. Around the brow is a plain circle and with narrow straps around the wrists. Worn over the hauberk is a long sleeveless surcoat, with the front of the skirt open and held around the waist by a narrow buckled belt. The plain sword-belt is broad with its square buckle placed to the left of the wearer and is attached to the scabbard by the diagonal thong method. The pommel of the sword is "pod-shaped", the grip oval, with the broad right quillon down-turned; the left quillon represented behind the shield.

Length: 5ft 10in.

Identification: Unknown. The effigy has been recorded by a number of antiquaries, most notably by Charles Stothard who published a drawing he made in 1812.[36] Holles remarked that locally the effigy was known as a "Bolle".[37] In Richard Gough's *Sepulchral Monuments*, it is recorded in its present position and the author remarks, "This is vulgarly called Bolls. It more probably represents some of the Ryes, lords here from the time of Henry III to Edward III, perhaps Nicholas who died 1292".[38] I have not discovered any member of the Bolle family holding land in Gosberton in the late thirteenth century or the early fourteenth century. The inquisition of Sir John de Rye in 1280 recorded he held 2 knight's fees at Gosberton,[39] leaving a son and heir Sir Ranulph who held one twentieth of a knight's fee there.[40] Ranulph held many positions in Lincolnshire being sheriff in 1311, summoned to serve against the Scots, 1296, 1297, 1298, 1300 and 1301 and was last recorded living in 1312.[41] Ranulph's son and heir John,

[33] Moor 1, p. 170.
[34] Moor 1, p. 171.
[35] Moor 1, p. 171.

[36] Stothard, p. 65.
[37] Holles, p. 173.
[38] Gough 1, pt. 2, p. 190.
[39] Moor 4, p. 61.
[40] Moor 4, p. 162.
[41] Brault 2, p. 369.

Fig. 34. Gosberton

Fig. 35. Gosberton

was dead 26 November 1334.[42] Given the above evidence the effigy is more likely to represent Ranulph. A number of the antiquaries who visited the church recorded a lost alabaster effigy with an inscription to Nicholas Rey.[43]

Commentary: A Lincolnshire effigy from the same workshop as Londonthorpe and Scrivelsby (nos.17, 18).

No.14: Caistor (1) (St Peter and St Paul) c.1315

Fig. 36. Caistor (1)

Current position: On a modern plinth, under a pointed arched recess in the north wall of the north aisle.

Condition: Defaced (top edge of the shield broken).

Heraldry: None.

Posture: Cross-legged (right over left) with the hands raised in prayer and the feet supported by a lion looking towards the effigy's left.

Description: Limestone. Two rectangular pillows, the upper positioned diagonally, support the head. Clad entirely in mail (realistically represented), wearing a separate coif, hauberk with mitten gauntlets, hose and a globular poleyn on the right (only one represented) with a central keel. Around the brow is a plain circle. Worn over the hauberk is a long surcoat, with the front of the skirt open and held around the waist by a narrow buckled belt. The plain sword-belt is broad, and has its buckle placed centrally. The sword is mostly concealed behind the shield; only the right quillon, which is slightly down-

turned, and pommel are just visible. The spurs are slender with small pricks.

Length: 5ft 5in.

Identification: According to Holles the effigy was known locally as a member of the Houndon family[44] and the church guide states it is Sir William de Hundon who founded a chantry, in what is now the Lady Chapel. A William de Hundone is recorded holding land in Nottinghamshire and Derbyshire and was summoned to serve against the Scots in 1297,[45] but I have not been able to discover if he had any connection with Caistor or land held in Lincolnshire. In 1324 there was an order to Matthew Broun, escheator in the counties of Lincolnshire, Rutland and Northampton, to take into the king's hand the lands of the late Philippa, wife of the late John de Hundon, tenant in chief.[46] In 1331 John Hundon (see Caistor (2) p. 88) had a grant of free warren in Hundon,[47] which is in the parish of Caistor, and he is very likely the son of John; therefore, the effigy may commemorate either William or John who died before 1324.

Commentary: The effigy is from the same workshop as South Kelsey, and not of high quality.

No.15: South Kelsey (St Mary) c.1315

Current position: Under a low arched recess in the north wall of the nave.

Condition: Damaged and defaced (surface worn with the loss of the right quillon).

Heraldry: Effigy, shield: *two mullets* [for Hansard] carved in relief; presumably the third mullet, which cannot be seen, is covered by the wall.

Posture: Cross-legged (right over left) with the hands raised in prayer and the feet supported by a lion looking towards the effigy's left.

Description: Limestone. Two rectangular pillows, the upper positioned diagonally, support the head. Clad entirely in mail (realistically represented), wearing a separate coif, hauberk with mitten gauntlets, hose and globular poleyns with a central keel. Around the brow is a plain circle. Worn over the hauberk is a long surcoat, with the front of the skirt open and held around the waist by a narrow belt. The plain sword-belt is of medium width, and has its buckle placed to the left, the loose end falling beneath the tip of the shield. The attachment of the belt to the scabbard is not fully shown as the shield partially covers it. The sword has a wheel-shape pommel and an oval grip. The right quillon was originally turned-down; the left is not represented. The spurs are slender, of which the only one fully visible (left) has a large down-bent prick.

Length: 5ft 9in.

Identification: The effigy can be identified with relative certainty from the heraldry on the shield as Sir Robert Hansard. In 1297 he is recorded as holding the manor of South Kelsey for one knight's fee and was

---

[42] Moor 4, p. 162.
[43] Gough 1, pt. 2, p. 60. Monson quoting Dodsworth, p. 149.

[44] Holles, p. 90.
[45] Moor 2, p. 251.
[46] *Cal. Fine Rolls* 3, p. 311.
[47] *Cal. Charter Rolls* 4, p. 230.

Fig. 37. Caistor (1)

Fig. 38. South Kelsey

Fig. 39. South Kelsey

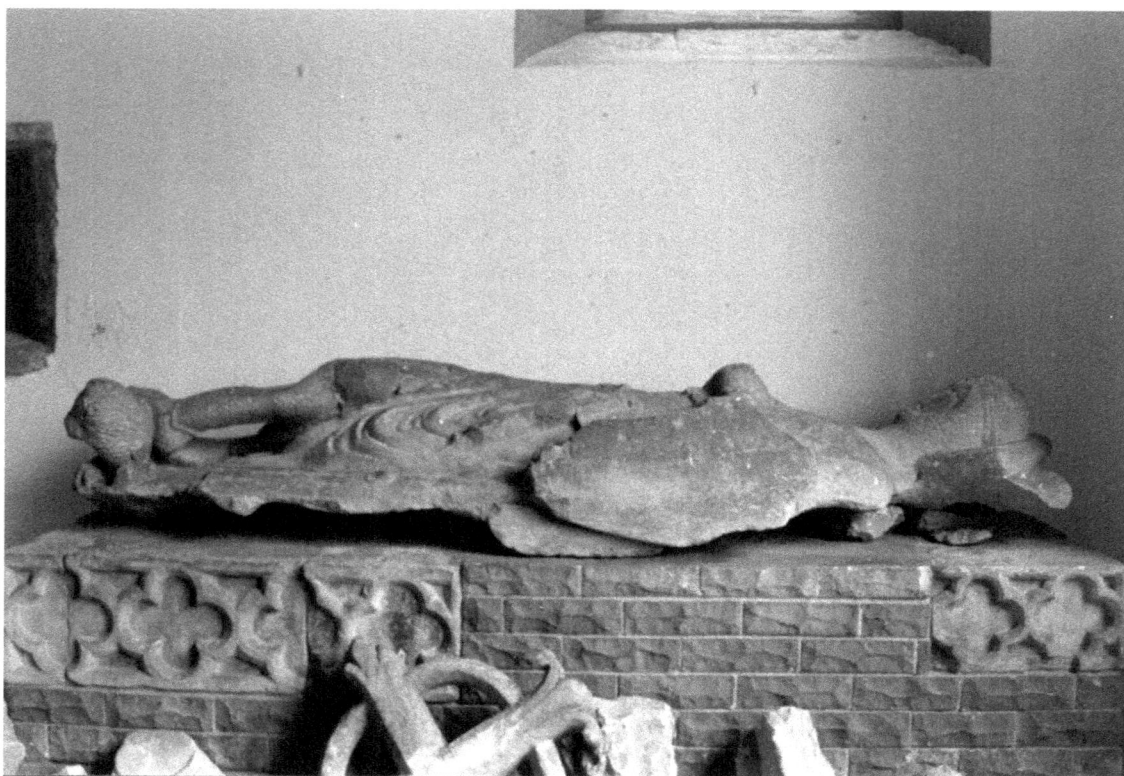

Fig. 40. Scotton

summoned to serve against the Scots in 1300 and 1301.[48] His arms; *gules, three mullets argent*,[49] have been recorded in various rolls: Galloway (1300), Stirling (1304), First Dunstable (1308) and Parliamentary (1312).[50] Rev. Henry Lawrence gives his date of death as 1313, but I have not been able to discover his source.[51]

Commentary: The effigy is not of high quality when being compared to others in the county, very little undercutting having taken place, and the appearance is fairly flat and ridged. A comparable effigy in the county, at Caistor (1), is also from the same workshop and is very likely a Lincolnshire product. In 1846 H. K. Bonney recorded the effigy positioned upright.[52]

No.16: Scotton (St. Genewys) *c*.1320

Fig. 41. Scotton

Current position: On a modern tomb-chest against the east wall of the south aisle.

Condition: Damaged (including the loss of the fingers, pommel, grip, quillons and lower scabbard).

Posture: Cross-legged (right over left) with the hands raised in prayer and the feet supported by a lion with its head turned away from the effigy.

Heraldry: None.

Description: Limestone. Two rectangular pillows, the upper positioned diagonally, support the head. Entirely in

mail (realistically represented), wearing a separate coif with a plain circle, hauberk with mitten gauntlets, hose and gamboised cuisses. Over the hauberk is a long sleeveless surcoat, with the front of the skirt open, held around the waist by a narrow belt, decorated with bar-shape plaques. The left arm passes through two enarmes of the shield. The sword-belt is of medium width, and is decorated with circular bosses and bar-shape plaques; its buckle placed centrally with the loose end of the belt passing behind the missing grip of the sword and falling near the point of the shield. The loose end has a D-shape chape. The scabbard is attached by the diagonal thong method.[53] On the left (only one remaining) is a slender down-bent prick spur.

Length: 6ft 7in.

Identification: Unknown. There is very little recorded regarding the manor of Scotton or who held it, therefore identification is difficult; however some accounts are worth mentioning. In 1242/43 both Simon de Vere[54] and John de Saunton[55] held small amounts of land, but the most prominent figure was Sir Philip de Nevill who held 1½ knights fee from Abbot de Burgo.[56] Philip had a grant of free warren in 1247[57] and died 1273.[58] His heirs are not known but a Philip de Nevill is recorded in 1303 holding 1¼ knights fee. Perhaps this Philip is also the same person selling wool in 1338[59] who sealed in 1346.[60]

Commentary: A Lincolnshire effigy, typically represented wearing the shield low on the left arm together with deeply cut folds of the surcoat. Comparable with other effigies in the county for instance: Kirton-in-Lindsey, Kingerby (1) and Wymondham (Leicestershire).[61]

No.17: Belleau (St John The Baptist) *c*.1320/25

Current position: Against the west wall of the nave, lying on a modern stone plinth.

Condition: Damaged (including the loss of the lower part of the scabbard and right leg).

Heraldry: None.

Pasture: Cross-legged (right over left), handling the sword and the feet supported by a lion looking towards the effigy's left.

Description: Limestone. Two rectangular pillows, the upper positioned diagonally, support the head, which is held by two headless angels. Clad entirely in mail, wearing a separate coif with a plain circle around the brow, the sleeve of the hauberk terminates at the wrist, with the hands bare. Clearly visible beneath the coif is an underlying bacinet with a central keel. It extends well down at the sides with a straight lower edge. Mail has not been represented on the coif, arms or legs; this was

[48] Moor 2, p. 179.
[49] College of Arms 1592, p. 47.
[50] Humphrey-Smith, p. 496.
[51] Lawrence 1946, p. 21.
[52] Bonney, p. 58.

[53] Blair 1993, p. 5.
[54] *B. F.* 2, p. 1086.
[55] *B. F.* 2, p. 1090.
[56] *B. F.* 2, p. 1079.
[57] *Cal. Charter Rolls* 1, p. 328.
[58] *Cal. Inq. Edw. 1* 2, p. 499.
[59] *Cal. Inq. Misc.* 2, p. 399.
[60] Moor 3, p. 257.
[61] Weatherley, p. 275.

Fig. 42. Belleau

presumably rendered in gesso, but no traces of this survive. Worn over the hauberk is a long surcoat, with the front of the skirt open and held around the waist by a narrow belt. The plain sword-belt is of medium width, and has its buckle placed centrally. The method of attaching the belt to the scabbard cannot be determined because of damage, but it was probably a ring. The fingers of the right hand hold the pommel and grip of the sword: the left hand holds the scabbard. The sword is cruciform with the quillons widening towards its oval grip; the pommel has a tall tang button. Covering the right knee (the only one fully visible) is a globular poleyn. A spur with a down-bent prick from a circular goad is on the left.

Length: 6ft ½in.

Identification: Unknown. Sir Adam de Welles (Baron), (*ob.* 10th September 1311[62]) held the manor and advowson of the church, his son and heir Robert also held the same lands as his father. He was born in 1297 and was dead on 29th August 1320.[63] Given the fact that the effigy is wearing an underlying bacinet, Robert would be a likely candidate.

Commentary: According to the church guide the effigy was found on the site of the Cistercian Priory of Greenfield. In 1847 H. K. Bonney recorded the effigy in the chancel.[64] The style of the lion supporting the feet of

the figure indicates that it is a product of the so-called "Westminster Workshop". It is of the type classified as "Westminster (B)" by the present author,[65] and has the following characteristics: an upturned, rather square face with pointed eyelids, Y-shaped nose, and downturned mouth; a body that is slightly slouched down on the crouched rear legs; a tail that is either represented running along the edge of the slab, parallel to it, (as here), or passing between the hind legs onto its back; and hair that is feather-like on the legs, and formed of incised S's set vertically on the mane. The refined style of the effigy, with its straight, ridged drapery, differentiates it from those produced locally, and is also characteristic of the "Westminster" workshop. A very closely related lion can be seen below the feet of the effigy of Aymer de Valence, died 1324, in Westminster Abbey, carved *c*.1325/30 and is very likely from the same hand. An interesting feature of this effigy is that he is handling his sword, and is the only example known to the author from this workshop. Claude Blair commenting in *Church Monuments*, suggests that shaped bacinets worn under or over the coif, shaped similar to the example worn by this effigy, seem first to appear in *c*.1315. The coif was then superseded *c*.1340-45 by a bacinet with an attached mail aventail. A number of military effigies are represented wearing an underlying bacinet, most notably those from the "Westminster Workshop": for instance at: Alderton (Northamptonshire), *c*.1315/20, Berrington (Shropshire) *c*.1320, Monk Sherborne (Hampshire) *c*.1320, Ashwell (Rutland) *c*.1315, Abergavenny (1) (Gwent) Sir John de Hastings died 1324/25,[66] Westminster Abbey (2) (London) *c*.1324 and Clifton-on-Teme (Worcestershire) *c*.1320/40.[67]

No.18 Fulstow (St Lawrence) *c*.1320/25

Current position: Upright against the east wall of the porch.

Condition: Very damaged (top of the shield broken; lower legs, quillons and lower scabbard missing).

Heraldry: None.

Posture: Cross-legged (right over left) with the hands raised in prayer and the feet supported by a lion.

Description: The type of material is unknown, as the effigy has been painted. Two rectangular pillows, the upper positioned diagonally, support the head. Clad in mail, wearing a separate coif with a plain circle, long sleeved hauberk with mitten gauntlets, the wrists encircled by narrow straps, and hose. The actual mail is not represented, and was presumably rendered in applied gesso. Worn over the hauberk is a long surcoat, with the front of the skirt open and held around the waist by a narrow buckled belt, with a long loose end falling to his right. The broad plain sword-belt, its rectangular buckle placed to the right, is attached to the scabbard by the diagonal thong method. The pommel is "wheel-shaped", and the grip oval. Over the knees are poleyns

[62] Moor 5, pp. 174-175.
[63] Moor 5, p. 175.
[64] Bonney, p. 93.

[65] Downing 1998, p. 22.
[66] Norman, p. 16.
[67] Downing 2002, Plate 19.

Fig. 43. Belleau

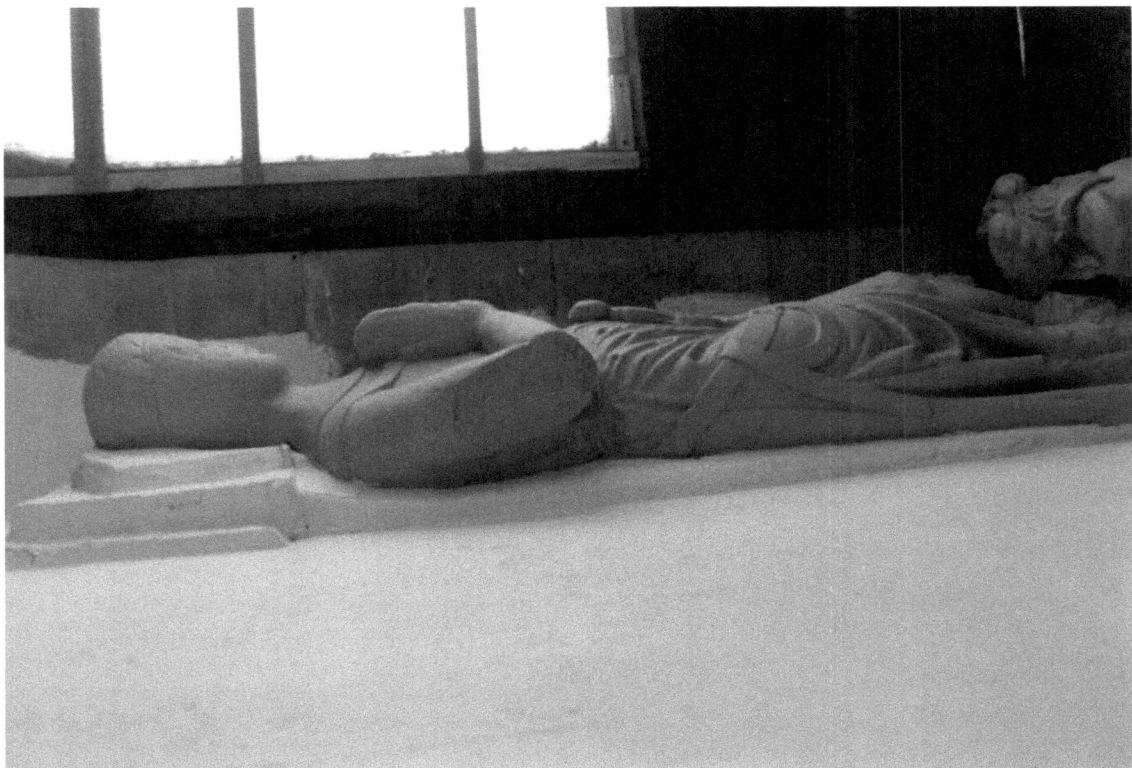

Fig. 44. Fulstow

Fig. 45. Fulstow

No.19: Londonthorpe (St. John Baptist) *c.*1320/25

Fig. 46. Londonthorpe

with a central keel; an incised circle is represented on either side of the central line.

Length: 5ft.

Identification: Unknown. At the end of the thirteenth century Philip de Marmyon, who died on 5th December 1291, held the manor.[68] In 1292 Roger de Lasceles (Baron) held two thirds of a knights fee at Fulstow,[69] of which in 1303 was held by Robert Tilliole,[70] also in the same year John Beek held half a knights fee formerly of Robert de Bolebek.[71] A writ on 27th June 1324 mentions William Beek of Fulstow,[72] who would be the most likely candidate for the effigy.

Commentary: In 1833 William Monson recorded the effigy thus;[73] "placed upright against the wall of the west end is the figure of a Knight Templar, his legs crossed, but broken at the bottom, his hands clasped, a shield on his arm. Over his head a lion couchant which may probably have been removed from under his feet. The whole is covered over with yellow ochre". The effigy bears resemblances to the effigies at Londonthorpe and Scrivelsby but in this instance no mail has survived. The baggy folds of the surcoat are deeply undercut around the thighs.

Current position: Under a pointed arched recess in the north wall of the north aisle.

Condition: Damaged and very broken (including the loss of the shield, lower legs, pommel and grip). The head is loose.

Posture: Cross-legged (right over left) with the hands raised in prayer.

Heraldry: None.

Description: Limestone. Two rectangular pillows, the upper positioned diagonally, support the head. The upper pillow was originally flanked by two supporting figures, presumably angels, of which the remains are just visible. Clad entirely in mail (realistically represented), wearing a separate coif, hauberk with mitten gauntlets and hose. Around the wrists are straps. The coif is tight-fitting, with a relatively deep cape covering the tops of the shoulders and around the brow is a circle decorated with flower heads, set at intervals. Over the hauberk is a long sleeveless surcoat, with the front of the skirt open, with a narrow belt around the waist. A guige passes over the right shoulder. The plain sword-belt is of medium width, and has a D-shape buckle placed to the left of the wearer. The loose end of the belt passes behind the sword's grip on the left, falling near the edge of the slab. The scabbard is attached by the diagonal thong method. The quillons, so far as one can judge from what remains of them, appear to have been down-turned. The globular poleyns have a central keel.

Length: 5ft 1in.

[68] Moor 3, p. 121.
[69] Moor 3, p. 17.
[70] *Cal. Inq. Edw. III* 5, p. 48.
[71] *Feudal Aids* 3, p. 146.
[72] *Cal. Inq. Edward II* 6, no. 524.
[73] Monson, p. 149.

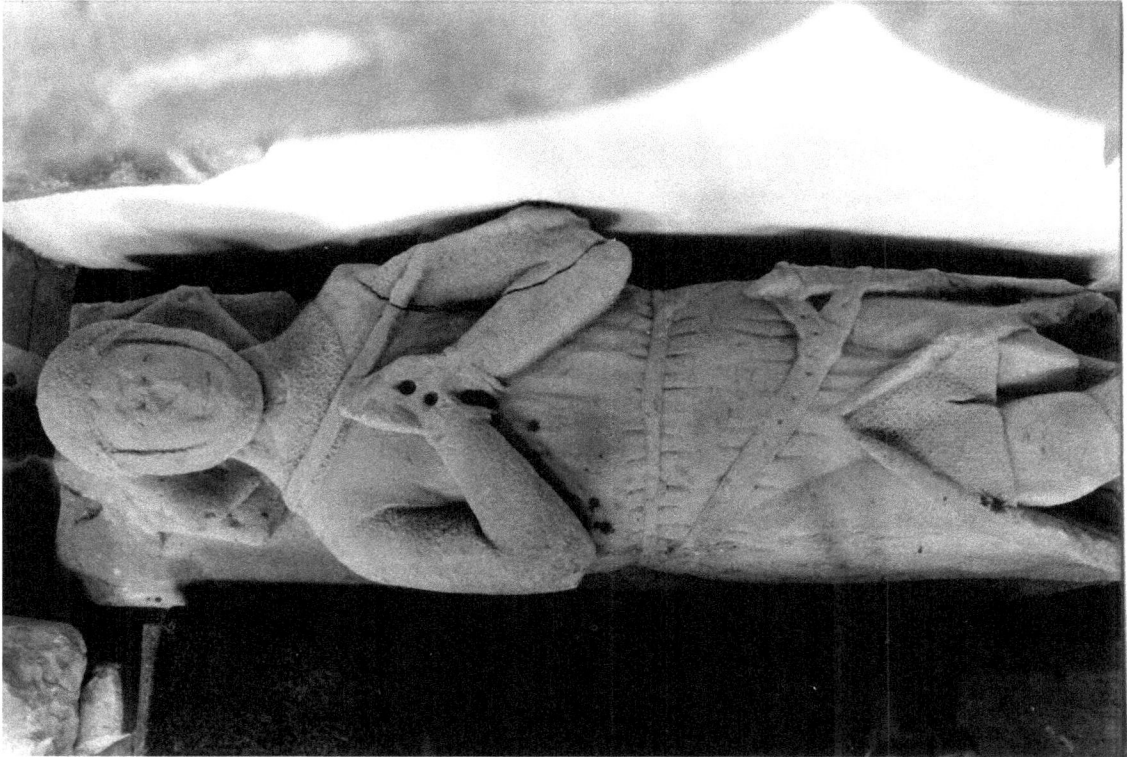

Fig. 47. Londonthorpe

Fig. 48. Old Somerby

Identification: Unknown. In 1242/3 Richard de Huwelle was tenant of Londonthorpe, and in the same year Nicholas de Lunderthorp held one part of a knight's fee.[74] In 1306 Hugo de Stowe held the part formerly held by William fitz Walter.[75] In the same year Nicholas de Stowe, son of Hugo of Lunderthorp, received a pardon.[76] The surname of Lunderthorpe, or some variant, appears frequently in the various rolls, especially Simon who is recorded in an inquisition 1297 holding Wellingore manor.[77] He was sheriff of Lincolnshire 1318/1319[78] and commissioner of gaol delivery in 1326,[79] which is when he is last recorded. Given the high position that Simon held, he would be a suitable candidate for the effigy.

Commentary: Holles recorded the effigy in its current position.[80] It is very likely from the same workshop as Scrivelsby.

No.20: Old Somerby (St Mary Magdalen) *c*.1320/25

Fig. 49. Old Somerby

Current position: Against the north wall of the chancel.

Condition: Damaged (including the loss of the squire's head and functional parts of the spurs; shield broken).

Fig. 50. Old Somerby. Detail of horse footrest

Heraldry: None. Holles recorded, *or, a chevron between ten crosses botony sable* [for Sleyt].[81]

Posture: Cross-legged (left over right) with the hands raised in prayer and the feet supported by a saddled kneeling horse.

Description: Limestone. Two rectangular pillows, the upper positioned diagonally, support the head. To the left of the horse is a kneeling figure, which presumably represents an attendant esquire. Clad entirely in mail (realistically represented), wearing a separate coif, hauberk with fingered gauntlets, hose and poleyns with a central keel. Around the brow is a plain circle. Worn over the hauberk is a surcoat, its hem falling below the knees, with the front of the skirt open and held around the waist by a narrow belt. The plain sword-belt is of medium width, and has its buckle placed centrally, its loose end passes behind the grip to the left, looping around the rear portion, and is attached to the scabbard by the diagonal thong method. The pommel is wheel-shaped and the grip tapering towards the quillons, which are straight.

Length: 6ft 4in.

Identification: Henry Sleyt? The coat of arms recorded by Holles was borne by the Sleyt family,[82] who held land at Old Somerby and in 1303 Henry de Sleyt is recorded tenant.[83] It is very likely he had two sons, Roger and John, with both being recorded together in 1330,[84] and John in 1346.[85]

Commentary: In 1839 William John Monson recorded the effigy in its present position.[86] The effigy is not of very good quality, and the carving has little undercutting. The lower folds of the surcoat are straight and ridged. Clearly the most interesting feature is the saddled-horse footrest, a unique feature, but its significance is not certain. Two other three dimensional monuments with representations of war horses are recorded in Exeter Cathedral[87] where an esquire holds the horse's reins and at Minster-in-Sheppey, (Kent),[88] where only the head is seen on the right of the slab. Both are dated to *c*.1330.

[74] *Book of Fees* 2, p. 1038.
[75] *Feudal Aids* 3, p. 161.
[76] *Cal. Patent Rolls Edw. I* 4, p. 481.
[77] *Cal. Inq. Edw. I* 3, p. 317.
[78] Moor 3, p. 83.
[79] Moor 3, p. 83.
[80] Holles, p. 246.

[81] Holles p. 201.
[82] Woodcock, Grant and Graham, p. 328.
[83] *Feudal Aids* 3, p. 171.
[84] *Cal. Patent Rolls Edw. III* 1, p. 481.
[85] *Feudal Aids* 3, p. 225.
[86] Monson, p. 331.
[87] Situated in the north wall of the north aisle at the east end.
[88] Stothard, p. 38.

Also at Hampstead Norris (Berkshire), is a mid thirteenth century Purbeck marble coffin lid, representing a mounted knight.

No.21: Rippingale (1) (St. Andrew) *c*.1300/25

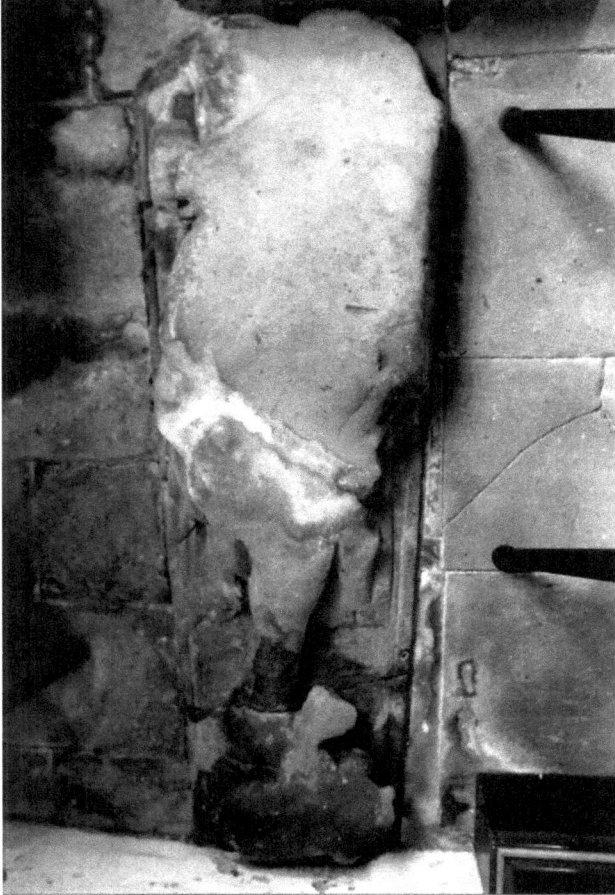

Fig. 51. Rippingale (1)

Current position: On the floor at the east end of the south aisle.

Condition: Extremely mutilated (including the loss of the head and right lower leg).

Heraldry: None.

Posture: Cross-legged (right over left).

Description: Limestone. No mail visible. The effigy wears a long surcoat, with its hem falling to the calf. What remains of the shield is on the left, and the waist-belt and sword-belts are on the right hip.

Length: 4ft 8in.

Identification: Unknown. In 1282 Sir John Gobaud held one knight's fee at Rippingale, who died in 1310.[89] His son and heir Guy who died in 1314 held land here together with his son Sir John (recorded as overlord in 1321), who was still living in 1324.[90] Sir Adam Fitz John was a minor in 1298,[91] recorded holding the manor of Rippingale in 1310 and 1318,[92] and was a summoned as a knight for Lincolnshire to the Great Council of

Westminster in 1324.[93] His date of death is not known. In 1302 Sir Roger de Pedwardyn held 1½ knights fee at Rippingale.[94] Due to the incomplete state of the effigy no conclusion can be drawn as to an attribution.

Commentary: Because of the effigy's mutilated condition no meaningful commentary on it is possible. However in 1831 William John Monson visited the church and recorded "On the north side of the Communion Table is the effigy of a knight in mail, completely armed, with his legs crossed, his head resting upon a helmet, and his feet upon a lion. It is in tolerable preservation, and the rings of the mail are plainly to be distinguished. Tradition gives it to one of the Brownlow family". It is quite possible that this is the effigy that he recorded: the presence of a helm under the head would point to a date after *c*.1330.

No.22: Saleby (St Margaret) *c*.1320/25

Current position: Under a low pointed arched recess in the north wall of the chancel.

Condition: Very well preserved.

Heraldry: Effigy, shield: *a cross engrailed, in the first quarter a martlet* [for Hardeshull] carved in relief. Canopy; on either side are these arms rendered in paint (modern); (right), *a chevron between an orle of martlets*; (left), *a cross engrailed, in the first quarter a martlet*.

Posture: Cross-legged (right over left) with the hands raised in prayer and the feet supported by a lion looking towards the effigy's left.

Description: Limestone. The effigy lies on a bed of leaves. Two rectangular pillows, the upper positioned diagonally, support the head. The effigy is clad entirely in mail (realistically represented), wearing a separate coif, hauberk with mitten gauntlets and hose. Around the brow is a plain circle and narrow straps around the wrists. On either side of the head are two loose figures, which belong to this monument. Worn over the hauberk is a long surcoat, with the front of the skirt open and held around the waist by a narrow buckled belt, decorated with bar-shaped plaques, its long loose end has a chape and falls to the hem of the surcoat on the right. The left arm passes through an enarme of the shield. The plain sword-belt is of medium width, and its rectangular buckle placed to the left, two small rivets secure the buckle to the short portion of the belt from the scabbard. The loose end passes behind the grip of the sword, falling to the edge of the slab on the left; it has a D-shape chape secured to the belt by two small rivets. The scabbard is attached by the diagonal thong method. The pommel is wheel-shaped with the visible face shaped like a truncated cone; the grip is of hexagonal section and the quillons slightly curve towards the blade. On the tip of the scabbard is a D-shape chape decorated with two small quatrefoils. On the right knee (the only one fully visible) is a poleyn with a tall domed cup. Small rivets surround the base of the cup, which presumably indicate that the poleyn is attached to the lower edge of the cuisse. The spurs are slender with the only one remaining (left) having a rowel.

---

[89] Moor 2, p. 121.
[90] Moor 2, p. 122.
[91] Moor 2, p. 42.
[92] Moor 2, p. 42.

[93] Moor 2, p. 42.
[94] Moor 4, p. 28.

Fig. 52. Saleby

Fig. 53. Saleby

Along the edges of the slab are small plain shields hanging off pegs, eight are represented on the front, also on each corner are human heads. Some light blue paint remains on the pillows and the grip of the sword.

Length: 5ft 11in.

Identification: The effigy can be identified from the heraldry on the shield as Sir William de Hardeshull, who married Juliana, daughter and heir of Sir Eustace de Hatch (died 1306),[95] a Wiltshire and Dorset knight who became one of his men-at-arms, adopting the Hatch coat-of-arms differenced with a martlet in preference of his father's.[96] His son John however reverted to his grandfather's arms; *a chevron sable surmounted by a orle of martlets gules*.[97] William de Hardeshull held the manor of Saleby jointly with his wife for 1 knight's fee, and had a licence for a market there in 1285.[98] He was summoned to serve against the Scots in 1300, 1301, died in 1303[99] and was the son and heir of John de Hartshill, (died 1274) of Hartshill, Warwickshire.[100]

Commentary: The representation of the effigy lying on a bed of leaves is only found on one other figure, so far as I know, that of Sir Robert Neville died 1318 at Brancepeth (Durham).[101] The arrangement of the small shields along the edge of the slab is also very unusual. It shows stylistic similarities to Caistor and South Kelsey, but is more competently carved, with more attention to detail. According to the church guide, it was once in the south side of the chancel, covered in whitewash; the latter was removed when the church was rebuilt in 1850. As mentioned above some fragments of paint survive, but much more was present, when in 1910 the Architectural & Archaeological Society of Lincolnshire visited the church, and recorded that the outer surface of the surcoat was painted red; the inner green and the waist-belt white with blue fretwork with a black edge.[102]

No.23: Scrivelsby (St Benedict) *c*.1320/25

Current position: On a modern stone plinth in the north aisle.

Condition: Damaged (including the loss of the scabbard and lower legs).

Heraldry. None.

Posture: Cross-legged (right over left) with the hands raised in prayer.

Description: Limestone. Two rectangular pillows with tasselled corners, the upper positioned diagonally, support the head. Clad in mail (realistically represented), wearing a separate coif, hauberk with mitten gauntlets with narrow straps around the wrists, hose and poleyn. Around the brow is a plain circle. Worn over the hauberk is a long surcoat, with the front of the skirt open. Around

Fig. 54. Scrivelsby

the waist is a narrow buckled belt with a long loose end falling to the right of the wearer. The plain sword-belt is broad, and has its square buckle placed centrally, the long loose end terminating in a D-shape chape, and is attached to the scabbard by the diagonal thong method. The sword is cruciform, with a wheel-shape pommel and tapering grip. The long tapered right quillon is slightly down-turned, whereas the left is represented behind the shield.

Length: 4ft 10in.

Identification: Unknown. Traditionally the effigy is thought to represent a member of the Marmyon family. Sir Philip de Marmyon was a large estate holder in various counties of England, including Lincolnshire[103], who held a knight's fee at Scrivelsby in 1252, and continued to hold the manor until his death in 1291.[104] His heirs were his daughters and granddaughter. Apparently it was his third wife Mary (died 1312), who held the manor as dower.[105] Her daughter Joan inherited her mother's estate and held the manor with her first husband Sir Thomas de Ludelowe (died 1314)[106] and second husband Henry Hillari.[107] Sir Thomas de Wylughby was overlord in 1317[108] and in 1318 Sir Robert de Wilughby held the manor from him.[109] Given the number of people holding the manor during the time

---

[95] Brault 2, p. 218.
[96] Coss 2003, p. 60.
[97] Brault2, p. 218.
[98] Moor 2, p. 187.
[99] Brault 2, p. 218.
[100] Brault 2, p. 218.
[101] Blair, C. H. Hunter, p. 22, Plate 5, figs. 2, 3. The effigy survived a huge fire on 16th September 1998.
[102] *Associated Architectural Societies Reports and Papers*, Vol. 30, pt. 2, p. 338.

[103] Moor 3, p. 121.
[104] Moor3, p. 121.
[105] Moor 3, p. 121.
[106] Moor 3, p. 55.
[107] Moor 3, p. 55.
[108] Moor 5, p. 199.
[109] Moor5, p. 198.

Fig. 55. Scrivelsby

Fig. 56. Kingerby (1)

span when the effigy was probably made, certain identification is impossible.

Commentary: An effigy from the same workshop as Londonthorpe and Gosberton (nos.17, 20).

No.24: Kingerby (1) (St. Peter) *c.*1325

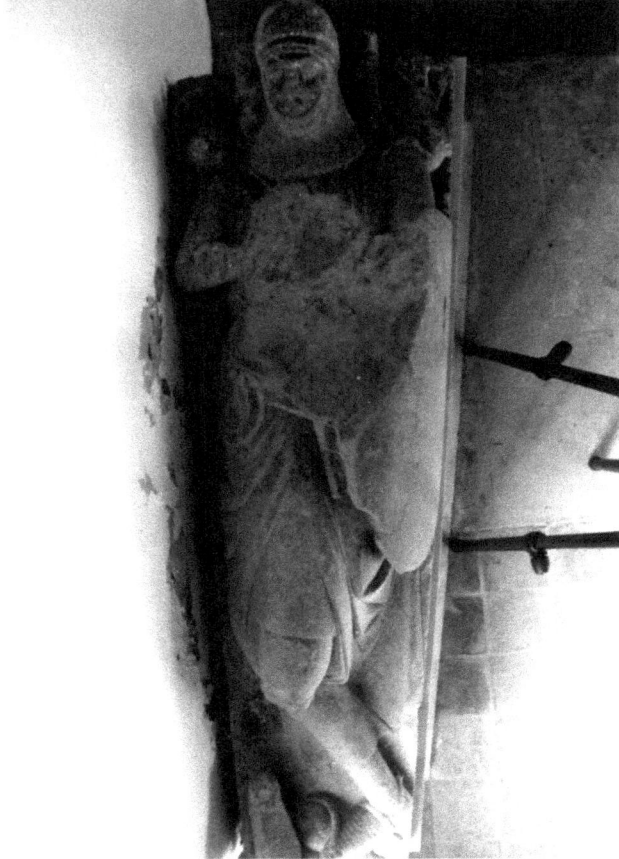

Fig. 57. Kingerby

Current position: On a tapering slab, which now rests on a modern limestone plinth against the south wall of the south aisle. In 1982 the church was vested in the Churches Conservation Trust, which undertook the conservation of the effigy.

Condition: Damaged (hands, left leg, lower scabbard and parts of the shield are missing).

Heraldry: Tomb-chest: south side, at either end, presumably once forming part of the original tomb-chest, each set within a quatrefoil; (left) *a maunch* [for Hastings] (right) *a chevron between three martlets* [for Argam].

Posture: Cross-legged (left over right) with the hands originally raised in prayer, and the feet, left resting on a head-less animal, and the right on a mutilated creature.

Description: Limestone. A rectangular pillow supports the head and on either side are sleeping puppies, a very unusual feature. Entirely in mail (realistically represented), wearing a separate coif with a plain circle, hauberk, hose and gamboised cuisses. Judging from the shape of the coif above the circle, there is an underlying spherical bacinet. Over the hauberk is a long sleeveless surcoat, with the front of the skirt open, held around the waist by a narrow belt (only visible on the right) its loose

end hangs directly below, passing behind the sword-belt. The sword-belt (only visible on the right) is plain and of medium width, the loose portion is looped back over the belt with the end falling to the right of the effigy. The prick spurs are slender and down-bent.

Length: 6ft 4in.

Identification: Unknown. The church guide states that the effigy is thought to represent a member of the Disney (or d'Isini) family who held the manor until the fifteenth century. Holles recorded two effigies, both cross-legged, and lying on a tomb-chest decorated with five heraldic shields, however only the cross-legged effigy under discussion survives: "(1) *a chevron between 3 birds*. (2) *three leopards passant* (Amundeville). (3) *three leopards passant with a label of three* (Amundeville). (4) *a maunch*. (5) *barruly of fourteen pieces, three chaplets* (Greystoke) [Fitzralph]".[110] A number of people held land in Kingerby at the period when the effigy was made, so identification is problematic, also the pedigree of the Disney family is very difficult to establish as they were a large family, with monuments both at Kingerby and Norton Disney (see p. 75). There were also junior branches of the family, which were recorded in documents as "of Dirrington" (Dorrington is twelve miles west of Norton Disney) and "of Fosham" (Yorkshire, East Riding).[111] A study published in 2002 by Hugh Disney on the Disney family has revealed much information on this family from the earliest documented evidence in 1150 up to 1461. To complicate matters, between *c.*1240-1461 seven heads of the family had the Christian name William.[112] What is evident in the fourteenth century is that the head of the family was known as "Lord of Kingerby" and in 1331 there were two Lords Disney, father and son.[113] Disney states that out of ten charters issued between 1329-1358, nine were sealed at Kingerby and only one at Norton Disney, therefore he believes that the power of the family was at Kingerby and not Norton Disney during this period.[114] It is worth mentioning how the Disneys became in possession of Kingerby. In the middle of the thirteenth century Sir William Dive had interest at Kingerby and elsewhere in the county. He was married to the only daughter of Peter Amunderville before 1233. They had three children, John, Elizabeth and Joan. Upon John's death in 1293, Joan and Elizabeth were his co-heirs, aged at this time between 30 and 40. Elizabeth who also died in 1293 was first married to Sir John D'Aubeny, and secondly to Sir Lambert de Bussy who left a son Sir Hugh de Bussy.[115] Joan was married first to Alexander Kyrketon and secondly to Ralph de Trehampton, both before 1288.[116] Joan married her third husband Adam de Swillington of Yorkshire in 1312; he died shortly after 1328[117] and was recorded in the same year as having a grant of free warren

---

[110] Holles, p. 68.
[111] Disney, pp. 55-57, 70.
[112] Disney, p. V.
[113] Disney, p. 63.
[114] Disney, p. 96.
[115] Moor 1, p. 298.
[116] Disney, pp. 50-51.
[117] Brault 2, p. 408.

and Kingerby.[118] Some sources/pedigrees state that Joan Dive's first husband was William (3) Disney who died in 1316, however Hugh Disney believes this is incorrect as she was would have been married three times before William died; therefore he believes that the Disneys were not related to the Dives, but Joan sold her land to William (4) (known in documents as "the elder" Lord Kingerby), before 1329, and that William (3) was married to another person called Joan.[119] William (2) apparently inherited Norton Disney in 1265 and died in *c.*1299, he was married to Constance,[120] his son William (4) (the elder), died 1339, and was married to Constantia. William (5) (known in documents a "the younger" Lord Kingerby), inherited his father's lands in 1339 and died in 1349, was possibly married to Eustachia, daughter of Lord Grey of Ruthin.[121] This William also had a son called William (6), who died in 1361 and was married to Joan daughter of Nicholas de Langford and a semi-effigy commemorates her, he is also commemorated at Norton Disney. There are records of William's (2) sons, John, in 1303 and 1346 holding land at Croxton (12 miles north of Kingerby).[122] The inquisition to William de Cateby death in 1322 records that he held land, which he then rented to John de Bussy.[123] The effigy cannot represent Sir Hugh Bussy given he is commemorated by the effigy at Hougham (see p. 33) and his son John was still alive towards the middle of the century, which would discount him also. It is unlikely it represents Adam de Swillington as his principal lands were in Yorkshire. At Norton Disney there is an indent of a brass, originally representing a cross-legged knight, which has been dated *c.*1340.[124] If this is the case the brass can only represent William (4), who died in 1339, which would mean that the effigy under discussion could represents his father William (3), who died in 1316 and the lost cross-legged Kingerby effigy was perhaps to William (2) who died in 1296. The effigies and the tomb-chests have been moved around the church, very likely on a number of occasions, and we do not know for certain how they were originally arranged, especially the heraldry as it may have been collected together, and it is difficult to assign the heraldry recorded by Holles on the sides of the tomb-chest to families who may have been connected with the Disneys. If William (5) was married to Eustachia daughter of Roger de Grey, Lord of Ruthin, her mother may have been Elizabeth Hastings,[125] which would account for the *maunch*. The *three leopards passant* recorded by Holles, which R. G. Cole attributed to Amundeville, is doubtful, as Amunderville arms are *azure fretty argent, a fess gules* [Richard Amundeville *c.*1255].[126] The earliest recorded arms for Disney *c.*1340 is given as; *argent three lions passant gules.*[127]

---
[118] *Cal. Charter Rolls* 4, p. 68.
[119] Disney, pp. 51-52.
[120] Disney, pp. 39-48.
[121] Disney, pp. 76-84.
[122] *Feudal Aids* 3, pp. 206, 216.
[123] *Cal. Inq. Edw. II* 6, p. 208.
[124] Binski 1987, fig. 130.
[125] *Complete Peerage* 6, p. 153.
[126] Humphrey-Smith, p. 367.
[127] Chesshyre and Woodcock, p. 283.

Commentary: The effigy is comparable to the effigy at Kirton-in-Lindsey and Rippingale (2) with the folds of the surcoat represented deeply cut around the thighs, whereas the hem is caught underneath the lower legs. It must be stated that the presence of the two puppies asleep at the pillow is typical of the individuality of the Lincolnshire carvers and is evidence of a local workshop.

No.25: Kirton-in-Lindsey (St. Andrew) *c.*1325

Current position: On a modern brick tomb-chest, underneath an arch between the nave and south aisle.

Condition: Damaged and surface very mutilated (including the loss of the left leg).

Heraldry: None.

Posture: Cross-legged (right over left), originally handling the sword, the right foot (turned on its side) rests on a dragon.

Description: Limestone. Supporting the head is a rectangular pillow. The slab tapers slightly from head to foot. Entirely in mail (realistically represented), wearing a separate coif with a plain circle, long sleeved hauberk, hose and gamboised cuisses. Over the hauberk is a long surcoat reaching to the calf; edging the right armhole is a plain border. Rather unusually the shield is suspended at hip level. To the right of the waist are two separate portions of belts. One appears to be the loose end of the waist-belt and the second is slightly diagonal, presumably the sword-belt. The prick spur is slender and down-bent.

Length: 5ft 10in.

Identification: Unknown. In 1601 Francis Thynme recorded an inscription, written in Anglo-Norman French:[128] CY GIST EMVIN GASCELIN SEYNUR DI MARHAM MONS DE RI ALME DIEV AIT MERCYS PATER NOSTER, which translates:[129] "Here lies Edmund Gascelin formerly Lord of Marham, on whose soul may God have mercy". Unfortunately Thynme did not state where he recorded the inscription or for that matter on what. Sally Badham has informed me that he got his notes muddled-up as the inscription he records was that of a brass (now lost), formerly at Peterborough Cathedral; he must have mistakenly labelled the note Kirton instead of Peterborough Cathedral. Dugdale, who also recorded the inscription at Peterborough, identified the brass to Sir Joscelin de Marham, however Nigel Saul's research attributes it to Sir Edmund Gascelin who held Marham (Northamptonshire) and died 1307.[130] The church guide remarks that the effigy may represent Gilbert Waterhouse, from the reign of Henry III. Burke's *General Armory* mentions Sir Edward Waterhouse, of Kirton in Lindsey, *temp* Henry III, but gives no reference. I have not been able to discover any information of this family in Lincolnshire.

Commentary: The effigy is very likely a product from one of the workshops operating in the county, comparable in style to the effigy at Kingerby (1) and that at Scotton. Typically the folds of the surcoat have been represented

---
[128] B. L. Sloane, 3836, fol.21v, p.54.
[129] I am grateful to Professor Brian Kemp for this translation.
[130] Badham 1997, p. 13. Whittemore, p. 31, fig. 19.

Fig. 58. Kirton-in-Lindsey

Fig. 59. Kirton-in-Lindsey

deeply cut around the thighs, whereas the hem is caught underneath the lower legs. Another unusual feature is the dragon footrest more commonly found on ecclesiastical effigies, it derives from Psalm 91, v. 13.[131] The 1996 church guide states that in 1862 the church was restored and the effigy was discovered buried beneath the chancel floor.[132] Holles recorded the effigy near the east window of the chancel.[133]

No.26: Rippingale (2) (St Andrew) *c*.1325

Fig. 60. Rippingale (2)

Current position: At the east end of the south aisle.
Condition: Damaged (including the loss of the shield and scabbard).
Heraldry: None.
Posture: Cross-legged (right over left) with the hands raised in prayer and the feet supported by a headless lion.
Description: Limestone. A rectangular pillow supports the head. Clad entirely in mail (realistically represented), wearing a separate coif, hauberk with mitten gauntlets, hose and gamboised cuisses, with a strap below its lower edge. Around the brow is a plain circle and with straps around the wrists. From the bulging appearance of the coif, it would appear that he is wearing an underlying spherical bacinet. Worn over the hauberk is a long surcoat, with the front of the skirt open. Around the waist

is a medium width belt with a buckle of D-shape, the long loose portion falling to the calf on the right. The shield was originally suspended on the left forearm by two straps. The plain sword-belt is of medium width, and has a D-shape rectangular buckle placed centrally, its loose end is looped over itself on the right. The method of attaching the sword-belt to the scabbard has been destroyed. The sword has a wheel-shape pommel, tapering grip and straight quillons. The spurs are slender; the only one fully visible (left) has a slender down-bent prick.
Length: 6ft 2in.
Identification: Unknown. See Rippingale (1 p. 45) for references to the manor and who held it.
Commentary: The effigy is comparable with other effigies in the county, at Harrington, Kingerby (1), Kirton-in-Lindsey, also nationally at West Tanfield[134] (North Yorkshire), and Wymondham,[135] (Leicestershire). It is typically represented wearing the shield low on the left arm, together with the folds of the surcoat deeply cut around the thighs, whereas the hem is caught underneath the lower legs. Another characteristic of this effigy is a baggy fold, seen at the side of the neck on the coif. In my opinion (and also of Brian and Moira Gittos) this effigy is a Lincolnshire product.[136]

No.27: Harrington (St Mary) *c*.1325/30

Fig. 61. Harrington

Current position: Under a shallow-pointed recess in the south wall of the nave.
Condition: Fair but cracked across lower legs, and worn (the base of the shield and quillons missing, also the shield's chief is a modern replacement). The scabbard is very damaged and the attachment to the belt also worn.
Heraldry: None.
Posture: Cross-legged (left over right) with the hands raised in prayer and the feet supported by a lion with its tongue out.
Description: Limestone. A rectangular pillow supports the head. The knight is clad entirely in mail (realistically represented), and wears a separate coif, hauberk with mitten gauntlets and hose. Around the brow is a plain

---

[131] Meara, p. 442.
[132] St. Andrew's Parish Church Kirton In Lindsey, Revd. I. D. Walker, (Easter 1996).
[133] Holles, p. 118.

[134] I'Anson 1926, figs. 33, 34.
[135] Weatherley, p. 275.
[136] Gittos 2003, p. 163.

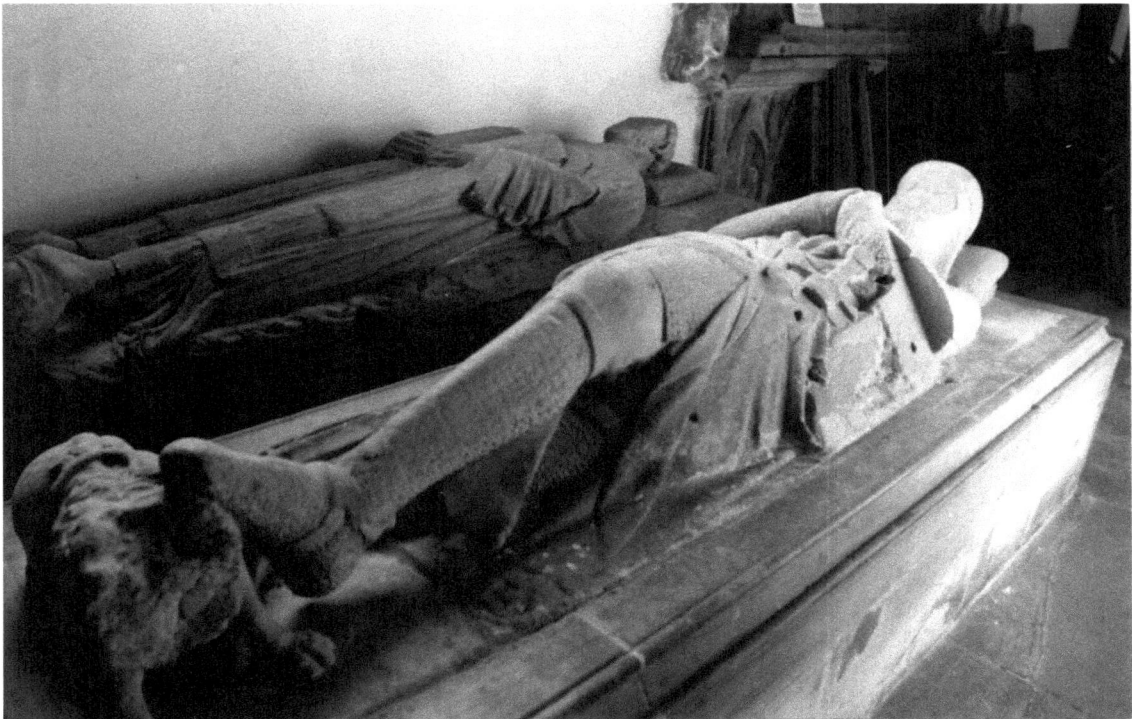

Fig. 62. Rippingale (2)

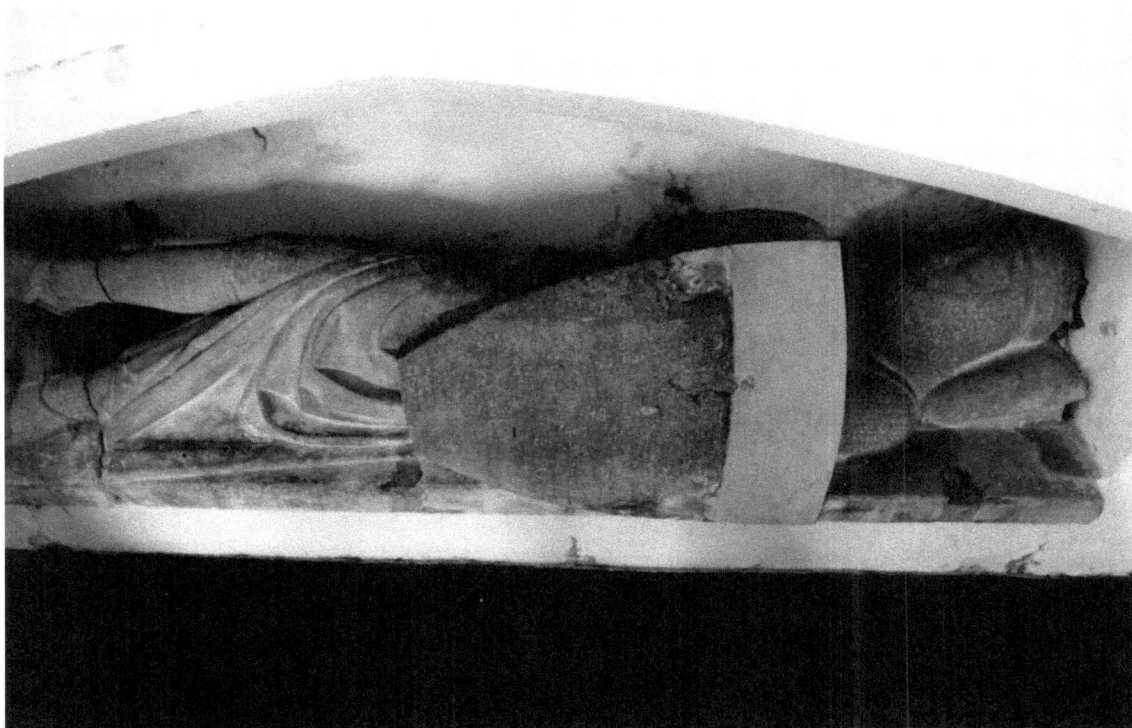

Fig. 63. Harrington

circle and on the wrists a strap. Worn over the hauberk is a surcoat, its hem falling to the ankles, the front of the skirt open and held around the waist by a narrow-buckled belt with a D-shape chape on the loose end. The shield is attached to the left arm by two enarmes. The plain sword-belt is of medium width, and has its buckle placed centrally, the loose end has a pointed-chape. The pommel of the sword is wheel-shape. Covering the left knee (the only one fully visible) is a poleyn. The spurs are slender with curved arms; on the right (the only one remaining) is a down-bent prick.

Length: 6ft 3in.

Identification: Unknown. The effigy is thought to represent Sir John de Harrington, who in 1313 held two knight's fees at Harrington.[137] In 1322 he was summoned as a knight of Rutland to serve against the Scots, recorded as over eighty years old, and a knight of Leicestershire, Lincolnshire and Rutland to the Great Council of Westminster in 1324. According to Moor he was recorded as dead 3rd June 1326.[138]

Commentary: The effigy is comparable stylistically with other effigies in the county from the same period, at Rippingale (2), Kingerby (1), Kirton-in-Lindsey, also nationally at West Tanfield (North Yorkshire), and Wymondham, (Leicestershire). It is typically represented with baggy folds of the surcoat, left foot lying flat on the slab, and with some fine undercutting of the right leg. Holles recorded the effigy in its current position.[139]

No.28: Careby (2) (St Stephen) *c.*1327

Current position: On a stone plinth against the north wall of the chancel.

Condition: Well preserved (angel's heads missing).

Heraldry: Effigy, shield: *two bars*, carved in relief.

Posture: Cross-legged (right over left) with the hands raised in prayer and the feet supported by a lion looking towards the effigy's right.

Description: Limestone. Two rectangular pillows, the upper positioned diagonally and held by two kneeling angels, support the head. The knight is clad entirely in mail (realistically represented), wearing a separate coif, hauberk with fingered gauntlets, hose and poleyns with a central keel. Around the brow is a circle decorated with flower heads, and around the wrists wide straps joined together by laces. Worn over the hauberk is a surcoat, its hem falling below the knees, with the front of the skirt open and held around the waist by a buckled belt, decorated with flower heads. Although a guige passes over the right shoulder, there is no shield, however it may have been made of wood and attached separately, as for example on the effigy of Robert Bourchier *c.*1340 at Halstead (Essex).[140] The plain sword-belt is of medium width, and its hexagonal buckle placed centrally, the loose end passes behind the scabbard, falling near the edge of the slab, a D-shape chape is represented, and is attached to the scabbard by the diagonal thong method.

Fig. 64. Careby (2)

The pommel is wheel-shaped with a small tang button. Laces bind the oval grip, herringbone-wise; the quillons are straight. The spurs have wide straps with D-shape buckles and chapes; their arms are strongly bent with a rowel on the left.

Length: 6ft 1in.

Identification: Unknown. The Reverend H. Lawrence remarks "The second effigy in this church distinctly shows on the surcoat *a fess with three roundels in chief*".[141] This is incorrect: the charges are clearly *two bars*, and Lawrence's three roundels look more like semicircles, however the stone is too worn in this area to form any firm conclusion. The earlier of the two effigies in the church (see p. 29) represents Suspirius de Bayuse who died 7 April 1292. His son and heir Sir William died after 1351, which would appear to be stylistically too late. However, he may have commissioned the effigy during his lifetime.

Commentary: The drapery on this figure is arranged in more-or-less straight ridges, unlike the more flowing drapery found on many other effigies in the county. The figure is also unusual, though not unique, in apparently never possessing a shield. On a number of effigies the shield was made separately, very likely wood, and attached to the arm by dowels, for example Edmund Crouchback *c.*1300 and Aymer de Valence *c.*1325/1330 at Westminster Abbey.[142]

[137] Moor 2, p. 188.
[138] Moor 2, p. 188.
[139] Holles, p. 129.
[140] Bayley, Plate 1.

[141] Lawrence 1946, p. 3.
[142] Bayley, Plate V, figs. 1, 2.

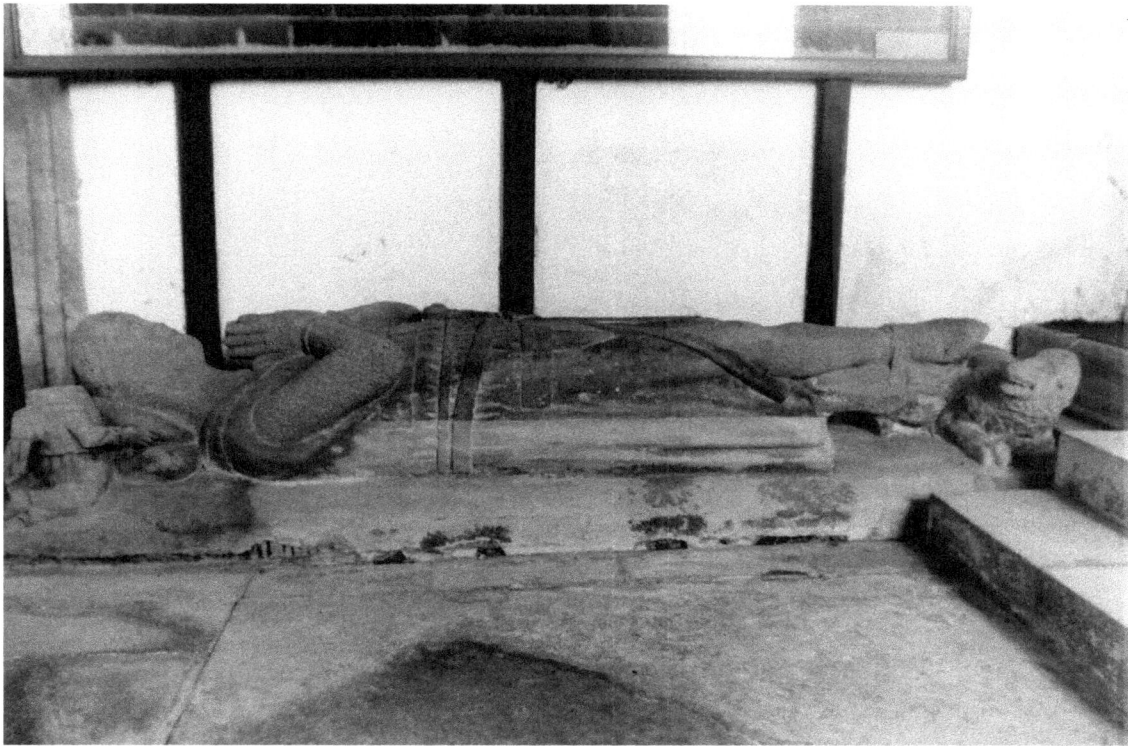

Fig. 65. Careby (2)

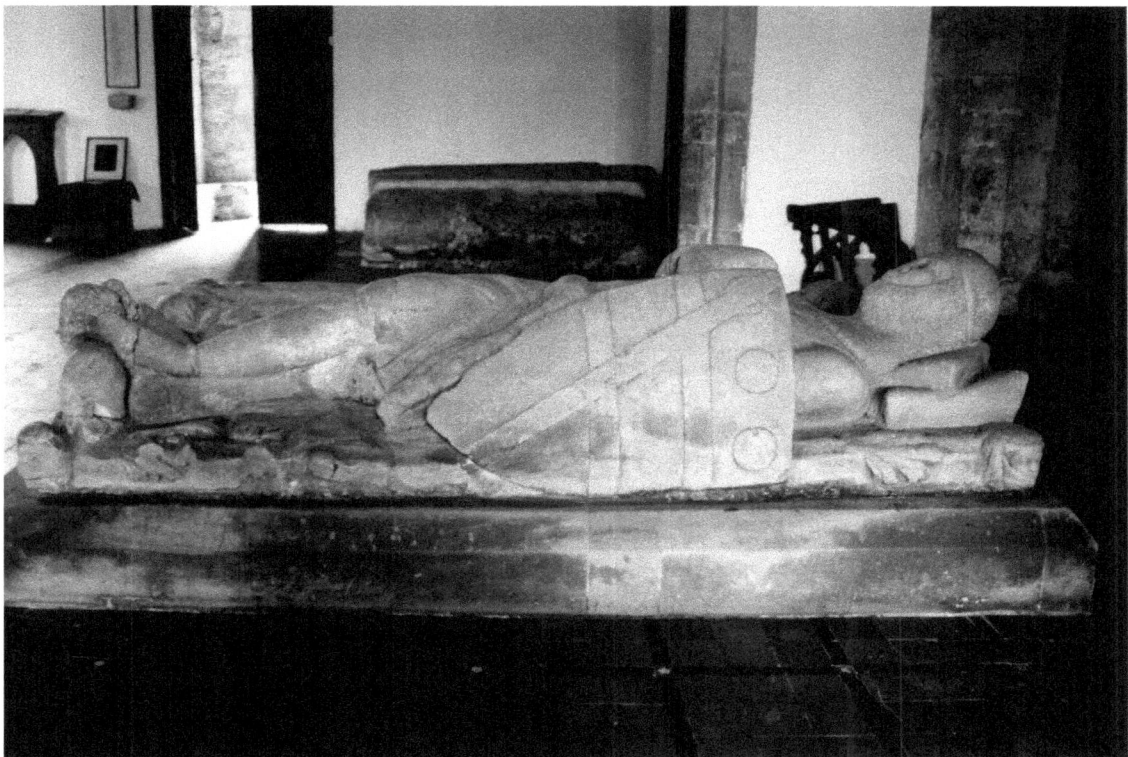

Fig. 66. Threekingham

No.29: Threekingham (St Peter) *c*.1330

Fig. 67. Threekingham

Current position: On a modern plinth, together with his wife, at the west end of the nave.

Condition: Lower right leg patched otherwise very well preserved.

Heraldry: Effigy, shield: *two bars, in chief three roundels, over all a bend* [for Threckingham] carved in relief.

Posture: Cross-legged (right over left) with the hands raised in prayer and the feet supported by two lions facing each other, and looking towards the effigy.

Description: Limestone. Two rectangular pillows, the upper positioned diagonally, support the head. Clad entirely in mail (realistically represented), wearing a separate coif, hauberk with mitten gauntlets, hose and globular poleyns. Around the brow is a plain circle and with narrow straps around the wrists. Worn over the hauberk is a long surcoat, with the front of the skirt open and held around the waist by a narrow buckled belt, decorated with bar-shaped plaques, the long loose end falling to the slab on the right. The sword-belt of medium width and is decorated with bar-shape plaques and large round-headed bosses, its buckle placed centrally, and a long loose end which passes behind the grip of the sword on the left and terminating with a D-shape chape. The attachment of the belt to the scabbard is of the diagonal thong type. The pommel appears to have been wheel-shaped and the left quillon straight (only one remaining). The damaged scabbard is decorated with applied bars and bosses. The spurs are slender, of which the only one fully visible (left) has a down-bent prick. On the corners of the slab are four human faces, two are ladies, another is a tonsured man and the fourth defaced. At intervals, the edge of the slab is decorated with leaves of foliage.

Length: 7ft 1in.

Identification: The effigy can be identified as member of the Threckingham family from the heraldry on the shield, however to which member is uncertain. Richard Gough suggests the effigy represents Sir Lambert de Threckingham who was the son of Lambert de Moulton, Baron Moulton, and bore the arms of his father, with a bend for difference.[143] Holles also states that the effigy represents Lambert.[144] Lambert was a King's clerk and Justice of the Bench between 1277 and 1331. Gough also mentions his lady beside him bore the arms of Spaygne.[145] In 1325 Sir Walter de Trikingham, son of Alexander de Trikingham,[146] obtained a licence for a chantry at Threekingham for the souls of himself, Lambert and his father and mother (deceased).[147] He was a knight of the shire in 1321, being summoned to the Great Council at Westminster in 1324 and fought at the battle of Boroughbridge, and reputedly died *c*.1331.[148] Given that he endowed a chantry chapel at Threekingham the effigy is most likely to represent him.

Commentary: Whether this effigy can be classified as a Lincolnshire product is questionable considering that there are four other similar related examples in neighbouring counties; those at Flintham, Gonalston (2) (both Nottinghamshire), Hornsea (East Yorkshire), Womersley (West Yorkshire) are contemporary with the effigy under discussion. The use of two lions to support the feet is very unusual, but other examples occur on the effigy of *c*.1320 at Georgeham (Devon) and the gilt copper-alloy figure of Queen Eleanor of Castile (*d*.1290) in Westminster Abbey.[149]

No.30: Maltby-le-Marsh (All Saints[150]) *c*.1330

Current position: On a modern brick support against the north wall of the chancel.

Condition: Damaged (angels heads, shield, pommel, grip and quillons are missing).

Heraldry: None.

Posture: Cross-legged (right over left) with the hands raised in prayer and the feet supported by a lion and dragon, engaged in a struggle.

Description: Limestone. Two rectangular pillows, the upper positioned diagonally and held by two seated angels, support the head. On either side of the shoulders are rectangular ailettes; no heraldry or paint remains on their surface. The knight is clad entirely in mail (realistically represented), wearing a separate coif, hauberk with mitten gauntlets and hose (no rings are represented underneath the foot). Around each wrist are buckled straps. Worn over the coif is a pointed bacinet with no sign of attachment. It has a shallow central keel

[143] Gough 1, pt. 2, p. 187.
[144] Holles, p. 217.
[145] Gough 1, pt. 2, p. 187.
[146] Cragg, p. 30.
[147] Moor 5, p. 49.
[148] Lawrence 1946, p. 43.
[149] Gardner 1951, Plate 425.
[150] The church is now redundant.

Fig. 68. Threekingham

Fig. 69. Maltby-le-Marsh

Fig. 70. Maltby-le-Marsh

with a deep U-shaped face opening with rounded corners. A narrow strip of a plain, unquilted garment is visible below the edge of the hauberk, above the knees, presumably intended to represent the lower edge of an aketon. Worn over the hauberk is a surcoat, its hem falling to the calf, the front of the skirt open and held around the waist by a narrow belt. The left arm passes through an enarme, visible at the inner corner of the elbow. The plain sword-belt is of medium width, and has its square buckle placed centrally, the loose end passing behind the scabbard on the left, falling near the edge of the slab, and is attached to the scabbard by the diagonal thong method. The upper edge of the poleyn overlaps the cuisses, which are longitudinally quilted, and the lower edge overlaps an additional lame. The prick spurs are slender with their arms downbent.

Length: 6ft.

Identification: Unknown. F. P. Bernard, who published an article on the effigy in 1909/10,[151] believed the effigy may represent either Robert de Tateshale or Sir William de Welle, between whom there was litigation as to the right of the patronage to the benefice. However this dispute occurred in 1265, which is much too early for either of them to be considered.[152] In 1331 Peter de Lekeburn had a grant of free warren at Maltby, also in the same year William Fraunceys of Tathewelle held part of a knight's fee.[153] In 1343 John de Sutton of Holderness also

had a grant of free warren,[154] however this person can be discounted as he is commemorated by an effigy at Sutton-in-Holderness (Yorkshire, East Riding) and it would be highly unlikely that he would have had two monuments.[155] The Welle family were overlords of the manor in the second half of the thirteenth century until the first quarter of the fourteenth century.[156] The effigy at Belleau possibly commemorates Sir Robert de Welles who died in 1320 therefore he can be discounted. Given the people holding land at Maltby when the effigy was probably made, the most likely candidate is Peter de Lekeburn.

Commentary: Though damaged, a good quality effigy, with much undercutting, especially the legs, which are carved fully in the round. The folds of the surcoat around the waist are portrayed being pulled to the right. This is the only effigy in the county wearing ailettes, a rare feature on effigies with only twenty-six other examples known in England. The fight between the lion and dragon is also a rare feature.

No.31: Somerby (St Margaret) *c*.1330

Fig. 71. Somerby

Current position: Under an arched recess in the south wall of the nave, at the west end.

---

[151] Bernard, p. 367.
[152] Moor 5, p. 10.
[153] *Cal. Charter Rolls* 4, p. 225.

[154] *Cal. Charter Rolls* 5, p. 19.
[155] Harvey, A. S., pp. 462-472, Plate to face p. 462.
[156] Moor 5, pp. 173-175.

Condition: Broken in four places and damaged (including the loss of the angels heads, pommel, quillons and lower scabbard).

Heraldry: Effigy, shield: *a chevron between three martlets* [for Ergum] carved in relief.

Posture: Cross-legged (right over left) with the hands raised in prayer and the feet supported by a lion looking towards the effigy's right.

Description: Limestone. Two rectangular pillows, the upper positioned diagonally and held by two seated angels, support the head. The knight is clad entirely in mail (realistically represented), wearing a separate coif, hauberk with mitten gauntlets, hose and globular poleyns with a central keel. Around the brow is a plain circle, and on the wrists are straps with buckles. Worn over the hauberk is a surcoat, its hem falling below the knees, with the front of the skirt open and held around the waist by a narrow belt and square buckle. The plain sword-belt is of medium width, and has its circular buckle placed centrally, the loose end, which has a D-shape chape, passes behind the scabbard on the left, falling near the edge of the slab, and is attached to the scabbard by the diagonal thong method. A sennet-knot is represented. The tip of the scabbard was supported by a small dog, which is licking its hindquarters. The arms of the prick spurs are bent.

Length: 5ft 7½in.

Identification: The effigy can be identified with relative certainty from the heraldry on the shield as William de Ergum. The first record of William was in 1314, when he held half a knight's fee in Somerby aged 40, being joint heir with Thomas de Ouneby, and a kinsmen of Maud de Percy.[1] The last record of him is in 1346 and he probably died shortly after this date.[2] He most likely commissioned the monument before his death. It would appear that William was the son of Ralph who was recorded in 1295 and dead by 1317.[3] William was holding the manor of Thorpe Bassett, until Robert (who was Ralph's grandson), came of age.[4]

Commentary: Once a fine effigy, well undercut around the legs and with finely carved detail on the hem of the surcoat. As with the effigy at Ashby-cum-Fenby and Buslingthorpe, the most interesting feature is the scabbard support. The fact that the dog is licking its backside is presumably merely an example of the kind of uninhibited humour that was common in the marginal art of the Middle Ages. The effigy was discovered in 1884, being used as part of the foundation of the east portion of the south wall, and was broken in four pieces.[5]

No.32: Halton Holegate (St Andrew) *c.*1335/40

Current position: Against the south wall of the south aisle, at the east end.

[1] *Cal. Inq. Edward III* 5, pp. 54 & 315.
[2] *Cal. Fine Rolls* 5, p. 504.
[3] *Cal. Fine Rolls* 2, p. 329.
[4] *Cal. Fine Rolls* 2, p. 329.
[5] Hall, p. 58.

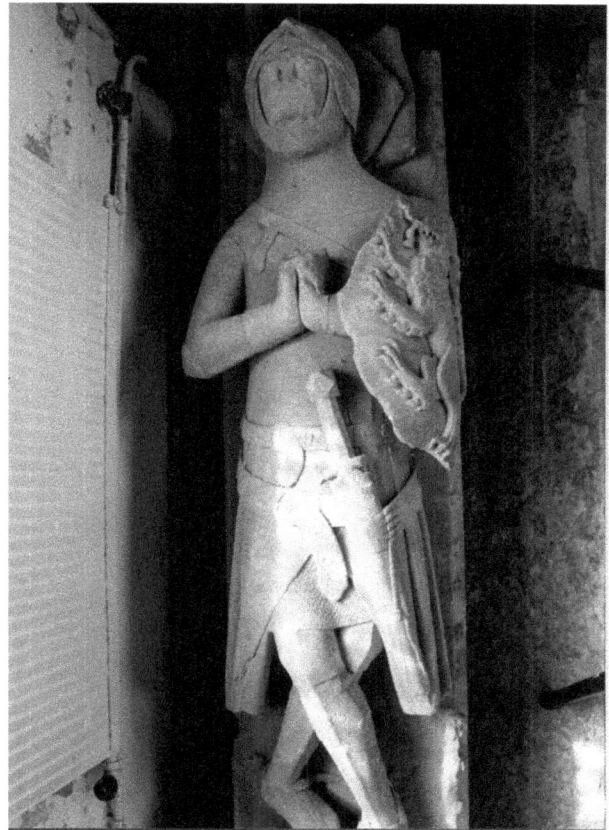

Fig. 72. Halton Holegate

Condition: Defaced (including the loss of the fingers, dexter and base of the shield and the head of the lion at the feet).

Heraldry: Effigy, shield: *a lion rampant*, carved in relief.

Posture: Cross-legged (right over left) with the hands raised in prayer and the feet supported by a lion.

Description: Limestone. Two rectangular pillows, the upper positioned diagonally, support the head. Clad in mail (realistically represented) supplemented by plate defences, with a separate coif, hauberk and hose. Worn over the coif is a bacinet with a raised pivoted visor. It has a shallow central keel with a deep U-shaped face opening with rounded corners. Around the face opening and lower edge, is a border decorated with quatrefoil-shaped flowers. The visor from the front is ogee-shaped and has a sharp central keel with a horizontal sight, and has curled ends (slightly incised), its lower edge is damaged, and just visible are two cross for ventilation. The heads of the pivots are also in the form of flower heads. Worn over the hauberk is a long sleeveless surcoat, partly open on the visible (right) side to reveal the mail of the hauberk, its hem falling to the calf, the front of the skirt open and held around the waist by a wide belt with a circular buckle, the short loose end with a D-shape chape. The supplementary plate comprises: rosette-shaped plates over the points of the elbows (that on the left concealed by the shield); plain poleyns and schynbalds, each of the latter a single solid plate, shaped to the bottom of the ankle-bone, and secured round the back by four narrow straps each attached to it by a rivet; bluntly-pointed sabatons, covering the tops of the feet

Fig. 73. Somerby

Fig. 74. Halton Holegate

only, and formed of a series of small rectangular plates, each with a central rivet. The gauntlets with short cuffs consist of a lining-glove reinforced over the back and sides of the hand with plates exactly like those on the sabatons, and secured round the underside of the wrist by two straps attached to the plates by rivets; the fingers, which are badly damaged, appear to be covered with small convex plates, those over the knuckles larger than the others. The rivets throughout have large, slightly-domed, circular heads. The exceptionally-wide sword-belt is decorated in the same manner as the waist-belt and has a D-shape buckle placed centrally, and terminates in a D-shape chape, and is attached to the scabbard by the diagonal thong method, incorporating a sennet-knot. The pommel is polyhedron shaped with a tall pyramidal tang button. The grip is hexagonal in section; the quillons down-turned. The arms of the spurs are bent in a V-shape with circular buckles and a rowel on the left (only one remaining). The bevelled edge of the slab is decorated with slipped quatrefoil-shape flowers.

Length: 6ft 1in.

Identification: Unknown. Holles, who recorded the figure against the south wall of the choir, mentioned that it was known locally as Sir Henry Halton.[6] In 1338 Henry de Halton was appointed a collector of scutage in Lincoln,[7] also being a commissioner in 1341[8] until 1344.[9] In 1345 he was exempt from military service in Scotland and elsewhere because of age.[10] The church guide also mentions that the effigy represents Henry de Halton, whereas the revised edition of Pevsner, *The Buildings of England, Lincolnshire*, remarks that it may be Sir John de Fenes.[11] Sir John de Fenes bore the arms, *argent a lion rampant sable*, being recorded in rolls of arms in 1280 and 1312.[12] I have not been able to discover who held the manor at the time the effigy was made.

Commentary: The effigy provides an unusually detailed representation of armour of the so-called "transitional" period in England, when mail was beginning to be supplanted by plate. The sabatons and gauntlets illustrate what are clearly versions of the "plates" construction, best known from the defence for the torso of that name (also "coat-of-plates"), which was made of hoops riveted to the interior of a textile or leather garment, instead of, as here, the exterior.[13] The latter form was probably chosen for the feet and hands because it gave more flexibility. Of particular interest is the fact that no attachments are depicted on the sabatons, which must mean that they were fixed to the top of the feet of the hose, and not to the lower edge of the schynbalds. It should be noted also that the mail of the hauberk is visible through the slit in the surcoat suggesting that plates did not accompany it on the torso. The representation of the visor on an effigy, which was a

normal fitting on a bacinet, is rare, but it occurs on a number of more-or-less contemporary figures: for example, Aldworth (nos.1, 2[14]) (Berkshire); Alvechurch[15] (Worcestershire); Chew Magna[16] (Somerset), Edington (Wiltshire); Bisley with Lypiatt and Forthampton Court (Gloucestershire); Sefton (no.2) (Lancashire); Warkworth[17] (Northumberland); and the brass of Sir Hugh de Hastings, at Elsing[18] (Norfolk) all are dated *c*.1330/1350. Comparable reinforced mail armour is also shown on the Pebmarsh brass to Sir William Fitz Ralph,[19] *c*.1330-1340,[20] (Essex) and on an effigy at Furness Abbey (Lancashire). As far as I am aware the polyhedron-shaped pommel is the only known sculptured representation on an effigy. The figure includes so many unusual features, rendered in such detail as to suggest that it might have been copied from existing armour, perhaps owned by the person represented. The posture of the effigy is very straight and rigid, as are the folds, the latter differing noticeably from the flowing folds found on most other Lincolnshire figures. I have not been able to link the effigy with any other examples, but it is, nonetheless, likely to be a local product. The effigy was discovered under the floor of the church during the restoration of 1846,[21] which would account for its good state of preservation.

No.33: Winteringham (All Saints) *c*.1335/45

Current position: Under an arched recess in the north wall of the chancel.

Condition: Damaged (the head of the right angel, pommel and lower scabbard missing).

Heraldry: None.

Posture: Cross-legged (left over right) with the hands raised in prayer and the feet supported by a lion looking towards the effigy's right.

Description: Limestone. Two rectangular pillows support the head; the upper positioned diagonally, being held by two kneeling angels. Clad entirely in mail (realistically represented), wearing a separate coif, hauberk with fingered gauntlets and hose. Around the brow is a plain circle and with a knotted tie around each wrist. Worn underneath the hauberk is a longitudinally quilted aketon. Over the hauberk is a sleeveless surcoat, its hem falling to the knees, the front of the skirt is open and held around the waist by a narrow belt with a rectangular D-shape buckle, the loose end falling to the left of the waist. The plain sword-belt is of medium width, and its rectangular D-shape buckle is placed centrally. The loose end passes behind the grip of the sword, and is attached to the scabbard by the diagonal thong method. The left quillon (the only one remaining)

---

[6] Holles, p. 164.
[7] *Cal. Fine Rolls* 5, p. 63.
[8] *Cal. Inq. Misc.* 2, pp. 435-436.
[9] *Cal. Patent Rolls Edw. III 6*, p. 299.
[10] *Cal. Patent Rolls Edw. III 6*, p. 299.
[11] Pevsner and Harris, p. 360.
[12] Humphrey-Smith, p. 63.
[13] See Blair, pp.8-10.

[14] Gardner 1951, fig. 416.
[15] Downing 2002, Plate 26.
[16] Gardner 1951, fig. 430.
[17] Lawrence 1946, Plate to face p. 13.
[18] Binski 1987, fig. 120.
[19] Moor 2, p. 55.
[20] Binski 1987, fig. 91.
[21] Associated Architectural Societies Reports and Papers, vol. 8, p. 64.

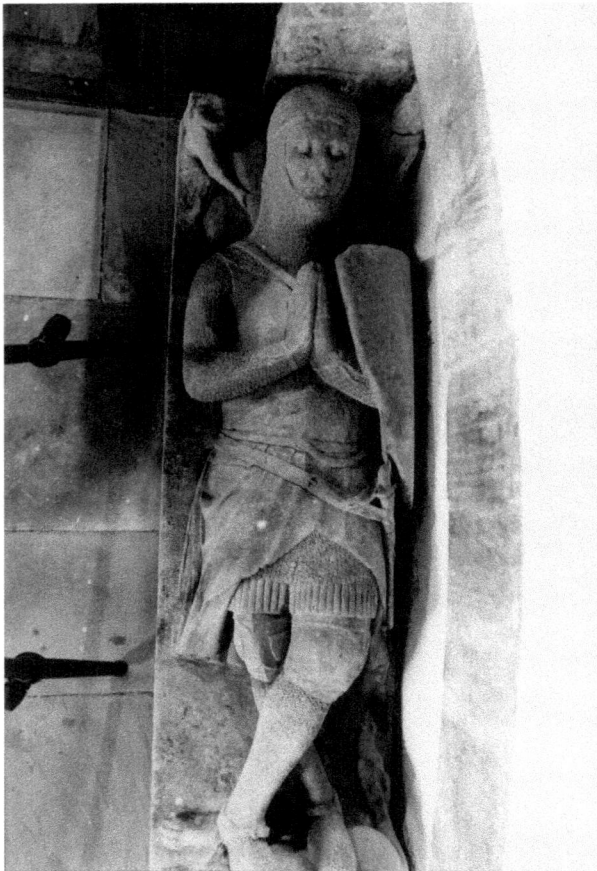

Fig. 75. Winteringham

is straight. The poleyns have central keels, which have small shields set on either side of the central line. A very unusual small detail is a series of stitches represented along the lower edge, which presumably attached the poleyn to a strap that passes behind the knee. The spurs have wide straps and D-shaped buckles.

Length: 5ft 9in.

Identification: The manor of Winteringham was held by the younger branch of the Marmion family of Scrivelsby (see p. 47).[22] William Marmion who died in or before 1276 sided with Simon de Montfort, whose lands were seized, who was later pardoned.[23] His son and heir Sir John, was a summoned to Parliament from 1313 to 1322,[24] and summoned to serve against the Scots in 1300 and 1301.[25] In 1310 he obtained a licence for a chaplain to celebrate in the chapel of St Nicholas, Winteringham, for the souls of himself and wife Isabella.[26] He died in 1322 and would be the most likely candidate for the effigy.

Commentary: The effigy has a rather straight and rigid posture and is very likely from the same workshop as the effigies at Harrington and Careby (pp. 52, 54). The surcoat is unusually short, its hem falling to the knees.

No.34: Burton-upon-Stather (St Andrew) *c.*1340

Current position: Underneath a pointed arch with ballflower decoration, in the north wall of the chancel.

Condition: Very worn and damaged (arms, lower legs, pommel, grip, right quillon and angel's heads missing).

Heraldry: Effigy, shield: *a chevron between three garbs* [for Sheffield] carved in relief.

Posture: Cross-legged (right over left), with the hands raised in prayer.

Description: Limestone. Two rectangular pillows, the upper positioned diagonally and held by two seated angels, support the head. The bacinet is pointed with an aventail, attached by the vervelle and cord method. The knight is clad in mail (realistically represented), wearing a hauberk, hose and globular poleyns with a central keel. It is not clear whether the hands were protected by mail mufflers, made in one with the sleeve of the hauberk, or plate gauntlets. Above the left knee can be seen the lower edge of a longitudinally quilted garment which may represent the lower edge of an aketon or cuisse. Worn over the hauberk is a surcoat, its hem falling to the knees, the front of the skirt open and held around the waist by a narrow-buckled belt. The sword-belt is plain and of medium width with a buckle placed to the left of the wearer, the loose end has a chape passing behind the sword on the left, falling near the edge of the slab. The belt is decorated with diamond-shape bosses and is attached to the scabbard by the diagonal thong method, incorporating a sennet-knot. The left quillon is straight.

Length: 5ft 6in.

Identification: According to Lawrence the effigy represents Sir Robert Sheffield, who acquired Butterwick by the marriage to the heiress of Alexander Lownde.[27] In 1332 he held a lease of land at Kirketon[28] and in the same year was exempt from holding office.[29]

Commentary: Again a transitional effigy, and the first effigy in the county to be represented wearing a bacinet with an attached aventail. It is reputed that John, Earl of Mulgrave removed the effigy from Owston Priory during the rein of Charles II, which is when the damage occurred,[30] but Lawrence believed it came from Butterwick.[31]

No.35: Buslingthorpe (St Michael) *c.*1340/45

Current position: On the north side of the nave. In 1987 the church was vested in the Churches Conservation Trust, which undertook the conservation of the effigy.

Condition: Very well preserved.

Heraldry: None.

Posture: Cross-legged (right over left) with the hands raised in prayer and the feet supported by a lion looking towards the effigy's right.

Description: Limestone. Two rectangular pillows, the upper positioned diagonally and held by two seated angels, support the head. The knight is clad in mail

---

[22] Wagner, p. 160.
[23] Brault 2, p. 282.
[24] Wagner, p. 160.
[25] Brault, 2, p. 281.
[26] Moor 3, p. 120.

[27] Lawrence 1946, p. 33.
[28] *Cal. Patent Rolls Edw. III* 2, p. 332.
[29] *Cal. Patent Rolls Edw. III* 2, p. 376.
[30] Jarvis, p. 55.
[31] Lawrence 1946, p. 33.

Fig. 76. Winteringham

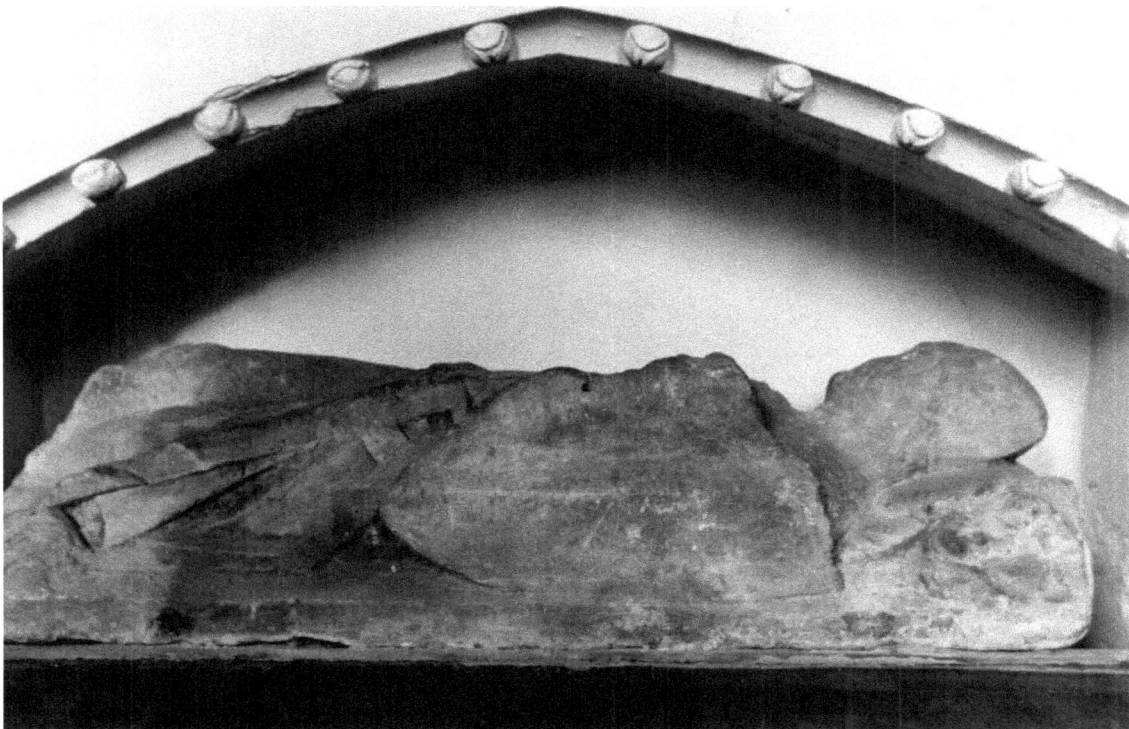

Fig. 77. Burton-upon-Stather

Fig. 78. Burton-upon-Stather

Fig. 79. Buslingthorpe

Fig. 80. Buslingthorpe

(realistically represented), wearing a separate coif, hauberk, hose and globular poleyns, decorated on either side of the central keel with a small plain shield. The mail is secured around the wrists by buckled straps; the hands are bare. The mail has not been completed underneath the right calf. Over the coif is a bacinet with a central keel fore-and-aft, and is attached to the coif by four laces; it has a shallow arched face-opening with the lower edge straight. Worn underneath the hauberk is a longitudinally quilted aketon, and over the hauberk is a long surcoat, its hem falling to the calf, the front of the skirt open and held around the waist by a belt with a rectangular buckle. The effigy was conserved in 1988, and during the conservation traces of medieval graffiti were found on the shield, (which is an un-tinctured shield): a number of crested helms, and a profile of a bearded man wearing a kettle-hat. They can be dated to the fourteenth century and were very likely executed by the workshop that carved the effigy, which was then covered over when the shield was painted. The sword-belt is plain and of medium width, with a rectangular buckle lying in the centre of the wearer, and the loose end of the belt passes behind the scabbard on the left, falling near the edge of the slab. The attachment of the belt to the scabbard, which has a tasselled fringe, (see also Norton Disney p. 75) is by two suspension bands. The sword has a wheel-shaped pommel with a tang button, the grip tapering towards the quillons and oval in section. The left quillon (the only one remaining) is straight and of hexagonal section. The tip of the scabbard rests on a small tailed-creature with an imp's face. The cuisses are

longitudinally-quilted. The rowel spurs are large, their arms slightly curved.

Length: 5ft 5in.

The effigy lies on tomb-chest made of limestone and decorated with shields set within quatrefoils, with no traces of paint or heraldry. Between the effigy and the tomb-chest is a Purbeck marble slab with a worn Lombardic inscription recorded by E. J. Willson in 1812. It reads with his additions in square brackets, [+ICY . GYS] T . SIRE . IOHAN . DE . BVSSEL[YNGTHOR]P . DE . EG...HAN...[LERE]   (Here lies Sir John de Bussleyngthorp of Eg...han...Knight (*chevalier*).[32]

Identification: The worn inscription identifies the effigy as Sir John Buslingthorpe, born 1277 and died between 1341[33] and 1344.[34] He is the only member of the family to hold the manor of Buslingthorpe, bearing the name John, and was married twice, Eva de Holbeach being his first wife who died 1321, and Maud his second wife, still living in 1346.[35] His son Richard died between 1361 and 1369 and is represented in the church by a half-brass effigy, set up during his lifetime between *c*.1325 and 1340.[36]

Commentary: There are two interesting features on this effigy, the medieval graffiti on the shield and the inscription, which is the only known instance where a freestone effigy and tomb are associated with inlaid latten letters.[37] John Blair states that the letters are the type used by the London brass-makers, but used here by a north-eastern workshop.[38] The creature supporting the tip of the scabbard is another example of the creativity of the Lincoln monumental sculptors; two other instances in the county can be seen at Ashby-cum-Fenby and Somerby (pp. 29, 71).

No.36: Lea (St Helen) *c*.1350

Current position: On a modern stone tomb-chest, under the easternmost arch between the north aisle and chancel.

Condition: Although the figure is well preserved the originality of some parts is questionable, as it has been re-painted, and partly restored (the shield and sword have been replaced and the face re-cut).

Heraldry: Effigy, shield: *a bend and a border gobony* [for Trehampton] carved in relief. Tomb; represented by paint (modern), the coat-of-arms illustrate the descent of the Andersons, who bought the manor in the seventeenth-century, from the Trehamptons. Also in the centre of the tomb-chest is a modern inscription, mentioning also descendants of the Trehamptons.

Posture: Cross-legged (right over left) with the hands raised in prayer and the feet supported by a lion looking towards the effigy's right.

Description: Freestone. Two rectangular pillows, the upper positioned diagonally with the lower pillow having

---

[32] Blair, J. 1975-9, p. 266.
[33] *Cal. Patent Rolls Edw. III* 5, p. 272.
[34] Blair, J. 1975-9, p. 267.
[35] Blair, J. 1975-9, p. 267.
[36] Blair, J. 1975-9, p. 269.
[37] Blair, J. 1975-9, p. 265.
[38] Blair J. 1975-9, p., 268.

Fig. 81. Lea

Fig. 82. Lea

tasselled corners, support the head. The bacinet has a central keel and a deep U-shaped face-opening; an aventail on which the vervelle and cord attachment is represented. Clad in mail (realistically represented) supplemented by plate defences, wearing a hauberk with mitten gauntlets and hose; the mail is secured around the wrists by buckled straps, their ends terminating in D-shape chapes. The supplementary plates comprises: couters each secured to the elbow by two straps, articulated by four additional lames above and below, and with circular side-wings; poleyns each with a central keel with a shallow additional lame below; and schynbalds, each of a single solid plate, secured round the back by five narrow straps. Worn underneath the hauberk is a longitudinally quilted aketon and over it a long surcoat, its hem falling to the calf, the front of the skirt open and held around the waist by a belt with a rectangular buckle, its long loose end falling to the right on the slab. The sword-belt is plain and of medium width, with a circular buckle lying in the centre of the wearer, its loose end passing behind the scabbard on the left, falling on the edge of the slab, where it terminates in a pointed chape. Rowel spurs are worn of which only one (on the right) is fully visible; their arms are slightly curved.

Length: 5ft 9½in.

Identification: According to the modern tablet inscription, the effigy traditionally represent Sir Ralph de Trehampton, whereas the revised edition of Pevsner, *The Buildings of England, Lincolnshire*, remarks that it is said to represent Sir John de Trehampton died *c*.1350.[39] Holles recorded the figure and heraldry in support of Trehampton.[40] Sir Ralph de Trehampton was the son and heir of Sir Roger de Trehampton, who served under Henry de Lacy Earl of Lincoln against the Welsh in 1277 and 1282 and who died before 24th January 1312.[41] His heir is not recorded but was probably Sir Ralph de Trehanton who in 1318 held 2 knight's fees at Lee and Burton.[42] In 1335 John de Trehampton, (son of Ralph de Trehampton) held two parts of the manor, and was a rebel siding with Thomas Earl of Lancaster, whose parts were then given to William de Anne for good service.[43] The third part, which Philip de Nevill and Agnes his wife held in dower of Agnes.[44] John de Trehampton's heir was his sister Margaret died 1355,[45] who was firstly married to John de Brewes, and secondly to Norman de Swynford.[46] In 1335 John de Brewes obtained a grant to hold two fairs at Lea.[47] John and Margaret's son also called John (recorded an idiot), was the heir of Margaret, but after a dispute with Norman de Swynford relinquished any claim to the manor, which in 1355 Norman held.[48] Sir John de Trehampton died between 1st October 1348[49] and 30th

September 1349,[50] being the last of the male line. He was a very prominent figure for the county, being a sheriff from 1334[51] until 1346[52] and an escheator until his death, also representing the counties of Rutland and Northampton.[53]

Commentary: Due to the fact that the effigy has been so much restored, possibly during the restoration of the church in 1849, it is difficult to obtain a clear picture of its originality. The figure may be from the same workshop as the knight at Maltby-le-Marsh.

No.37: Surfleet (St Lawrence) *c*.1346/7

Current position: On a stone plinth against the north wall of the sanctuary.

Condition: Fair, (covered in whitewash) but the sword and the attendant angels heads are missing.

Heraldry: None.

Posture: Cross-legged (left over right) with the head turned to the right and the hands raised in prayer, the feet supported by a grinning lion looking towards the effigy's right.

Description: Limestone. Two tasselled rectangular pillows, the upper positioned diagonally support the head. The bacinet is spherical with an aventail, on which the vervelle and cord attachment is represented. Wearing a mail haubergeon (mail realistically represented) supplemented by plate defences. The coat-armour is short in the front and long at the back (formerly known as a cyclas by antiquaries), the front presumably terminating underneath the sword-belt. No guige is represented. A smooth garment is worn below the hauberk, which presumably is an aketon. The supplementary plate comprises of four-lame spaudlers, upper and lower cannons are not represented with any buckled straps or hinges; couter (the only one visible) with a circular side-wing, and is articulated to the upper and lower cannons by a narrow lame. The gauntlets with short cuffs consist of six narrow lames, and over the back of the hand by a broad lame, articulated by a narrow lame below. The fingers are covered by small convex plates, those over the knuckles larger than the others. Projecting from underneath the coat-armour are four lames of the coat-of-plates, tapering tile-wise. The cuisses are smooth and project below the poleyns, which have cusped edges and lobed side-wings. The schynbalds consist of a front and back plate and are secured together by two buckled-straps, both on the inside and outside and are presumably worn over hose, which can be seen through the open joint at the sides; the sabatons consist of seven lames. The rowel spurs have arms bent in a V-shape. Decorating the right-hand edge of the slab are lions faces, alternating with quatrefoils. Built into the east wall, below the effigy's feet, appears to be part of a tomb. Whether it was part of the effigy's tomb is difficult to determine it comprises a vaulted cusped gablette.

Length: 5ft 11in.

---

[39] Pevsner and Harris, p. 429.
[40] Holles, p. 146.
[41] Brault 2, p. 421.
[42] Moor 5, p. 45.
[43] *Cal. Close Rolls Edw. III* 3, p. 460.
[44] *Cal. Close Rolls Edw. III* 3, p. 460.
[45] *Cal. Inq. Edw. III* 5, p. 189.
[46] *Cal. Inq. Edw. III* 5, p. 189.
[47] *Cal. Charter Rolls* 4, p. 335.
[48] *Cal. Inq. Edw. III* 5, p. 189.
[49] *Cal. Fine Rolls* 6, p. 84.

[50] *Cal. Fine Rolls* 6, p. 154.
[51] *Cal. Fine Rolls* 4, p. 422.
[52] *Cal. Fine Rolls* 5, pp. 13, 446, 461.
[53] *Cal. Fine Rolls* 6, pp. 25, 26, 37, 40, 50, 51, 58, 69, 84.

Identification: Sir Hugh de Cressy. Holles recorded the effigy on the north side of the chancel, together with heraldry; a lion rampant with its tail duplicated.[54] The Cressy family bore *argent a lion rampant queue fourchée sable*, which was recorded on the effigy's chest, and also in the window above.[55] William de Cressy held the manor of Risegate in Surfleet from 1318,[56] until his death in 1334.[57] His son and heir Sir Hugh, born 20th September 1313,[58] did fealty for his father's lands in the same year,[59] having protection beyond the seas on the king's service in 1337,[60] being a commissioner for Lincolnshire in 1343/1344,[61] and received a pardon for good service in the war with France on November 20th 1346,[62] dying shortly before 16th January 1347[63] aged 33, possibly from illness or injuries received during the Crécy campaign. His will dated 1st May 1346, states that if he should die in England his body was to be buried in Surfleet.[64] He was married to Maud, who died 9 August 1355.[65] His son and heir, John, who died in 1383 was also buried in the church.[66]

Commentary: An extremely interesting effigy depicting the lower four lames of the coat-of-plates, is a rare feature on English military effigies.[67] A similar representation can be seen on the effigy attributed to Sir Thomas Cresacre died 1348[68] at Barnburgh[69] (Yorkshire, West Riding), Northmoor (Oxfordshire), Winterbourne (1) (Gloucestershire), and later at Etchilhampton (Wiltshire) and Isleham (Cambridgeshire) both *c*.1370/80. Other representation of the coat-of-plates can be seen through the side openings of the coat-armour on two effigies, Ash, *c*.1345/1350 (Kent)[70] (see fig. 143) and Pershore Abbey, *c*.1280/1300 (Worcestershire),[71] and also the outline of transverse plates can be seen beneath the surcoat on the earliest alabaster effigy at Hanbury, *c*.1340, (Staffordshire).[72] On a number of effigies including brasses dated to the 1340's plain or rosette-shape studs are visible, which indicate that the metal plates are riveted to the inside of a textile cover; for instance Horley[73] (Surrey), and Coberley (Gloucestershire), attributed to Thomas Berkeley died 1344[74] and two brasses at Westley Waterless,[75] to Sir

John de Creke and at Stoke D' Abernon,[76] to Sir John III D' Abernon. Another interesting feature is the way the body is slightly reclining to the right, which is uncommon, but it occurs also on the effigies of Edmund Crouchback died 1296 at Westminster Abbey[77] and Sir John de Freville died 1312, Little Shelford[78] (Cambridgeshire), both are from the so-called "Westminster Workshop". Other effigies from this workshop dated to the 1340s do not show this feature; therefore it may be possibly cautiously to attribute the effigy under discussion to that workshop.[79] The effigy is one of only two in the county to be wearing coat-armour, which is long at the back and short in the front, the other being Spilsby (1). An unpublished drawing of the effigy by the eminent antiquarian Charles Alfred Stothard is in the British Museum, Department of Prints and Drawings.[80]

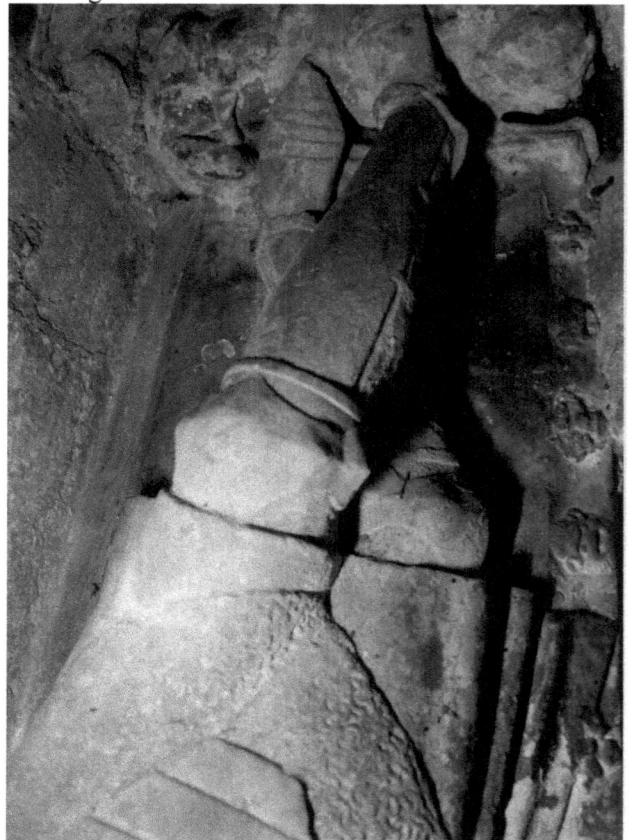

Fig. 83. Surfleet

No.38: Spilsby (1) (St James) *c*.1348

Current position: In the northeast corner of the north (Willoughby) chapel together with his wife. The tomb-chest is decorated with fleuron panels, each having two shields set within quatrefoils and divided from each other by pillars. Each corner is raised into two tall Gothic gabled-pinnacles, with statues of saints underneath gabled

---

[54] Holles, p. 173.
[55] Holles, p. 173.
[56] *Complete Peerage* 3, p. 529.
[57] *Cal. Fine Rolls* 4, p. 427.
[58] *Complete Peerage* 3, p. 529.
[59] *Complete Peerage* 3, p. 530.
[60] *Cal. Patent Rolls Edw. III* 3, p. 527.
[61] *Cal. Patent Rolls Edw. III* 6, pp. 89, 184.
[62] *Cal. Patent Rolls Edw. III* 7, p. 502.
[63] *Cal. Fine Rolls* 5, p. 480.
[64] Gibbons, p. 15
[65] *Complete Peerage* 3, p. 530
[66] *Complete Peerage* 3, p. 530.
[67] For a complete discussion on the coat-of-plates, see Thordeman, pp. 285-328.
[68] I'Anson 1927, p. 63.
[69] Fryer 1924, Plate XVII, figs. 38 & 39.
[70] Stothard, p. 54.
[71] Downing 2002, Plate 5.
[72] Blair 1992, p. 6.
[73] Waller, Plate to face p. 187.
[74] Gittos 2003, pp. 155-158.
[75] Binski 1987, fig. 102.

---

[76] Binski 1987, fig. 103.
[77] Tummers, pls. 123, 126.
[78] Blair, 1995/6, pp .36-38.
[79] For other effigies from this workshop see Downing, pp. 20-28.
[80] Lankester 2004, p. 8.

Fig. 84. Surfleet

Fig. 85. Surfleet

Fig. 86. Spilsby (1)

recess. According to Holles, they were in a very bad condition and were included in the restoration of 1825.[81]

Condition: Although well preserved, it was extensively restored and re-cut by C. R. Smith in 1825.[82] There is a horizontal crack below the knee.

Heraldry: Effigy, shield: *a cross Moline* [for Willoughby] carved in relief.

Posture: Cross-legged (right over left) with the hands raised in prayer and the feet supported by a lion looking towards the effigy's right.

Description: Limestone. Two rectangular pillows with tasselled corners, the upper positioned diagonally, which is held by two seated angels, support the head. On the head is a bacinet with an aventail, and suspended from a cord, which secures the aventail to the bacinet, are scale pendants. Across the brow of the bacinet is a band decorated with small flower-heads. The coat-armour is tight fitting, being short across the front and long at the back, beneath which is the coat-of-plates with a scalloped fringe at the hem. Worn beneath the coat-of-plates is a mail haubergeon and a vertically quilted aketon. The right spaudler (the only one visible) consists of four narrow lames, and a besagew decorated in the form of a lion's mask with its tongue exposed. The cannons of the upper and lower vambraces are hinged. The couter on the right elbow has three narrow articulating lames above and two below, the side-wing is a lion's mask. The gauntlets with long cuffs have an additional hinged plate on the inside, and secured to the forearm by a narrow strap, and over

the back of the hand by a broad lame, articulated by three narrow lames above and one below. The fingers are covered with small convex plates, those over the knuckles larger than the others. Around the waist is a narrow belt, decorated with flower-heads, with a D-shape buckle placed centrally.

The broad sword-belt has a large D-shape buckle, lying slightly to the right of the wearer, the loose end of the belt passes behind the quillons falling to the left near the base of the slab, a pointed chape is represented. The belt is decorated with two *crosses moline* and three lions faces each set within a square mount. The method used to secure the sword-belt to the scabbard is by two rings. The scabbard has two raised mounts, positioned at intervals, which are decorated with a lion's face; a *cross moline* is positioned halfway down the scabbard, the lower part is a restoration. The pommel is wheel-shaped and is decorated with a lion's mask. The hexagonal grip is concave and the quillon straight with curved ends. Over the knees are globular poleyns, each reinforced across the front with an I-shaped strip, and two narrow articulated lower lames, and the lowest lame has small tassels. Incised vertically down the inside and outside of each leg respectively presumably indicates that schynbalds or closed greaves were represented, but it is not clear which since no straps or buckles are shown. The sabatons consist of six lames. The rowel spurs have wide straps with strongly down belt necks.

Length: 5ft 10½in.

Identification: John, Lord Willoughby. He was the son and heir of Baron Robert de Willoughby (died shortly before 25th March 1317), born 6th January 1306/7, and having seisin of his lands on 29th January 1327, made a knight Banneret on 20th January 1327.[83] He was summoned to Parliament from 27th January 1332 to 10th March 1349, and for service in Scotland, 1333, 1335, 1340 and 1341.[84] He was with the king at Antwerp, July 1338, and fought at Crécy 26th August 1346, marrying in 1323 Joan Roscelyn.[85] He died 13th June 1349[86] aged 45 and was buried at Spilsby.

Commentary: In 1348 John Lord Willoughby endowed a chantry chapel at Spilsby where his tomb originally lay (now the present chancel),[87] but after the dissolution of the chantries, and enlargement of the church, the tomb was moved to the choir, as recorded by Holles between 1638-1642.[88] It was probably moved to its present position when it was restored in 1825. There is no doubt that the effigy is from the "Westminster Workshop" and is closely related[89] to the effigies at Ifield (Sussex), Sir John Ifield,[90] c.1340/45, died between 1341[91] and 1343;[92] Ingham (Norfolk),[93] Sir

[81] Lord, pp. 89-90.
[82] Lord, pp. 89-90.

[83] *Complete Peerage* 7, p. 658.
[84] *Complete Peerage* 7, p. 659.
[85] *Complete Peerage* 7, p. 659.
[86] *Cal. Inq. Edw. III* 9, p. 181.
[87] Lord, p. 86.
[88] Holles, p. 89.
[89] For others in this group see Downing 1998, p. 23.
[90] Stothard, p. 53.
[91] *Cal. Close Rolls Edw. III* 6, p. 129.
[92] *Cal. Close Rolls Edw. III* 7, p. 175.
[93] Badham 2007, pp. 9-23

Fig. 87. Spilsby (1)

Fig. 88. Spilsby (1)

Oliver Ingham, died 1344;[94] Waterperry (Oxfordshire), Robert Fitz-Elys, *c*.1340/45, died in or before 1346[95] and Westminster Abbey, John of Eltham Earl of Cornwall, *c*.1340, died 1336,[96] and was very likely the work of the Royal Mason, William Ramsey III *fl*.1323 – +1349[97] or under his influence. This workshop has produced some of the finest military effigies in the country, with close attention paid to the fine detail of the armour and other equipment.

No.39: Wilsthorpe (St Faith) *c*.1350

Fig. 89. Wilsthorpe

Current position: In the northeast corner of the sanctuary.

Condition: Damaged (lower legs, lower scabbard, right foot and head of the supporting hound are missing).

Heraldry: Effigy, shield & surcoat: *two bars, on a chief three mullets* [for Mortimer] carved in base relief and decorated with a diaper of pimples with vine scrolls.

Posture: Cross-legged (right over left) with the right hand holding the dexter corner of the shield and the left hand resting on the scabbard and the left foot resting on a hound.

Description: Limestone. A rectangular pillow supports the head. The aventail is attached to the bacinet by the

vervelle and cord method (the mail realistically represented). The figure wears a small moustache. Clad in mail, supplemented by plate defences, wearing tight-fitting coat-armour, which falls to the knees and has a scalloped fringe at the bottom. On the hem, between two horizontal lines, is a textualis inscription in Middle English, which reads; BETTER IS PYS THAN WERS (i.e. better is peace than wars). Incised mullets separate the words. The supplementary plate comprises: single lame spaudlers, upper cannon of the vambrace, which only covers the outside of the arm and secured over the mail haubergeon by two straps whereas the lower cannon totally encloses the forearm and cup-shaped couters. A gutter-shaped plate covers the top of the thighs and legs, secured over the mail hose by straps. Over the knees are poleyns with a central keel. The gauntlets with long cuffs, consists of four lames, and over the back of the hand by a broad lame, the fingers although worn, appear to be covered with small plates. Around the waist is a medium-width belt decorated with rosettes, which is joined by a rosette-shaped buckle on the right hip, its loose end terminates by a chape in the form of a floral-C, also on the right, and secured by a small-knotted lace. Attached to the waist-belt by a vertical strap is a circular purse, which was formerly secured to the strap by a buckle, as Edward Blore (1787-1879) indicated in an unpublished drawing preserved in the British Library.[98] Also attached to the waist-belt by a single band is a very long dagger, its grip octagonal in section with slightly down-turned quillons. The scabbard was originally decorated with a lozengy trellis. The sword-belt is plain and of medium width, and has a circular buckle lying in the centre of the wearer. The loose end of the belt is looped around the portion carrying the buckle, and then passes over the scabbard. The attachment of the belt to the scabbard is concealed by the left hand. The large pommel of the sword is wheel-shaped with a long flattened octagonal grip and straight quillons. The sabaton of the left foot consists of six lames; the strap of the spur remains.

Length: 6ft 1in.

Identification: The heraldry of the figure identifies it as a member of the Mortimer family, who were subtenants of the Wakes, and bore arms based on their overlords, but which individual is represented is problematic to determine. Very little is recorded concerning the Mortimers of Lincolnshire. The effigy probably represents one of the four sons of Walran de Mortimer and very likely the eldest, Ralph. In 1347 Ralph, Thomas and William are recorded carrying off at Wilsthorpe the goods belonging the parson of Passenham, Buckinghamshire. In 1340 Thomas Mortimer of Wilsthorpe was accused of assault, and in 1357 he acknowledges that he owes to Michael, bishop of Lincoln, 20 marks, levied in default of payment of his land in Northampton. Ralph, together with his son John, held half knight's fee at Wilsthorpe, who is last recorded in 1349.

Commentary: The effigy is unique in the context of English monumental military effigies, in having the

[94] *Cal. Inq. Edw. III* 8, p. 374.

[95] *V.C.H. Oxfordshire* 5, p. 298.

[96] Southwick, pp. 7-21.

[97] Harvey, J. 1987, pp. 46-47.

[98] Blair and Goodall, p. 40.

Fig. 90. Wilsthorpe

Fig. 91. Edenham

inscription on the hem of the surcoat. The reason for the inscription is difficult to determine. Claude Blair, who published the effigy in *Church Monuments*,[99] believes the person commemorated may have been a disillusioned veteran of the Hundred Years War or was the inscription intended for an expression of deep religious or social belief ? This Christian sentiment was known in the thirteenth and fourteenth centuries. The *Buildings of England* series (Lincolnshire), describes the effigy as a seventeenth-century fake "The crossing of the legs is improbably done, and the surcoat and its carved pattern is also improbable. The way the hand lies instead of holding the shield has no parallel";[100] both these statements are completely wrong. There are three other effigies surviving in England and Wales with their right hand holding the dexter edge of the shield; Iddesleigh[101] *c*.1250, Lustleigh[102] *c*.1320, (both Devon), and Hinchingbrook House *c*.1250/1300, Huntingdonshire, and the statement regarding the crossing of the legs is complete nonsense as this feature is very common, but unusual at this period. Rather interestingly a shield is represented, which at this period is uncommon, also it is the first sculptured effigy in the county to be shown wearing short coat-armour, but not as short as those a few years later, which wear the so-called "jupon".

No.40: Edenham (St Michael) *c*.1350/60

Current position: On a high tomb-chest together with his wife, underneath the west tower, against the north wall. The tomb-chest, made of limestone, is from the sixteenth century (not belonging to the effigies) and the shields are set within elaborate foiled and cusped panels. Upright shafts, decorated with small standing figures under canopies, divide the shields from each other. A moulded plinth runs along the bottom of the tomb-chest, which has crenellations above it.

Condition: The surface of the stone is very worn and damaged (including the loss of the top half of the shield and the scabbard's attachment to the sword).

Heraldry: Effigy, shield: *a fess of three fusils*, carved in relief. Tomb; from left to right: (1) *a fess three cross-crosslets*, (2) as no.1, (3) *a bend between six martlets*, (4) *quarterly 1 & 4 fusils, 2 & 3 three dolphins*.

Posture: Straight-legged with the hands raised in prayer and the feet, slightly turned to the left, supported by a dog looking away from the figure's left.

Description: Limestone. The tall pointed bacinet, which rests on two rectangular pillows, the upper positioned diagonally, has an aventail (mail represented realistically). The knight is clad in a mixture of mail and plate, wearing short coat-armour, which is tight fitting around the torso, whereas the skirt is flowing with a scalloped hem, falling above the knees. Visible below the coat-armour is the hem of the mail haubergeon (mail realistically represented). The edge of the cuisses extends below the foliated poleyns, which are secured around the

Fig. 92. Edenham

knee by a strap. Worn on the lower legs are closed greaves, consisting of front and back gutter-shaped plates, secured together by straps over a mail hose, which is visible between the two plates, and the feet by sabatons. The spaudlers consist of two lames. There is no guige to support the shield. Due to the damaged nature of the stone, it is not possible to determine whether the arms are covered by vambraces. The right couter (the only one visible) has a circular side-wing. The fingered gauntlets have short cuffs, and are secured round the underside of the wrist by two straps; the fingers appear to be covered with small convex plates, those over the knuckles larger than the others. The sword-belt is broad and decorated with square floral bosses. Hanging off the sword-belt, by a cord is a ballock dagger. The pommel of the sword is wheel-shaped with a long grip and straight quillons. The rowel spurs have short necks.

Length: 6ft 2in.

Identification: Unknown. Due to damage, it is not possible to know for certain whether there was any additional heraldry on the shield therefore identification is problematic. Edward Blore, who made two drawings of the effigy, attributed it in one drawing to Roger de Neville *c*.1320[103] and in a second to John de Neville *c*.1335[104] of Grimsthorpe, but did not give any source. According to William Dugdale the effigy, was brought from the Cistercian abbey of Vaudey, Grimsthorpe, after

---

[99] Blair and Goodall, p. 40.
[100] Pevsner and Harris, p. 802.
[101] Rogers, Plate II.
[102] Rogers, South Devon section Plate VI.

[103] British Library Add. Ms. 42013, drawing no. 58.
[104] British Library Add. Ms. 42011, drawing no. 40.

the dissolution of the monasteries,[105] and the person holding the manor during the 1340's until his death on 27th May 1359 was Gilbert de Nevill of "Grymesthorpe".[106] I have not been able to discover his coat of arms, however the Nevill family of Scotton, Leicestershire, bore on a seal the arms; *gu three fusils in fess arg a border engrailed or*.[107] Therefore it is quite probable that the effigy represents Gilbert de Nevill, the last of the male line, whose daughter, Elizabeth and heir, was married to Simon Simeon.[108]

Commentary; In March 1646 the effigy and tomb-chest were recorded by Dugdale on the north side of the chancel[109] and on the south side of the chancel in the nineteenth-century by D T. Powell,[110] also it was recorded in the churchyard *c*.1808. An interesting feature also is the schybalds and the way the feet slightly turn to the left. The brass of Sir John Wantone, *c*.1347 at Wimbish (Essex)[111] shows similar armour, as do the figures represented in the side panels of the brass of Sir Hugh Hastings, *c*.1347, at Elsing (Norfolk).[112]

No.41: Norton Disney (St Peter) *c*.1350

Current position: On a high limestone tomb-chest under an arch between the north chapel and altar. The north and south sides are decorated with three shields set within quatrefoils; no heraldry or paint survives.

Condition: Defaced (quillons and lower scabbard missing).

Heraldry: Effigy, shield: *three lions passant* [for d'Isini] carved in relief.

Posture: Straight-legged with the hands raised in prayer and the feet supported by a dog looking away from the figure's left.

Description: Limestone. The bacinet, which is supported by lozenge-shaped pillow, has an aventail, attached by the vervelle and cord method, not in the usual method across the lower edge in a straight line, but in the V-shape. The mail of the aventail is realistically represented, but rather crudely executed. On the upper-arms is a vambrace, and the elbows a couter. The palms of the hourglass gauntlets are bare and the fingers covered with small plates. The cuisse, greaves and poleyns are plain. The sabatons consist of nine lames. The functional parts of the spurs are not shown. The coat-armour is short and tight fitting, with the hem falling to the top of the thighs. No guige has been represented to support the shield. Around the waist is medium-width belt with a large circular buckle, positioned in the centre of the wearer; a long loose end falls to the right, and has a large circular chape. The sword-belt is also plain and of medium width, and it is attached to the scabbard by a series of narrow thongs passing through the mouth of the

scabbard, with their ends hanging in vertical strips. The pommel is wheel-shape with a tapering grip.

Length: 5ft 10in.

Identification: The effigy probably represents William Disny who was dead by 2nd December 1361.[113] In 1336[114] and 1350[115] he was a collector of subsidies (fifteenth and tenth tax) and sheriff of the county between 1341 and 1346.[116] He was the son of William de Isny, who obtained a grant of free warren in 1331 in his lands of Norton Isny.[117]

Commentary; This is a poor quality effigy when compared to others from a similar date in the country, and probably from a local workshop in the East Midlands. The sides of the slab have a downward slope; while unusual, it is a feature found on two other civilian monuments in the church. No undercutting has taken place; also no attention has been paid to fine detail, however this may have been rendered by paint. The Buildings of England series (Lincolnshire), states that because the effigy is straight-legged it is late thirteenth century.[118] This statement is incorrect, as no effigy would be wearing a bacinet with an aventail until the 1330's at the earliest; also the short coat-armour indicates a date after *c*.1345/50. Thirteenth century straight-legged military effigies in England are rare and those that survive total about seventeen and this posture did not become fashionable until the 1340's, previous to this date cross-legged effigies were in vogue. It is a very early example of sculptured hourglass gauntlets, which were introduced *c*.1350.[119]

No.42: Holbeach (All Saints) *c*.1350/60

Current position: On a high tomb-chest made of limestone at the west end of the north aisle. The slab has a hollow chamfer along the edge, which is decorated with alternating square flower-heads of four petals and lions faces with their tongues out. Also the top edge of the tomb-chest has a chamfered edge and is decorated on the north side in the same manner as the edge of the slab, whereas the remaining sides are decorated with running foliage. The north and south sides of the tomb-chest are decorated with four deep niches with trefoiled ogee arches. Pinnacles divide each niche from one other. The walls of the niches on the south side are decorated with flower-heads of four petals. Carved between each gable and pinnacle is a shield hanging from a bracket. The west and east ends have upright shafts with two trefoiled ogee arches.

Condition: Very well preserved apart from the loss of the lower part of the sword-scabbard, dagger; and damage to the edge of the shield and sword.

Heraldry: Effigy, shield: *two lions passant guardant* [for Littlebury] carved in relief. Crest; a man's head wearing a net-like coif. Tomb; on the south side are eight

[105] Bodleian Library, Oxford, Ms. Dugdale 11, fol. 159v.
[106] *Cal. Inq. Edw. III* 10, p. 391.
[107] Loyd and Stenton, p. 18.
[108] *Cal. Inq. Edw. III* 10, p. 391.
[109] Bodleian Library, Oxford, Ms. Dugdale 11, fol. 159.
[110] British Library Add. Ms. 17462, fol. 64.
[111] Binski 1987, fig. 121.
[112] Binski 1987, fig. 120.

[113] *Cal. Fine Rolls* 7, p. 200.
[114] *Cal. Fine Rolls* 4, p. 481.
[115] *Cal. Fine Rolls* 6, p. 234.
[116] *Cal. Fine Rolls* 5, p. 491.
[117] *Cal. Charter Rolls* 4, p. 224.
[118] Pevsner and Harris, p. 590.
[119] Blair, Claude, 1972, p. 66.

Fig. 93 Norton Disney

Fig. 94. Norton Disney

Fig. 95. Holbeach

shields, five show *two lions passant guardant* and three *barry of six* [for Kirton]; north side eight shields, four *two lions passant guardant* and four *barry of six*.

Posture: Straight-legged with the hands raised in prayer and the head supported by a great helm, and the feet supported by a lion looking away towards the figure's right.

Description: Limestone. The bacinet has an aventail, attached by the vervelle and cord method (mail realistically represented), its junction decorated with trefoils. The spaudlers consist of three lames. The coat-armour is short and tight-fitting with the hem decorated with oak leaves, below is the lower edge of the mail haubergeon. Visible between the leaves are small rivets, indicating that a coat of plates[120] is worn beneath the coat-armour; the small plates that cover the shoulders are just visible above the top lame of the spaudler. The upper and lower cannon vambrace has two hinges on the inside, a couter (the right only one represented) with a small circular side-wing, which is articulated to the upper and lower cannons by a narrow lame. The gauntlets have short cuffs, each consist of two lames, and over the back of the hand by a broad lame, articulated by a narrow lame below. Small convex plates, those over the knuckles larger than the others, cover the fingers. The guige is decorated with rectangular plaques, set at wide intervals.

The hip-belt consists of square pyramidal bosses, each decorated around its edge with small pimples and the centre with a quatrefoil flower. Its large circular buckle

lies to the right of the wearer and is decorated with small flower-heads, the eyelets are large circular bosses decorated with a dimple border. The loose end of the belt is looped underneath itself and then pulled through, forming a knot. The sword-belt passes diagonally across the waist from the right hip, and is decorated at wide intervals by quatrefoils; its circular buckle lies to the left of the wearer near the sword. The method of attaching the belt to the scabbard is by two rings, the locket is decorated with a crocketed gable; the chape of the sword's scabbard remains on the edge of the slab. The pommel and grip appear to be represented, bound with a diamond-shaped pattern. The quillons are down-turned with their ends slightly rolled over. The cuisse are decorated with small flower-heads, indicating that in reality the studs would have held metal plates to the inside lining. On the knees are poleyns, which have a reinforced riveted cup covering the kneecaps; a mail fillet can be seen underneath the knee. The greaves have two hinges on the inside whereas the outside, appear to be plain. The sabatons consist of rectangular plates. The rowel spurs are small with bent arms; the eyelets of the straps have small circular bosses.

Length: 6ft 3in.

Identification: Sir Humphrey de Littlebury. He bore the arms *argent two lions passant guardant gules*[121] and was married to Elizabeth Kirton, heiress of Sir John de Kirton,[122] who bore the arms *barry of six ermine and gules*;[123] both these coats appear on the tomb. Humphrey was a king's yeoman and forester of Sherwood in 1310 and in 1315 he was Captain and Admiral of the king's fleet.[124] He was summoned as a knight of Lincolnshire to the Great Council in 1324 and chosen as a Commissioner of Array.[125] An inquisition dated 13th August 1323 at Boston, where Reynald le Ceu and others ware guilty of robbery at the manor of Sir Humphrey de Littleberey at Holbeach.[126] Humphrey died shortly after July 1339, and his heir was his eldest son Sir Robert who died in 1351.[127]

Commentary: The monument is one of the finest and best preserved in the country, with fine detail rendered to the armour and tomb decoration. A very rare feature is the deep niches on the tomb-chest, but whether these originally contained standing statues is questionable. Julian Luxford believes different people made the tomb-chest in two sections and that it is earlier than the effigy at *c*.1340-45.[128] The tomb-chest of Edward II *c*.1340 at Gloucester cathedral,[129] and the tomb-chest dated *c*.1330 in the Chapel of St Stephen Bures, also have deep niches,[130] which are associated with shrine style construction. A drawing by Daniel King, dated 1653,

---

[120] A similar coat-of-plates construction was discovered in 1905 on the site of the battle of Wisby fought in 1341. See Thordeman, pls. 93-95.

[121] Burke, p. 612.
[122] Gough 1, pt. 2, p. 97.
[123] Chesshyre and Woodcock, p. 90.
[124] Moor 2, p. 52.
[125] Moor 2, p. 52.
[126] *Cal. Inq. Misc.* 2, p. 171.
[127] Luxford, p. 167.
[128] Luxford, p. 169.
[129] Morganstern, pls. 48, 49.
[130] Morganstern, Plate 50.

Fig. 96. Holbeach

Fig. 97. Holbeach

shows that the Bures tomb-chest originally contained figures (possibly apostles)[1] decorating the walls of the niches, whether these were carved or painted is unclear.

Some authors are of the opinion that the effigy is of Lincolnshire, however I believe that the style of the lion supporting the feet of the figure indicates that it is a product of the so-called "Westminster Workshop" and classified under the my lion footrest research as "Westminster type D".[2] Other lions in this group are at Reepham (Norfolk), Sparsholt (2) (Berkshire) and Spratton (Northamptonshire). Also given the fact that the tomb-chest has deep niches, which are also found at Gloucester and Bures, again points to the "Westminster Workshop". That the figure is made from limestone does not necessarily mean Lincolnshire sculptors carved it. Other types of material effigies used for carving effigies from this workshop are alabaster and wood, therefore the type of material used for the Holbeach effigy should not detract from the possibility that it was made elsewhere. It is a unique effigy, with no others in the country like it, and is from a period when workshops were producing individualistic high quality effigies. Armour was advancing rapidly, studded cuisses being a feature shown on effigies and brasses for only a short period *c*.1350-70, however, the shield is a very late occurrence on an effigy.

No.43: Great Grimsby (St James) *c*.1360/70

Fig. 98. Great Grimsby

Current position: On a stone plinth in the north transept.

Condition: Defaced, damaged and worn (including the loss of the fingers, dagger's pommel, sword's lower scabbard and damage to the sabatons).

Heraldry: Effigy, coat-armour: *six lions rampant* [for Heslarton] carved in relief. Crest; a lion's head.

Posture: Straight-legged with the hands raised in prayer and the head supported by a great helm and the feet supported by a lion looking towards the figure's right.

Description: Limestone. The bacinet has an aventail (mail realistically represented), attached by the vervelle and cord method. The spaudlers consist of four lames. The coat-armour is short and tight-fitting, with a fork on the right-hip revealing a garment with a scalloped fringe and small rivets. This represents the lower edge of the coat of plates. Below the scallops can be seen rings of mail, presumably representing the lower edge of the hauberk. The upper cannon of the vambrace has a strap and buckle on the inside, whereas the lower appears to be plain. The couters, which have a small bi-lobate side-wing, are articulated to the upper and lower cannons by a narrow lame. The hourglass gauntlets are strapped around the forearm. The hip-belt consists of plaques decorated with square flower-heads; each set between three small studs, the clasp or buckle is placed centrally. The loose end of the belt passes behind and hangs directly below. Lying at an angle from the right hip-belt is a dagger; the quillons are short and slightly down-turned. The pommel of the sword has not been represented as the sculptor has placed the elbow over it. The grip is hexagonal in section, with the left quillon (the only one remaining) straight; the locket is decorated with a quatrefoil. The cuisse are studded, indicating that in reality the studs would have held metal plates to the inside lining. Below the poleyn is a forked fringe, presumably the lower edge of the cuisse. The greaves have two straps on the inside and a line on the outside. The rowel spurs are large and have strongly curved arms.

Length: 6ft 6in.

Identification: Heslarton (the name is recorded indifferently). The effigy is traditionally thought to represent Sir Thomas Heslarton;[3] however this attribution is tentative as it may commemorate another member of this family. The Heslartons were mainly a Yorkshire[4] family who held, including others, the manor of Lowthorpe in the East Riding,[5] where members of this family are buried and have monuments. The church of Lowthorpe contains amongst others the effigy of Sir John Heslarton, dead 1348,[6] together with his wife Margeria who had five sons, and a fragment of a very elaborate brass is thought to represent Sir Thomas. It is possible that Thomas may have been commemorated by two monuments, but this is purely speculative. John's four other sons were, John & Nicholas *o.s.p.*1348, Walter

[1] Morganstern, Plate 50.
[2] Downing 1998, p. 25.

[3] Holles, pp. 6-7.
[4] They also held land in Cambridgeshire. *Cal. Charter Rolls* 4, p. 328.
[5] Salmarsh, p 50.
[6] Saltmarsh, p 50.

Fig. 99. Great Grimsby

Fig. 100. Ewerby

Fig. 101. Ewerby

Fig. 102. Friskney

*o.s.p.*1349 and Sir Simon *o.s.p.*1376-7,[7] both Thomas and Walter bore the same arms,[8] however it appears that only Walter, Simon and Thomas achieved knightly status therefore it is more likely that the effigy represents one of them. I have not been able to discover if this family held land in Lincolnshire, but Holles states that he had seen a deed stating that Euphemia de Heslarton held land at Aylesbry near Grimsby,[9] and that she was married thirdly to Walter de Heslarton (son of Walter) dead 1368.[10] It is very difficult to date the effigy; however, considering the coat-armour is tight fitting around the torso and the skirt is slightly flared, a date between 1360-1370 seems probable. If the effigy represents Simon, it must have been set up during his lifetime.

Commentary: While the effigy is damaged it is very interesting, showing rivets of the coat-of-plates and detail on the cuisses, similar to that at Holbeach and shown also on a number of brasses dated to the 1360s.[11]

No.44: Ewerby (St Andrew) *c.*1370

Current position: On a modern stone plinth, underneath a gabled recess in the north wall of the north chapel. There is a steep gable surmounting the arch, which has a great helm within the gable with mantling flowing at the back. The crest is missing, but appears to have been an animal with a long spiralling tail hanging at the back. Below the helm is a shield without any heraldry. The gable is flanked by pinnacles (broken).

Condition: Damaged and broken (the great helm's crest, arms, toes, sword, dagger and the functional parts of the spurs missing).

Heraldry: None.

Posture: Straight-legged with the head supported by a great helm and the feet on a lion looking towards the effigy's right. Originally the hands were represented in the conventional praying position

Description: The bacinet has an aventail, attached by the vervelle and cord method. The rings of the mail are represented by gesso, and are now only visible on the back of the neck. The spaudlers consist of four lames. The coat-armour is short and tight-fitting, below of which is a garment now smooth, presumably representing the lower edge the mail haubergeon. The hip-belt is plain, with the buckle to the wearer's right which is decorated with a *lion statant guardant*. Attached to the cuisses and greaves by rivets, are cup-shaped poleyns with a central keel. On the outside of the greave is a shallow incised line with two hinges. Sabatons protect the feet. The spurs have strongly-curved arms.

Length: 6ft 3½in.

Identification: According to Holles, who recorded the effigy in the north of the choir, and above the tomb the arms *ermine, on a fess gules three crosses botonee or* (Aunsell),[12] the effigy represents Sir Alexander Aunsell

who died without issue. In 1330 Alexander together with others, was accused of unlawful entry into land at Willoughby. In 1346 he held ½ a knight's fee at Ewerby,[13] was a commissioner for Lincolnshire in 1351[14] and paid the king for alienation in mortmain for a rood at Ewerby in 1353.[15] He purchased land at Ewerby from Ranulph de Rye.[16] In 1370 John Aunsell held a fifth part of a knight's fee in Ewerby,[17] but I have not been able to discover how they were related. Alexander's date of death is not recorded, but he most likely died between 1353 and 1370, although the church guide states 1360.

Commentary: The effigy appears to be a Lincolnshire product, and is from a period when effigies are depicted wearing armour of the type that remained in fashion until the early fifteenth century.

No.45: Friskney (All Saints) *c.*1370/80

Fig. 103. Friskney

Current position: On a coffin in the northwest corner of the chancel.

Condition: Very damaged and broken with many pieces loose (the arms, lower legs, sword and dagger missing).

Heraldry: None.

---

[7] Saltmarsh, p 50.

[8] Chesshyre and T. Woodcock, p. 315.

[9] Holles, pp. 6-7.

[10] *Cal. Close Rolls Edw. III* 12, p. 417.

[11] Boutell, p. 30.

[12] Holles, p. 216.

[13] *Feudal Aids* 3, p. 194.

[14] *Cal. Patent Rolls Edw. III* 9, p. 81.

[15] *Cal. Patent Rolls Edw. III* 9, pp. 81, 408.

[16] Maddison 3, p. 839.

[17] *Cal. Inq. Edw. III* 12, p. 293.

Posture: Straight-legged with the hands originally in the conventional praying position.

Description: Limestone. Two cushions, the upper positioned diagonally, support the head. The bacinet has an aventail, attached by the vervelle and cord method. The mail is rendered by gesso, which only survives on the gusset on the right armpit. The spaudlers consist of three lames. The coat-armour is short and tight-fitting, below which is a deep smooth fringe, presumably representing the lower edge of the mail haubergeon. The upper cannon is loose, and on the elbow is a couter, which has a small circular side-wing, and is articulated to the upper and lower cannon by a narrow lame. There are no visible straps or buckles. The hip-belt is joined by a bilobate-buckle; and the loose portion passes behind the belt and is pulled through it forming a knot. The cuisses are plain and the poleyns globular, with a bilobate side-wing and an additional lame below. The inside of the upper part of the greaves has a strap and buckle, also the loose lower portion of the greave has a strap and buckle. A loose piece of the lion's tail remains.

Length: 5ft 1½in.

Identification: It is not known whom the effigy represents; however in 1303 Sir Ranulph de Friskeney obtained a licence to crenelate his dwelling at Friskney, therefore this family had strong association with the village, though other people also held land. In 1349 William de Friskeney was a collector of subsidy, who was also recorded in 1377. Thomas de Friskeney is recorded protecting the Friskeney coastline in 1368 and in 1372 John de Wylughby held land at Friskeney for 1 knight's fee. William de Michell is recorded of Friskeney in 1381 and 1388.

Commentary: Holles did not record the effigy under discussion, but he did record a cross-legged effigy (now missing) with the arms; "*a saltire between four cross formée*, Friskney",[18] which may have represented Ranulf de Friskney.[19]

No.46: Saxilby (St Botolph) *c.*1370/80

Current position: The effigy, together with his wife, is on a table-tomb made of a dark limestone, against the north wall of the north chapel. The tomb-chest is later than the effigy, probably of sixteenth century date, and is decorated on the south side by two large foliated squares with a small shield in the centre.

Condition: Defaced and damaged (the arms, feet, sword, dagger and helm's crest missing). In 1993 it was conserved by Harrison Hill Ltd, at a cost of £10,500.

Heraldry: Effigy, coat-armour: *four fusils in fesse* [for Daubeney] carved in light relief. Crest; *a lion*.

Posture: Straight-legged, with the head resting on a great helm, and the feet on a lion looking towards the effigy's right. The hands were originally represented in the conventional praying position,

Description: Alabaster. The bacinet has an aventail, attached by the vervelle and cord method (mail realistically represented). Encircling the scull is an orle,

Fig. 104. Saxilby

decorated with large flower-heads, quatrefoils and lozenges, set within a wide border. The figure wears a drooping moustache. The coat-armour is short and tight-fitting and joined by lacing on the right. The spaudlers consist of five lames and are riveted on the inner corners; a portion of the left upper of cannon remains. The hip-belt consists of square pyramidal plaques, decorated with lozenges and set between small pimples; the clasp or buckle placed centrally. The cuisses and greaves have two hinges on the outside whereas the inside appears to be plain. On the knees are poleyns with small bilobate side-wings, which are articulated to the greave by a narrow and a broad lame. The broad lower lame is secured to the greaves by a turning-pin on the corner. Part of the right spur strap is visible together with a rowel.

Length: 6ft.

Identification: From the heraldry on the coat-armour, the effigy could commemorate either Sir Ralph Daubeney who was still living in December 1378[20] or his son Sir Giles, who died on 24th June 1386 at Barrington, (Somerset),[21] both were styled of South Ingleby, Lincolnshire, and South Petherton, (Somerset). Giles's widow Alianore died in 1400 and was buried at Kempston, Bedfordshire, together with their son Giles, who died 22nd August 1403.[22] Ralph had an active military career, being knighted in 1326/7, performing

---

[18] Holles, p. 162.
[19] Brault 2, pp. 185-186.

[20] *Complete Peerage* 4, p. 97.
[21] *Complete Peerage* 4, p. 97.
[22] *Complete Peerage* 4, p. 98.

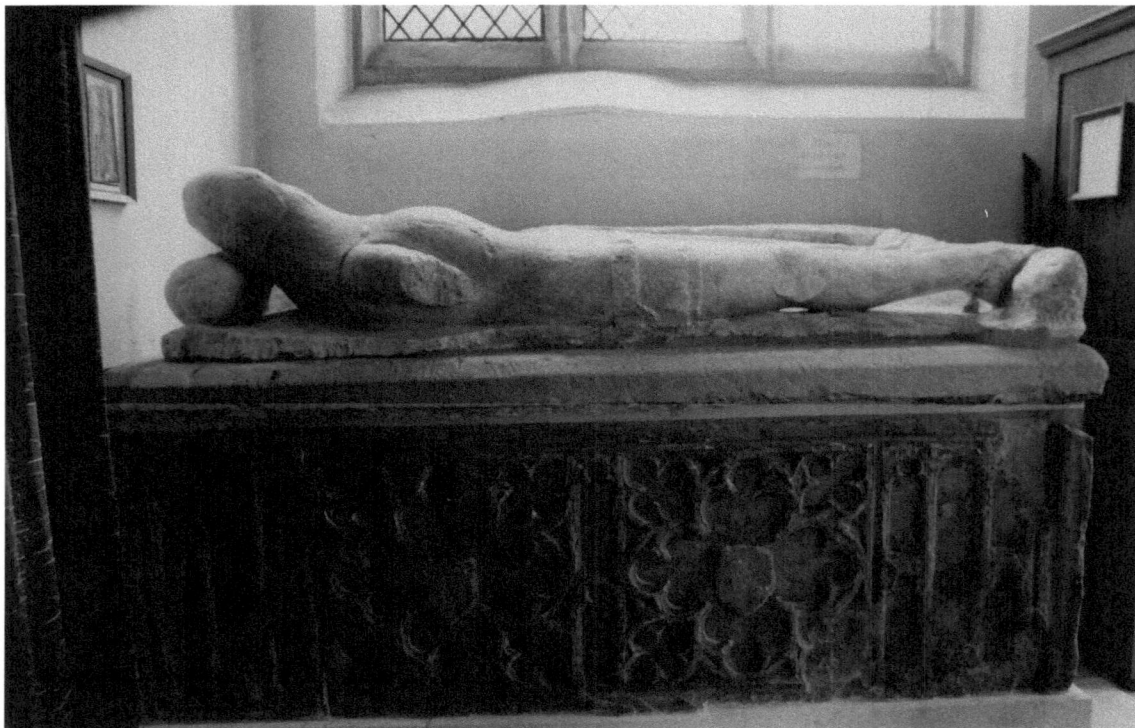

Fig. 105. Saxilby

Fig. 106. Spilsby (2)

military service in Scotland, being captured there in 1337, and fighting in the King's division at Crecy.[23] He was first married to Alice in 1332/3, and second to Katharine in 1345/6, who died between 1364 and 1374.[24] Giles was a sheriff of Bedfordshire and Buckinghamshire 1379-80, and a knight of the shire for Somerset 1382-4.[25] As a female effigy is present it is more likely to represent Ralph and his second wife Katharine as Giles's widow was buried elsewhere.

Commentary: According to the church guidebook the effigies were brought from the private disued chapel at North Ingleby, which lies one mile to the north of the village. The effigy is the earliest alabaster monument in the county and one of the earliest made of this material in the country. It has an early representation of an orle, and the extremely rare feature of lacing on the side of the coat-armour. It is difficult to say whether the effigy is a Lincolnshire product, with the alabaster being imported from Derbyshire where the material was quarried, and then carved in the church; but more likely it was in a finished state when transported to the church.

No.47: Spilsby (2) (St James) *c*.1375

Current position: On a high modern limestone tomb-chest, on the south side of the north chapel. Shields on the tomb-chest are set within foliated panels, and above the shields on the north and south sides, are small female heads, whereas the east and west ends have male angels holding the top of the shields. Both the north and south sides of the slab are decorated with four bedesmen, standing on pedestals under crocketed gables; the east and west ends have running foliage.

Condition: Although in very good condition some parts have been restored (dagger missing and sword replacement). The functional parts of the spurs are missing.

Heraldry: Effigy, coat-armour: *a cross moline* [for Willoughby] carved in relief. Crest; *two horns*. Tomb; south side from left to right: (1) *a cross engrailed* (2) *bezantée* (3) *per pale a cross sarcellée, a cross engrailed* (4) *six escallops* (5) *on a fess three rondels*; north side from left to right: (1) *a bend between six martlets* (2) *six mascles* (3) *a lion rampant queue fourchée* (4) *billettée, a fess dancette* (5) *crusilly, a pierced cinquefoil*; west end: *a cross recerecelée*; east end: *fretty*.

Posture: Straight-legged with the hands raised in prayer and the head supported by a great helm with a ducal coronet and strawberry leaves. A lion looking towards the figure's right supports the feet.

Description: Alabaster. The bacinet has an aventail (mail realistically represented), attached by the vervelle and cord method, with an orle encircling it, which is decorated with alternating circular flower-motifs and lozenge-shape plaques. The spaudlers consist of three lames. The coat-armour is short and tight-fitting with a foliated fringe and laced on the right side. Projecting from beneath the coat-armour is the extreme lower point

of the coat-of-plates, with two horizontal rows of small rivets, worn beneath is the lower edge of the mail haubergeon. The upper and lower cannons have two hinges on the inside, and couters with small bi-lobate side-wings are articulated to the cannons by a narrow lame. The hourglass gauntlets have short cuffs with small convex plates; those over the knuckles larger than the others cover the fingers. The hip-belt consists of square pyramidal plaques, decorated with alternating quatrefoils and multifoils, its clasp or buckle placed centrally. The sword's pommel is spherical and the oval grip decorated with a diamond-shape pattern. Each quillon has two scroll ends. The mouth of the scabbard has an ogee arch and is decorated with a *cross potent*. The cuisses are closed, indicated by two hinges on the outside and by two straps with buckles on the inside, and globular poleyns with a central keel, articulated to the greaves by a narrow lame. The greaves are closed, indicated by two hinges on the inside and outside. Below the greave is a mail fillet, the mail represented in the same manner as the aventail. The sabatons consists of five lames. The straps of the spurs are decorated with circular flower-heads, carved in low relief, and the arms slightly curved towards their terminals.

Length: 6ft 4in.

Identification: John, Lord Willoughby. He was the son and heir of John, Lord Willoughby (see Spilsby (1) p. 68), and was born at Eresby manor and baptised at Spilsby 1328/9, having seisin of his father's lands in 1349/50 and died 29th March 1372.[26] He was in the company of Edward, Prince of Wales, at the siege of Calais in 1347 and Poitiers in 1356, and summoned as a member of parliament from 1350 and 1370.[27] He married Cecily Ufford before 1349.[28]

Commentary: As with Spilsby (1), this effigy was restored, possibly in 1790, by the sculptor Thomas Brayne, whose work included "getting paint off with soap, sanding grounding and polishing" and in 1825 by the sculptor Charles Smith, who made new moulded alabaster bases.[29] In all probability the effigy under discussion has had its surface re-cut, which would account for there being no graffiti, and with new additions (nose, sword and hands). The figures on the edge of the slab are very unusual, particularly on this type of monument, and one must wonder if they have been added. However, they were there when Richard Gough published his book on *Sepulchral Monuments* in 1786, where he recorded the effigy on the north side of the choir, which would also account for the fact that no antiquarians recorded the coats of arms on the north side of the tomb-chest;[30] presumably it was against a wall. Holles also recorded the effigy in the choir between 1638-1642.[31] Alabaster effigies wearing orles that are represented in low relief are rare, others can be seen at Saxilby (p. 83) and Dorchester Abbey (Oxfordshire).

[23] *Complete Peerage* 4, p. 96.
[24] *Complete Peerage* 4, p. 97.
[25] *Complete Peerage* 4, p. 97.
[26] *Complete Peerage* 12, pp. 659-660.
[27] *Complete* Peerage 12, pp. 659-660.
[28] *Complete* Peerage 12, p. 660.
[29] Lord, pp. 90-91.
[30] Gough 1, pt. 2, pp. 187-189.
[31] Holles, p. 88.

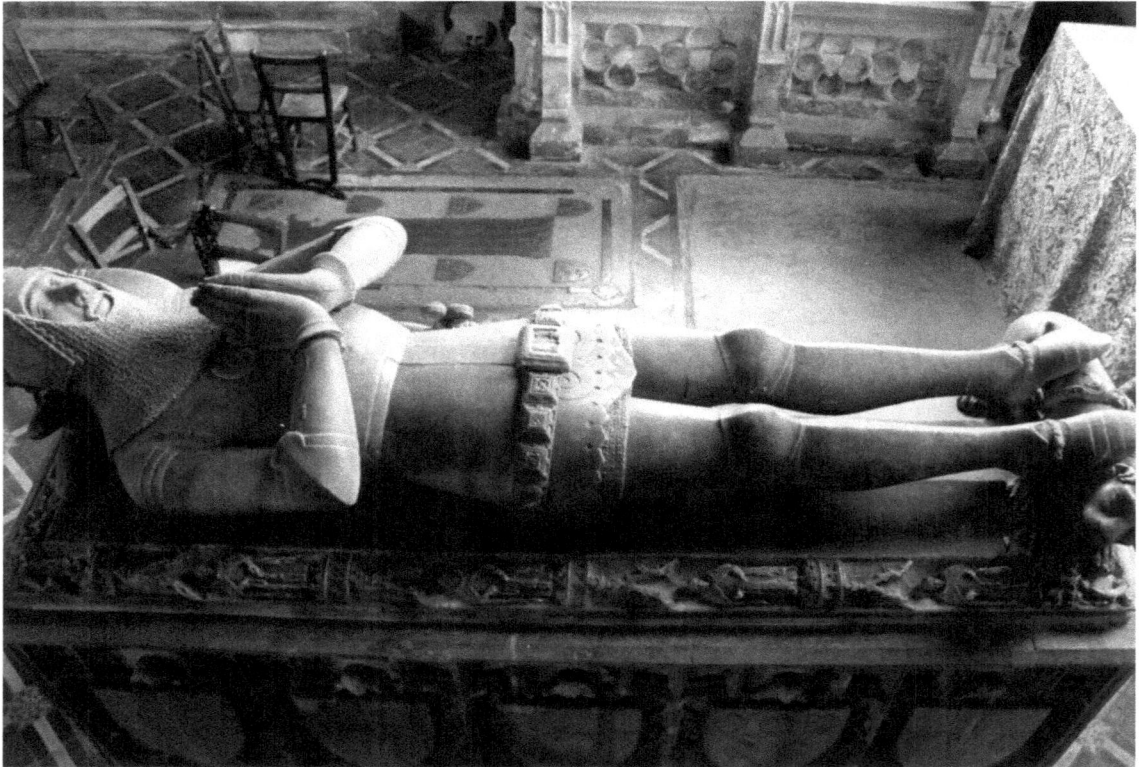

Fig. 107. Spilsby (2)

Fig. 108. Lincoln Cathedral (1)

Fig. 109. Lincoln Cathedral (1)

Fig. 110. Caistor (2)

No.48: Lincoln Cathedral (1) *c.*1375

Current position: On a high tomb-chest made of limestone, underneath an arch at the east end of the south aisle. The coping below the slab is made of Purbeck marble.

Condition: Very damaged and worn (head, right arm, hands, legs and footrest missing).

Heraldry: Effigy, coat-armour: *fess vair, between three leopards faces jessant-de-lis* [for Cantelope] carved in relief. Tomb-chest; three shields on the south side and one on the west end, all bear *a fesse checky, between three leopards faces jessant-de-lis*. Each shield is set within an octofoil. The north and east sides of the tomb-chest are plain.

Posture: Originally represented straight-legged, with the hands in the conventional praying position.

Description: Limestone. The tops of the shoulders are covered by the lower part of an aventail. The coat-armour is short and tight-fitting with a scalloped lower edge. Below the scallops can be seen rings of mail indicated by parallel rows of C's stamped in applied composition, this presumably represents the lower edge of the haubergeon. The left spaudler consists of three lames, and the upper cannon with a strap on the inside, whereas the lower cannon appears to be plain. The couter has a small bi-lobate side-wing, and is articulated to the upper and lower cannons by a narrow lame. Around the waist is a hip-belt, decorated with flower-head plaques and joined in the front by a large circular buckle; the loose end hangs below. On the left hip are the remains of the sword. The small remaining portion of the cuisses have round-headed rivets, indicating that in reality the studs would have held metal plates to the inside lining.

Length: 3ft 3in.

Identification: Nicholas Cantelope, died February 21st 1371 at Avignon.[32] He was the son and heir of Nicholas de Cantelope, third Baron Cantelope, Lord of Gresley, Nottinghamshire, who died 1355.[33] He was twice married, firstly to Joan,[34] who had a brass next to his monument,[35] and secondly to Katharine.[36] He was a justice for the Holland division of Lincolnshire[37] and a keeper of the peace for Nottinghamshire.[38]

Commentary: The figure has been recorded by a number of antiquaries and heralds, most notably by Sir William Dugdale who comments on the effigy as follows; "bacinet, helm and aventail painted steel coloured.[39] All armour gilt, face coloured. Crest of a swan's head beaked *or*. Arms on coat-armour: *gules a fess vair between three leopard's heads jessant-de-liz*. So bright and undamaged that I feel sure the figure must already have been painted". The footrest was recorded as a wolf.[40] The earliest documented evidence for the effigy is by John

Leland during his survey of England and Wales between 1535 and 1543,[41] who recorded it in the southeast chapel. During the eighteenth-century it was recorded by Brown Willis (1742)[42] and Richard Gough (1786),[43] then on the north side of the chapel.

No.49: Caistor (2) (St Peter and St Paul) *c.*1380

Fig. 111. Caistor (2)

Current position: Under a cusped arch in the north wall of the north aisle.

Condition: Defaced and damaged (fingers and attendant angels heads missing).

Heraldry: None.

Posture: Straight-legged with the hands raised in prayer and the feet supported by a lion looking away from the figure's right. The head rests on two tasselled cushions with the upper positioned diagonally and held by two angels.

Description: Limestone. Encircling the bacinet is a narrow orle decorated with alternating quatrefoils and cinquefoils, and an aventail (mail realistically represented) attached by the vervelle and cord method. The coat-armour is short and tight-fitting; has a scalloped lower edge and is laced on the right side. Below the scallops can be seen the lower edge of the mail haubergeon. The spaudlers consist of four lames, and upper and lower cannons closed, each having two hinges on the outside and couters with small bi-lobate side-

---

[32] *Cal. Inq. Edw. III* 13, pp. 76-78.

[33] *Dictionary of National Biography* 8, p. 447.

[34] *Cal. Fine Rolls* 8, p. 152.

[35] Gough 1, pt. 2, p. 130. Whittemore, p. 41, fig. 23.

[36] *Cal. Inq. Edw. III* 13, pp. 76-78.

[37] *Cal. Inq. Misc.* 3, p. 367.

[38] *Cal. Inq. Misc.* 2, p. 272.

[39] British Library Add. MS. 714, 74, fol. 99V.

[40] College of Arms 1634, fol. 11V.

[41] Smith 5, p. 122.

[42] Willis, p. 1, no. 12.

[43] Gough 1, pt. 2, p. 130.

Fig. 112. Kingerby (2)

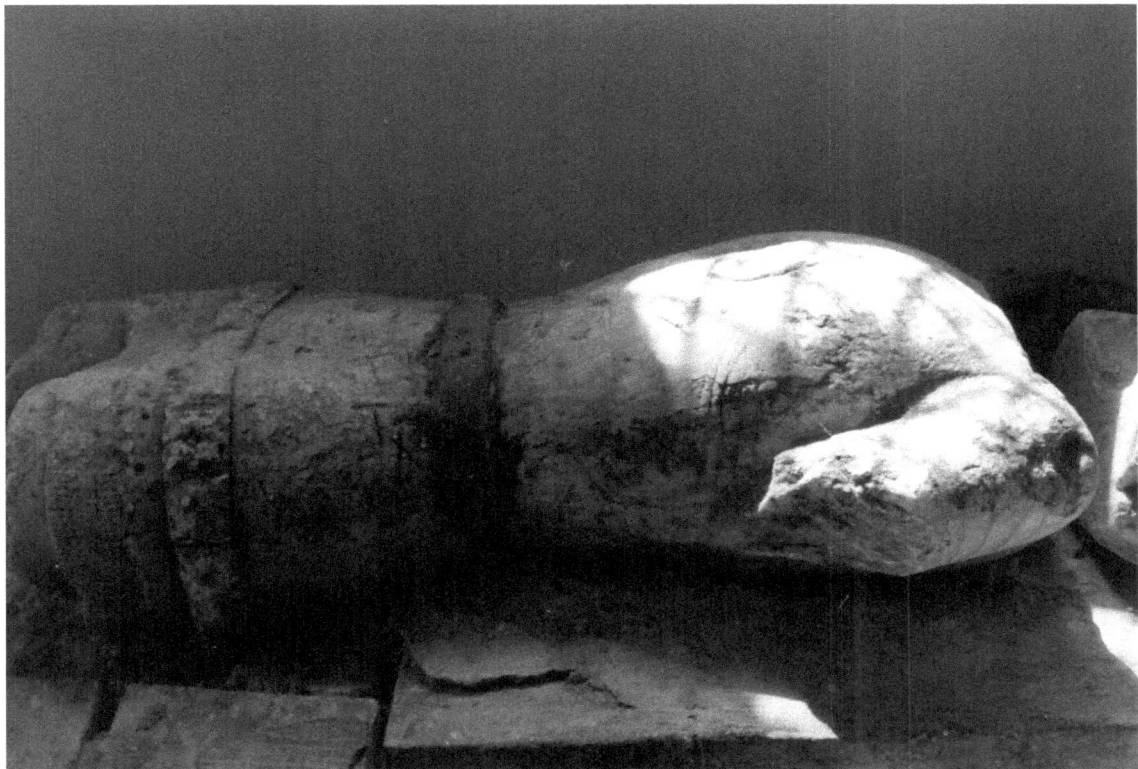

Fig. 113. North Cockerington

wings, articulated to the upper and lower cannons by a narrow lame. The hourglass gauntlets, while damaged, have a plate on the back of the hand, which is hinged. The hip-belt consists of square plaques, decorated with alternating quatrefoils and cinquefoils, its clasp placed centrally. A fragment of the dagger remains on the right hip. Passing diagonally from the right hip is a narrow sword-belt, which has a short loose portion. The pommel is wheel-shaped with a long grip and straight quillons. Poleyns with a central keel and a small bi-lobate side-wing, are articulated to the cuisse by a narrow lame and to the greave by two lames. The greaves have two hinges on the outside and a closing line on the inside. The sabatons consist of nine lames. The large rowel spurs have straight arms and straps decorated with square floral bosses and rectangular buckles.

Length: 6ft ½in.

Identification: Unknown. According to Holles the effigy was believed locally to represent Sir John de Hundon,[44] and the church guidebook also attributes the effigy to Sir John. The earliest record of him occurs in 1331 when he had a grant of free warren in Hundon,[45] in the parish of Caistor. He was an escheator for Lincolnshire and Rutland between 1342 and 1344,[46] sheriff for Lincolnshire 1342/43,[47] and commissioner in 1349 and 1350.[48] The last record of him is in 1359, he may have died shortly after. He was probably the son of John Hundon who died in or before 1324[49] (see Caistor (1) p. 36).

Commentary: The most interesting features on this effigy are the two attendant angels and the cushions, which are uncommon at this late date, and also the lacing on the coat-armour and the diagonal sword-belt.

No.50: Kingerby (2) (St Peter) *c*.1380

Current position: On a tomb-chest against the south wall of the south aisle. In 1982 the church was vested in the Churches Conservation Trust, which undertook the conservation of the effigy.

Condition: Defaced and broken (including the loss of the fingers, legs, lower sword's-scabbard, pommel, dagger's pommel and scabbard).

Heraldry: Effigy, coat-armour: *three lions passant a label of three points* [for d'Isini] carved in relief. Crest: a lion. Tomb: right-left (1) *barry of fourteen three chaplets* [for Greystoke/Fitzralph]*:* (2) *a maunch* [for Hastings]*:* (3) *three lions passant a label of three points* [for d'Isini]. The tomb is mainly modern with the shields set within quatrefoils.

Posture: Straight-legged with the hands raised in prayer and the head supported by a great helm. A lion supports the feet, looking away from the figure's right.

Description: Limestone. The bacinet has an aventail (mail realistically represented), attached by the vervelle

Fig. 114. Kingerby (2)

and cord method. The spaudlers consist of three lames. The coat-armour is short and tight-fitting with a scalloped lower edge. Below the scallops can be seen a smooth undergarment, very likely intended to represent the lower edge of the mail haubergeon, with the ring of mail originally represented by composition. The upper cannon is plain and on the elbows are couters, which have a small circular side-wings, and are articulated to the upper and lower cannons by a narrow lame. Although the rivet securing the strap inside the elbow is represented on the couter wing, the articulating-rivets required to hold all these plates together are not. The gauntlets have cuffs shaped like an hourglass, which have small studs bordering the edge of the cuff. Around the waist is a belt, decorated with incised large square flower-heads, and with a circular central buckle; the loose end, which passes behind the belt, and hangs vertically below, has a diamond-shape chape decorated with a flower-head. The grip of the sword and dagger are octagonal in section and their quillons short and straight. The locket of the sword is decorated with four quatrefoils set within rectangles. Part of the right cuisse remains, which is smooth. The sabatons consist of eight lames. The functional parts of the spurs are not represented.

Length: 4ft 2in.

Identification: The heraldry on the coat-armour is that of a Disney, but to discover which member it represents is problematic given how large the family was and that members of the family may have wished to be buried with their ancestors. As a label is represented on the coat-armour, this may be to *mark cadency* for the eldest son,

[44] Holles, p. 90.

[45] *Cal. Charter Rolls* 4, p. 230.

[46] *Cal. Patent Rolls Edw. III* 5, p. 574.

[47] *Cal. Fine Rolls* 5, pp. 303, 349.

[48] *Cal. Patent Rolls Edw. III* 8, pp. 236, 516.

[49] *Cal. Fine Rolls* 3, p. 311.

however some bore this in their own right (see Kingerby (1) p. 49 for an account of the Disneys). It is worth mentioning three members of a junior branch of the Disneys who are worth considering; John living 1346-1360, William living 1360-65, both of Dirrington (Dorrington) and Thomas Disney of Fosham, living between 1347-1394.[50] In 1345 John was involved in an inquisition regarding the late lands of Templars in Nottinghamshire and Lincoln.[51] Hugh Disney believes the effigy represents William (5) who died in 1349,[52] however the date of the effigy is too much later for him to be considered.

Commentary: Holles recorded the effigy in the vanished north aisle.[53] Stylistically the effigy appears to be a Lincolnshire product and although damaged it shows some fine detail to the armour and equipment.

No.51: North Cockerington (St Mary) *c.*1380/90

Fig. 115. North Cockerington

Current position: On the floor against the south wall of the south aisle. In 1981 the church was declared redundant and is now vested in the Churches Conservation Trust.

Condition: Very damaged with only the torso and the lion footrest remaining. It is broken across the waist, where it has been repaired with modern cement.

Heraldry: Effigy, coat-armour: *on a cross a mullet*, carved in low relief.

Posture: Straight-legged, with the hands originally in the conventional praying position.

Description: Alabaster. The coat-armour is short and tight-fitting with a scalloped hem; below is the lower edge of the mail haubergeon. On the left shoulder (the only one remaining) is a four lame spaudler. Around the waist is a hip-belt made of square pyramidal plaques. Only a small part of the plain cuisses remains.

Length: 3ft 5in.

Identification: The heraldry[54] on the coat-armour suggests that the effigy may represent John de Cockerington, who held a tenement in Cockerington for a part of a knight's fee, and who was a collector of tax in Lindsey, co. Lincolnshire in 1380.[55]

Commentary: Church notes taken in 1835 records the effigy in a similar state of preservation as it is today, except that the head remained, wearing a "gorget of mail".[56]

No.52: Stamford (St Mary) *c.*1400

Fig. 116. Stamford

Current position: On a limestone tomb-chest decorated with foiled arches and in the centre is a large shield set within an octofoil, and placed against the north wall of the north chapel.

---

[50] Disney, pp. 55-57, 70-72.
[51] *Cal. Patent Rolls Edward III* 6, p. 522.
[52] Disney, p. 98.
[53] Holles, p. 69.

[54] Burke, p. 209.
[55] *Cal. Fine Rolls* 9, p. 187.
[56] Monson, p. 88.

Fig. 117. Stamford

Fig. 118. Kirkby-cum-Osgodby

Condition: Very damaged (arms, hands, lower legs, feet, footrest, sword, dagger and attendant angels missing).

Heraldry: Effigy, coat-armour: *three lions paws couped and erect* [for Brown] carved in light relief.

Posture: Straight-legged, with the head resting on two cushions, the upper positioned diagonally and the lower held by two seated damaged angels. The hands originally were represented in the conventional praying position.

Description: Alabaster. The bacinet has an aventail (mail realistically represented); a band covers the junction between the aventail and bacinet with a row of feathering on its lower edge. The spaudlers consist of three lames. The coat-armour is short and tight-fitting with a fringed hem; below is the lower edge of the mail haubergeon. The hip-belt consists of square pyramidal plaques with indents, which presumably once contained glass or paste decoration; the clasp or buckle placed centrally, a dagger-tie is worn on the right. The cuisses have a closing line on the inside whereas the outside has a border decorated with a square floral-motif. On the knees are poleyns with a central keel and lobed side-wings.

Length: 5ft 4in.

Identification: John Brown. The effigy has been recorded by a number of antiquaries who have attributed the figure to either Brown[57] or Usher[58] from the heraldry. In various rolls the name Broun is recorded very frequently which make an attribution problematic, however in 1377,[59] 1388[60] and 1395[61] John Broun of Stamford is recorded and the only reference I have discovered to the Ushers in Lincolnshire is in 1396/7 when Richard Ussher held the manor of Lopynthorp (*sic*).[62] A Richard Ussher was under the captaincy of Humphrey Duke of Gloucester, during the Agincourt campaign in 1415.[63] The fact that a John Broun of Stamford is recorded suggests that it is more likely that the effigy represents a member of this family. In 1377[64] and 1388[65] John Broun was a commissioner to collect the tenth and fifteenth tax in Kesteven, co. Lincoln; also in an inquisition of 1395[66] John Broun of Stamford was recorded as husband of Maud (heir of Sarah Taverner, aged 24). We do not know if it is the same person who is recorded in 1371/88 and 1395, as there may have been father and son with the same name. In 1391 John the younger and elder were involved in an inquisition of land

in Cambridgeshire,[67] but this very likely refers to a different branch of the Browns.

Commentary: The effigy is a common design, but what is slightly unusual is the presence of pillows and angels at the head, rather than a great helm is normally represented. Holles recorded the effigy in its present position together with heraldry in stained glass; "*gules 3 lyons paws couped argent, Brown*".[68]

No.53: Kirkby-cum-Osgodby (St Andrew) *c.*1400

Fig. 119. Kirkby-cum-Osgodby

Current position: On a tomb-chest in the south-east corner of the sanctuary. His wife's effigy is on the opposite side of the sanctuary.

Condition: Well preserved (sword, dagger and functional parts of the spurs missing).

Heraldry: Effigy, coat-armour: *three boars passant* [for Wildbore] carved in light relief. Crest, *a boar sejant*. Tomb; the south-side has three shields each carved with, *three boars passant*, alternating with two escarbuncles; west end has one shield carved with, *three boars passant*. The tomb-chest was originally freestanding as the side panels from presumably the north and east sides are now fixed behind the effigy on the south wall, decorated with three shields, *three boars passant* alternating with three escarbuncles. A worn inscription runs around the top of the south and west sides, with crenellations above; *Hic Jacet Johannes Wildebor qui Obiit tertio nonas Octobis*

[57] British Library Lans. Ms. 99, fol. 29, p. 52.

[58] Butcher, p. 17.

[59] *Cal. Fine Rolls* 10, p. 55.

[60] *Cal. Fine Rolls* 10, p. 216.

[61] *Cal. Inq. Rich. II* 17, no. 563.

[62] *Cal. Inq. Rich. II* 17, no. 763.

[63] The details of Richard Ussher military career have been taken from the AHRC-funded 'The Soldier in Later Medieval England Online Database', www.medievalsoldier.org, accessed 16 July 2008.

[64] *Cal. Fine Rolls* 10, p. 55.

[65] *Cal. Fine Rolls* 10, p. 216.

[66] *Cal. Inq. Rich. II* 17, no. 563.

[67] *Cal. Patent Rolls Rich. II* 4, p. 471.

[68] Holles, pp. 200-1.

Ano Dni Millesimo trecentesimo Nonagesimo octavo Cujus anime & c. On the base of the tomb-panels are human and lion faces.

Posture: Straight-legged, with the hands in the conventional praying position, and the head resting on a great helm. The feet rest on a boar, looking away from the effigy's right.

Description: Limestone. The bacinet has an aventail, (mail realistically represented) with a band covering the junction between the aventail and bacinet. The spaudlers consist of three lames; small articulating rivets are on the inner corners. The coat-armour is short and tight-fitting with fringed lower edge, below which can be seen rings of mail, presumably the lower edge of the mail haubergeon. Both the upper and lower of cannons have two hinges on the outside, and couters with small bi-lobate side-wings, articulated to the upper and lower cannons by a narrow lame. On the hands are fingered hourglass gauntlets with short cuffs, small convex plates, those over the knuckles larger than the others, cover the fingers. The hip-belt consists of square pyramidal plaques decorated with quatrefoils and bordered by small square flower-heads; the centre clasp is lozenge-shape and is decorated in the same manner as the plaques; a dagger cord is worn on the right. The cuisses and greaves have two hinges on the outside whereas on the inner they are plain. The poleyns have large bi-lobate side-wings, which have a large flower-head rivet securing the strap underneath the knee. Each poleyn is articulated to the cuisse by a narrow lame, and to the greave by a broad lame. The sabatons consist of nine lames. The straps of the spurs are decorated with square plaques, with strongly curved arms. A mail fillet is between the lower edge of the greave and spur strap.

Length: 6ft 2in.

Identification: From the inscription on the tomb the effigy can be identified as John Wildbore who died 1398 and was married to Margaret Tourney.[69] There is little known about John, who in 1392 until his death held the manor of Exton from Thomas, Earl of Stafford.[70] In 1379 he was involved with others accused of causing damage to the lands of John, Duke of Lancaster.[71]

Commentary: The effigy is of standard design for the period, but the tomb-chest is very interesting/unusual and must be from a local workshop. An effigy virtually identical and from the same workshop can be seen at Catterick[72] (Yorkshire North Riding). The presence of the escarbuncles on the tomb-chest is probably a decorative feature and not heraldic. Burke gives the arms of Wildbore (Burghley, co Lincoln) *sable a fess, between three boars passant argent*, crest; *a boar sable bristled or*.[73] His wife's effigy is carved in low relief whilst he is carved in the round, which is a strange combination, as one would expect both effigies to be of similar composition. Holles recorded the tomb in the quire.[74]

[69] Holles, p. 70.
[70] *Cal. Inq. Rich. II* 17, nos. 217, 557, 1281.
[71] *Cal. Patent Rolls Rich. II* 1, p. 360.
[72] *V.C.H. Yorkshire, North Riding*, p. 311.
[73] Burke, p. 1110.
[74] Holles, p. 70.

No.54: Uffington (St Michael) *c.*1400

Fig. 120. Uffington

Current position: On a limestone tomb-chest underneath an ogee arch between the chancel and the north chapel.

Condition: Defaced and damaged (including the loss of the fingers and scabbard). The collar's pendant is very worn, and the cuisses have been re-cut.

Heraldry: Effigy, coat-armour: *on a bend a fess double cotised* [for Schropshire[75]] lightly incised. Crest; *a demi-peacock with its wings erect*. Tomb-chest south-side, three worn shields of which only the far right is legible and is the same as that on the effigy (q.v.). The shields are set within cusped panels and are divided from each other by two cusped gables. The floor of the north chapel has been raised covering the north side of the tomb-chest. Around the edge of the tomb-chest are crenellations.

Posture: Straight-legged with the hands raised in prayer and the feet supported by a lion looking towards the effigy's left. The head rests on a great helm with a coronet.

Description: Limestone. The bacinet has an aventail (mail realistically represented) with a band covering the junction between the aventail and bacinet. Around the neck is an SS collar. The coat-armour is short and tight-fitting with quarter length tasselled sleeves and tasselled

[75] Woodcock, Grant and Graham, p. 8.

Fig. 121. Uffington

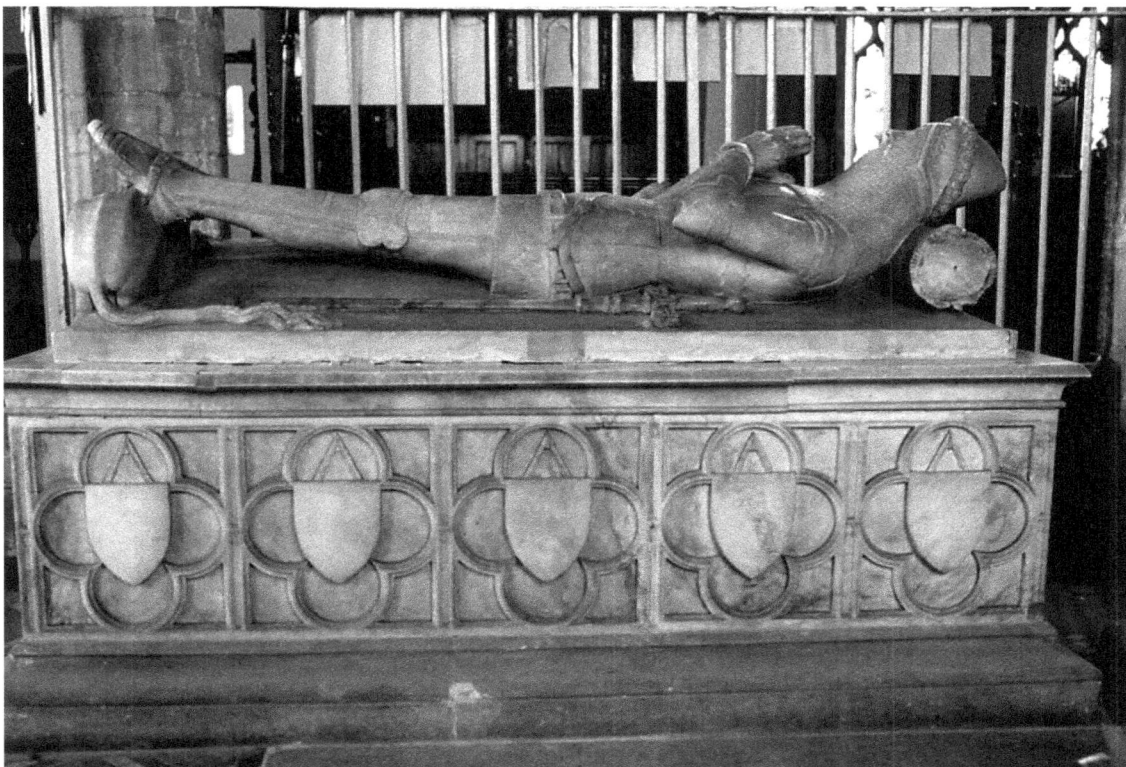

Fig. 122. Spilsby (3)

hem, below is the lower edge of the mail haubergeon. Projecting from below the sleeves is the lowest lame of the spaudler. Attached to the elbows by straps are couters with small bi-lobate side-wings, articulated to the upper and lower cannons of the vambraces by a narrow lame; a mail gusset closes the open joint. The fingered hourglass gauntlets have short cuffs; the metacarpal plate is carved in relief with two diamond-shape plaques. The hip-belt is decorated with incised lozenges; its loose end passes behind the belt and hangs directly below the central buckle. Only the locket of the sword, decorated with two Gothic arches remains. The cuisses comprise five broad lames with small rivets in the top outer-corners, and poleyns with a bi-lobate side-wings, small rivets secure the strap passing underneath the knee and are articulated to its cuisse and greave by a narrow lame. A gusset of mail closes the open joint under the knee. The greaves on the outside have a plain narrow border. The sabatons are comprised of nine lames, together with a large broad top-plate, which covers the first four upper lames. The spurs consist of large rowels, with straight arms.

Length: 6ft 8in.

Identification: Richard de Schropshire died sometime between 1416[76] and 1421,[77] and appears to have been the standard-bearer to Thomas lord Roos, who granted him the manor of Uffington for life for good service and the office of constable of Belvoir castle.[78] He is recorded on many occasions with the Lords Roos and, although it is pure speculation, he may have been killed together with Sir John lord Roos at the battle of Baugé in 1421.[79]

Commentary: The most interesting feature on the effigy is the quarter-length sleeves; it is one of only two three dimensional effigies recorded with this feature, the other being at Ashbourne (Derbyshire), attributed to Edmund Cockayne *ob.*1403.[80] The effigy resembles similar datable effigies made of alabaster, but does not have the same quality; very likely the sculptor has tried to emulate an alabaster effigy, but has failed with little undercutting, also the sides of the slab taper upwards giving an unrefined appearance.

No.55: Spilsby (3) (St James) *c.*1400

Current position: On a high modern alabaster tomb-chest together with his wife on the south side of the north chapel. The side panels are carved with shields represented as hanging off brackets, set within quatrefoils. There are five shields on the north and south sides and one on the west and east ends respectively.

Condition: Although in very good condition it has been restored (dagger and functional parts of the spurs missing).

Heraldry: Effigy, coat-armour: quarterly, 1 & 4 *a cross engrailed*, 2 & 3 *a cross moline* [for Willoughby impaling Ufford] carved in low relief. Crest; a bearded

[76] *Cal. Inq. Hen. V* 20, no. 376.
[77] *Cal. Inq. Hen. V* 21, no. 843.
[78] *Cal. Patent Rolls Edw. III* 15, p. 193.
[79] *Complete Peerage* 11, p. 104.
[80] Lawrence and Routh, Plate 1.

Fig. 123. Spilsby (3)

man. Holles recorded on the side of the tomb-chest four worn painted coats of arms, which are no longer visible; *six mascles, bezantée, six mascles, per pale a saltire with a cross patonce.*

Posture: Straight-legged with the hands raised in prayer and the feet supported by a lion looking towards the effigy's right. Supporting the head is a great helm with a ducal coronet decorated with strawberry leaves.

Description: Alabaster. The bacinet has an aventail (mail realistically represented) with a band covering the junction of the aventail and the bacinet. Encircling the scull is a broad orle carved in high relief and decorated with representations of small stones. Above the forehead is the Latin inscription IHC NAZAREN (Jesus Nazarenes). The spaudlers consist of three lames with small rivets in the inner corners. The coat-armour is short and tight-fitting with a scalloped hem, through which the edge of the mail haubergeon worn beneath is visible. The upper cannons of the vambraces have two buckled straps on the inside, whereas the lower cannons are plain, and couters with small bi-lobate side-wings decorated with running scrolls of foliage, and articulated to the upper and lower cannons by pairs of narrow lames. Gussets of mail are shown closing the open joins between the breastplate and the spaudlers under the armpit, also between upper and lower cannons at the elbow. The fingered hourglass gauntlets have short cuffs, small convex plates; those over the knuckles are larger than the others cover the fingers. The back of each hand is carved in relief, with four plaques of unequal diamond-shape, each framing an elaborate cross. The hip-belt consists of indented square plaques. Passing diagonally across the waist from the right-hip is the sword-belt, with a rectangular D-shape buckle, lying to the left of the wearer. The sword on the left is a complete replacement. The pommel is spherical and the grip oval and is decorated with a diamond-shape pattern, each quillon has two scroll ends.

The outside of the cuisses and greaves have borders decorated with a square floral-motif, also the front lower-edge of the greave has the same pattern. The poleyns are globular with a central keel, and are decorated with borders of running scrolls of foliage and articulated to the cuisses and greaves by a narrow and broad lame. The sabatons consist of eight lames and a large broad lame covering the top of the first four lames; also small riveted-plates cover the heel. On the heels, attached by straps are spurs, the straps decorated with square flower-heads carved in low relief. The arms of the spurs are plain and slightly curved towards their terminals.

Length: 6ft 5in.

Identification: Robert, Lord Willoughby. He was the son and heir of John, Lord Willoughby (see Spilsby (2) p. 85), and was born *c*.1349; having seisin of his father,s lands on 9 May 1372, and died on 9th August 1396.[81] He accompanied Richard II on his expedition to Scotland in 1385, served with Duke of Lancaster in France 1373, and Spain in 1386-87, and was summoned to Parliament between 1375-1394.[82] He married three times, first to Alice (said to have been daughter of Sir William de Skipworth), who died in or before 1370, secondly Margarey (daughter of William Le Zouche), who died 18th October 1391. His third wife was Elizabeth Latimer (widow of John de Neville, 3rd Lord Neville of Raby) who died 1395[83] and is represented also in alabaster on Robert's right.

Commentary: The presence of the Latin abbreviation for 'Jesus of Nazareth' on the bacinet is probably a practical manifestation of the belief that the inscribing of the sacred name on the forehead provided protection from sudden death. This is mentioned for instance in thirteen-century accounts of the life of St. Edmund of Abingdon, while a version of the belief described in the late twelfth-century account of "Vision of the Monk of Eynsham" implies that the presence of the sacred name would save the person so marked from the results of dying suddenly without being shriven by a priest.[84] Clearly, the protection claimed would have been the greatest importance to those likely to be involved in combat, as the majority of those commemorated by armoured effigies were. This being so, it seems plausible that the sacred name on helmets in the group of effigies listed below derives from real helmets used as models. No actual armour so inscribed appears to have survived, but a comparable inscription is found on the famous late-fourteenth century armour in the Churburg armoury:[85] *Jesus Autem Transiens Per Medium Illorum* [But Jesus passing through the midst of them went on his way].[86]

Inscriptions similar to the example under discussion cover a period between *c*.1400 and 1456, and are only found on alabaster knightly effigies. Considering that the contract for carving the effigy of Ralph Green and his wife at Lowick, Northamptonshire, by the Prentys/Sutton workshop specifies the composition in great detail we can say with relative certainty that the carvers were aware of the vision stated above. As with Spilsby (1) & (2) (pp. 68, 85), this figure has been restored and its surface re-cut to removed graffiti. In the opinion of the author the effigy is from the Prentys/Sutton workshop, which also produced Stamford. It is a common design, with other military effigies from the same date at, Acton (Cheshire), Layer Marney (Essex), Nuthall (Nottinghamshire), Swine (3) (Yorkshire East Riding) and Wolverley (Worcestershire).

No.56: Lincoln (Lincoln City & County Museum) *c*.1400/10

Current position: Currently in secure storage.[87]

Condition: Only the lower torso remains.

Heraldry: None.

Posture: Originally straight-legged.

Description: Limestone. The coat-armour is short and tight-fitting, with a scalloped hem, below is the lower edge of the mail haubergeon. Passing diagonally across the waist is a narrow sword-belt, joined on the left by a buckle. The hip-belt is wide and decorated with square plaques each consisting of pyramidal floral-boss. Below the mail haubergeon can be seen a small portion of one cuisse, which are plain.

Identification: Unknown.

Commentary: The fragment was discovered in 1958 in a load of building stone, which was delivered to the Old Bishop's Palace at Lincoln, and donated to the museum in the same year by Mr. F. J. Weare. It is believed that the load of stone possible originated from either Wellingore or Waddington.[88] The only indication of a positive date is the diagonal sword-belt, which seems to have been in use by *c*.1400, as a supplementary item for the hip-belt.

No.57: Broughton (St Mary) *c*.1410

Current position: On a freestone tomb-chest with his wife on his left, underneath an arched recess decorated with cusped oval panels, in the north wall of the chancel. Only the tomb-chest's south side is visible with shields set within a foiled panel. At the west end of the south side is a lion rampant within a foiled panel and at the east end is a rectangle with a hexagonal void, also set within a foiled panel. On the edge of the slab is a concave frieze, which is decorated with square and circular flower-heads motifs.

Condition: Defaced, damaged and worn (including the loss of the right hand, dagger, head of crest, spurs and pendant of collar).

Heraldry: Effigy, coat-armour: *fretty, a chief*, carved in low relief. Crest: a ram.[89] Tomb: left-right (1) *two lions passant* (2) *fretty, a chief* (3) *fretty, a chief impaling two lions passant* [for Retford impaling Strange].

Posture: Straight-legged, with the right hand originally holding his wife's right hand, the left holding the right gauntlet and below the feet a lion looking towards the effigy's right with a long scroll in its mouth. The head rests on a great helm.

Description: Alabaster. The bacinet has an aventail (mail realistically represented), its junction covered by a band decorated in relief with foliate scrolls, all between two narrow roped mouldings. On the top edge is a row of foliated points. Encircling the scull is a broad orle, carved in high relief with representations of

---

[81] *Complete Peerage* 12, pp. 660-661.
[82] *Complete Peerage* 12, pp. 660-661.
[83] *Complete Peerage* 12, p. 661.
[84] Kemp, pp. 203-204.
[85] The author is grateful to Claude Blaire for bringing this to his attention.
[86] Trap, O. G., and J. G. Mann, cat. no. 13.

[87] Lincoln City & County Museum registration number 42-58.
[88] Petch, pp. 24-25.
[89] *Topographer*, p. 62/3.

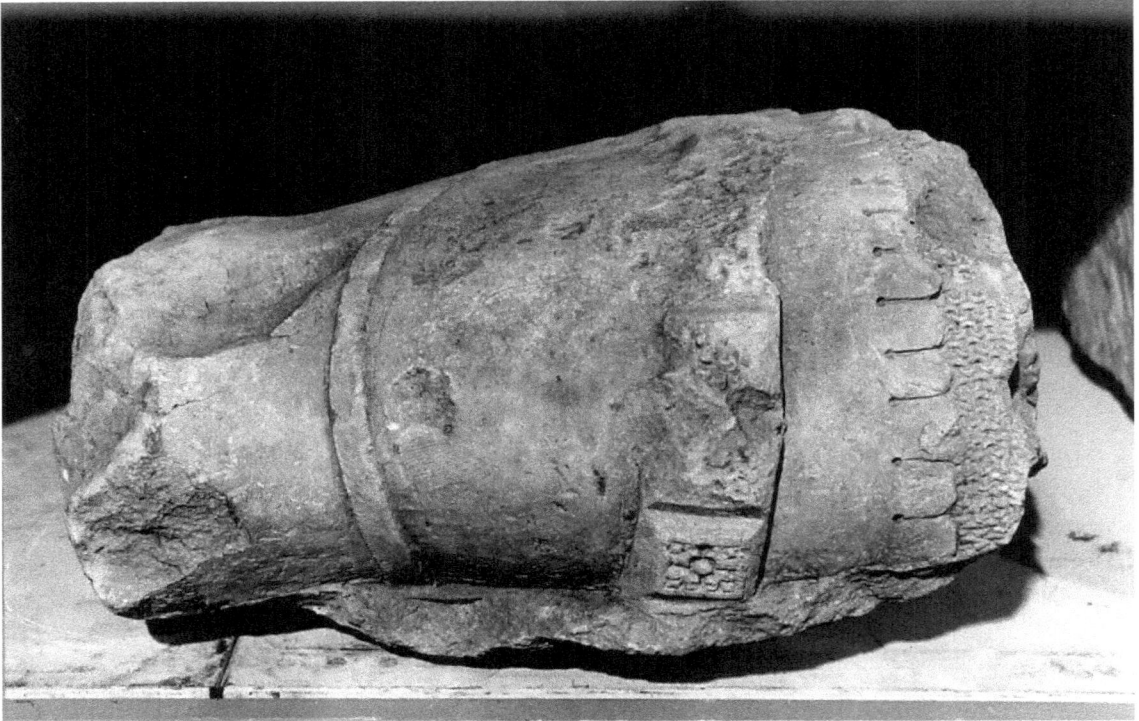

Fig. 124. Lincoln City & County Museum

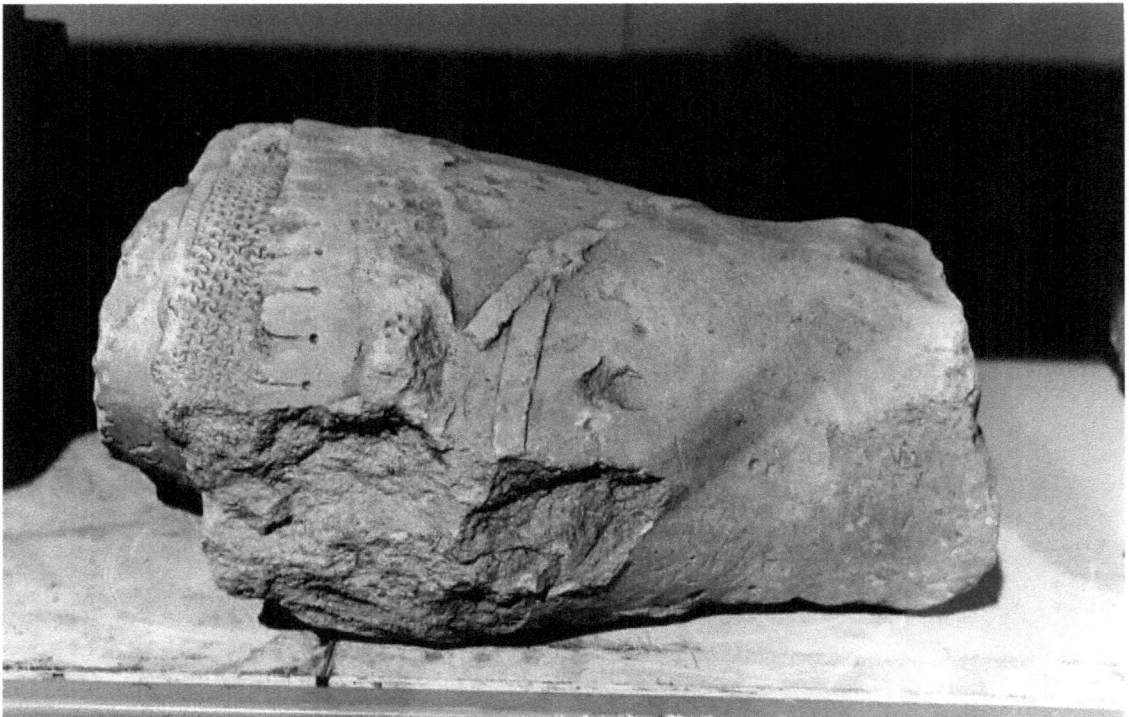

Fig. 125. Lincoln City & County Museum

Fig. 126. Broughton

Fig. 127. Broughton

small stones. Around the neck is an SS collar. The coat-armour is short and tight-fitting with a scalloped hem. Below the hem is the lower edge of the mail haubergeon, indicated by a small number of rings. The spaudlers consist of three lames, and couters with a border carved with running scrolls of foliage, and a small lobed side-wing, and articulated to the upper and lower cannons by pairs of narrow lames. Gussets of mail close the open joins between the breastplate and the spaudlers, also between upper and lower cannons at the elbow. On the left hand is an hourglass gauntlet. The hip-belt consists of round-head plaques, the dagger originally attached to the belt by a cord, worn on the right. Passing diagonally across the waist from the right-hip is the sword-belt, decorated with square floral plaques; a rectangular buckle lies to the left of the wearer. The sword on the left is complete, the pommel and quillons are concealed by the left hand. The outsides of the cuisses and greaves have borders decorated with square floral-motifs. On the knees are globular poleyns with a central keel; each is articulated to its cuisse by a narrow and a broad lame, and to its greave by two similar lames. The poleyns are decorated with borders of running scrolls of foliage. Beneath the greave is a mail fringe covering the upper part of the sabatons, the mail represented in the same manner as the aventail. The arms of the spurs are plain and are slightly curved. The eyes of the lion footrest have hollows, which presumably once contained paste or glass decoration.

Length: 6ft 3in.

Identification: Sir Henry Retford (*fl.* 1354-1409). Sir Henry held a diplomatic, political and military role, being sheriff of the county in 1389, 1392-3, 1397, 1406-7, M. P. attending the Great Council in 1401 and speaker of the Commons in 1402.[90] His career embraced the regimes of Richard II and Henry IV, being a soldier of some experience, as he accompanied Richard's expedition to Scotland in 1385, John of Gaunt's force to Spain in 1386 and Richard's expedition to Ireland in 1393.[91] He was knighted by 1384.[92] At the time he was speaker of the Commons he was fifty years old, dying in June 1409.[93] He was married twice, first to Katharine Strange (widow of Sir Ralph Paynel) in 1384,[94] and secondly to Mary, who married after Henry's death two more times.[95] He was possibly the son of Ralph Retford (*fl.* 1329-1374),[96] who is possibly commemorated by a brass in the church.[97] The female effigy represents his first wife whose arms are; *gules two lions passant argent*, and Sir Henry's arms; *argent a fret of six and a chief sable*, both of these coats of arms are on the side of the tomb-chest.

Commentary: The effigy is one of twelve three-dimensional military effigies represented holding hands with his wife. The other eleven can be seen at, Chichester

Cathedral[98] (Sussex) *c.*1370/80; Elford[99] (Staffordshire) *c.*1390/1410; Ingham[100] *c.*1405 (Norfolk); Kirkby-in-Cleveland (Yorkshire, North Riding) *c.*1425/50; Lowick[101] (Northamptonshire) *c*1419; Hoveringham[102] *c.*1403, Strelley[103] *c.*1390/1410 (both Nottinghamshire); Macclesfield[104] *c.*1470 (Cheshire); Warrington[105] *c.*1468 (Lancashire); Warwick[106] (Warwickshire) *c*1370 and Wimborne Minster[107] (Dorset) *c.*1444. Nine are carved from alabaster and those at Chichester, Ingham and Kirkby-in-Cleveland from freestone. The right hands of all knights mentioned above hold the hand of the lady; nine of the ladies are positioned on the knight's right, and three on the left: Macclesfield, Strelley and the figure under discussion. Brasses are more frequently represented with this posture. The explanation as to why effigies are portrayed in this manner is uncertain, although a number of suggestions have been put forward, but one theory is love, devotion and union. The effigy is from the Thomas Prentys/Robert Sutton workshop which produced many alabaster effigies, but why were there so few handholding effigies produced? Very likely it was stipulated in the contracts similar to Lowick; as it was the effigies of Richard II and Anne of Bohemia in Westminster Abbey.[108] The lion footrest is holding a scroll in its mouth, which is a very rare occurrence, and is indeed one of only three found in England and Wales, the others being at Ingham (1) (Norfolk) *ob.*1344[109] and Pickering (North Yorkshire) *c.*1410. The scroll would doubtless have been painted with a Latin inscription.

Holles recorded the tomb under an arch in the north side of the quire,[110] but it was removed to its present position during the seventeenth-century to accommodate the monument of Sir Edmund Anderson *ob.*1661.[111]

No.58: Deeping St James (St James) *c.*1410

Current position: On the floor in the south west corner of the chancel.

Condition: Extremely worn with the lower legs missing.

Heraldry: None.

Posture: Straight-legged with the hands raised in prayer and the head resting on a single rectangular cushion.

---

[90] Roskell, p. 141 note 1.
[91] Roskell, p. 141 note 1.
[92] *Oxford Dictionary of National Biography* 46, p. 508.
[93] *Cal. Patent Rolls Hen. IV* 4, p. 88.
[94] *Oxford Dictionary of National Biography* 46, p. 508.
[95] Roskell, p. 117.
[96] *Oxford Dictionary of National Biography* 46, p. 508.
[97] Clayton, Plate 7.

[98] Richardson restored the effigy and some doubt has been cast as to the authenticity of the hand holding pose. However as the left hand is holding the right hand's gauntlet, it would imply that it retains its original pose.
[99] Gardner, Plate 149.
[100] Stothard, p. 52 . I am grateful to Sally Badham, who informed me that the effigies were originally holding hands.
[101] Gardner, Plate 180.
[102] Fellows, Plate to face p. 12.
[103] Gardner, Plate 150.
[104] Gardner, Plate 66.
[105] Gardner, Plate 7.
[106] Gardner, Plate 148.
[107] Gardner, Plate 81.
[108] For a detailed discussion on the hand holding posture see Coss 1998, pp. 84-107.
[109] *Cal. Inq. Edw. III* 8, p. 374.
[110] Holles, p. 107.
[111] *Topographer*, p. 62/3.

Fig. 128. Deeping St James

Fig. 129. Boston

Description: Limestone. Wearing a bacinet with an aventail, short tight-fitting coat-armour, with, visible below its lower edge, some of the rings of the mail haubergeon worn beneath. The poleyns are globular with lobed-side wings. On the wrists are traces of two overlapping lames of the gauntlet cuff. The hip-belt is formed of square plaques. Faint traces of horizontal lines round the hips indicate that a plate skirt was once represented. The left edge of the slab on which the figure rests is decorated with dogtooth ornament.

Length: 4ft 4½in.

Identification: Unknown.

Commentary: Due to its poor condition, the effigy is difficult to date. The revised Lincolnshire edition of Pevsner dates it to the late fourteenth century, but as a plate skirt is represented together with a bacinet and aventail it can be dated with relative certainty to *c.*1410; see, for example, the brasses of J. Hauley, 1408, at St. Saviour, Dartmouth[112] and Sir P. Courtenay, 1409, Exeter Cathedral.[113]

No.59: Boston (St Botolph) *c.*1430/50

Current position: On a high alabaster tomb-chest underneath a recess with a pointed arch in the south wall of the south aisle. Only the south side of the tomb-chest is visible. It is decorated with four figures of angels, holding

shields in front of them, and standing under ogee arches separated by crocketed pinnacles.

Condition: Although very well preserved it has been totally restored and re-cut. The dagger is missing from the right, as are the sword's pommel and the functional parts of the spurs.

Heraldry: None.

Posture: Straight-legged with the hands raised in prayer and the feet supported by a lion looking away from the effigy's right. The head rests on a great helm.

Description: Alabaster. A broad orle encircles the great bacinet, carved in high relief with a spiral binding of ribbon, and running scrolls of foliage. The bevor of the bacinet consists of two plates and around the neck a chain, with a pendant; *a cross patée*. The pauldrons consist of five lames with small rivets on the upper lame, also a riveted border on the inside, continuing around the arm which appears to form part of the lowest lame. The outsides of the upper and lower cannons have a border decorated with a square floral motif and couters with lobed side-wings. The gauntlets, have long longitudinally boxed cuffs, which consist of five narrow lames over the back of the hand with the fingers covered by small convex plates. Upper and lower breastplates protect the torso, with the lower tapering upwards to a point high on the chest. The skirt consists of five upward pointing hoops and secured to the fifth lowest lame are four rectangular tassets, each has two straps with hexagonal buckles and with triangular chapes; the attachment of the strap to the skirt is not shown. The sculptor has only

---

[112] Clayton, Plate 14.
[113] Clayton, Plate 15.

Fig. 130. Deeping St James

Fig. 131. Boston

shown half of the rear tassets. A triangle of mail hangs from underneath the lowest lame of the skirt, presumably representing the hem of the mail haubergeon (mail realistically represented). The hip-belt is made of square plaques; each consists of four leaves in saltire with studs between the arms, its large central clasp has a raised plaque decorated with a flower-head and small stones in the outer corners. The sword on the left is a complete replacement, and is attached to the effigy by a screw. On the outside of the cuisses and greaves are borders, decorated with running scrolls of foliage and across the lower edge of the greave is a square floral motif. The poleyns are globular with a central keel and lobed side-wings, which are articulated to the greave by a pointed lame. The poleyn itself is decorated with a border of square floral flowers. The sabatons consist of four lames. The arms of the spurs are slightly curved.

Length: 5ft 7in.

Identification: Unknown. In 1430 Robert Petwardyn, who died in 1431, held the manor of Boston.[547] His heir was Roger, the son of his brother Walter who died in 1430.[548] Roger was a sheriff of Lincolnshire in 1441,[549] who was last recorded in 1449.[550] Given the period when the effigy was carved, although speculative, the effigy may represent Roger.

Commentary:[551] An etching of the effigy and tomb-chest under an arch, published in 1842 shows the effigy with no arms, but the standing angels on the side of the tomb-chest are present.[552] In 1850 the monument was restored by Abraham Kent of Boston, and an etching in a publication dated 1856, shows the monument in its present condition. It was apparently moved from the east end of the north aisle to its present position about 1760.[553] The monument was moved to St Botolph's from St John's church in the town, when the latter was demolished in 1626.[554] The *cross patée* on the chain around the neck has led some authors to suggest that the effigy represents a member of the Order of St John of Jerusalem,[555] but considering that the effigy has been restored, it probably was added by the whim of Abraham Kent.

No.60: Wellingore (All Saints) *c*.1430/40

Current position: On a high alabaster tomb-chest together with a female, against the north wall of the north aisle. The south side of the tomb-chest is decorated with three panels with shields set within quatrefoils and flanked on either side by double tiered, slim trefoiled-headed arches. The east end is virtually concealed by part of the organ, but a small amount can be seen to show it is decorated in a manner similar to the south side. The west

Fig. 132. Wellingore

end is covered with modern cement and painted white.

Condition: Defaced and worn (including the loss of the fingers, toes, dagger, sword and spurs). The legs are broken across the shins, which have been repaired with modern cement and supported underneath by a block of alabaster. A deep hole has been drilled in the nose of the figure.

Heraldry: Crest: *a lion sejant*.

Posture: Straight-legged with the hands raised in prayer and the feet supported by a lion looking towards the effigy's right. The head rests on a great helm.

Description: Alabaster. A broad orle encircles the great bacinet, which is carved in high relief with a spiral binding of ribbon studded with representations of small stones; stylised square roses and foliage on a hatched ground fill the interspaces. A broad band decorated with stylised leaves covers the junction of the bacinet and neck-plates. Pivoted to the sides of the bacinet are two gorget-plates, covering the throat and upper chest, also two plates cover the neck and shoulders. Across the forehead is a worn inscription, 'Ihc Nazaren', a Latin abbreviation for 'Jesus of Nazareth'. Around the neck is an "SS" Collar, of which the ends are joined to the tiret by buckles. He has a drooping moustache. The front-plate of the helm has a shallow central keel with two rectangular sights; the mantling is held around the helm by a twisted wreath. The spaudlers consist of four lames and small besagews protecting the armpits. The upper cannons of the vambraces are closed and joined by two buckled straps, their outer edges decorated with a square floral motif border, also the couters are decorated in the same manner. The couters have small fan-shaped side-

[547] *Cal. Inq. Henry. VI* 6-10, nos. 548, 633.
[548] *Cal. Inq. Henry. VI* 6-10, no. 436.
[549] *Cal. Fine Rolls* 17, p. 205.
[550] *Cal. Patent Rolls Henry. VI* 5, p. 275.
[551] The author is very grateful to Sally Badham who provided relevant material on St Botolph's church.
[552] *Descriptive & Historical Account of St Botolph's Church Boston*, (Boston, 1842), Plate to face p. 38.
[553] Thompson, p. 184, note 1.
[554] Thompson, p. 184, note 1.
[555] Jebb, p. 63. Lambert and Walker, p. 95.

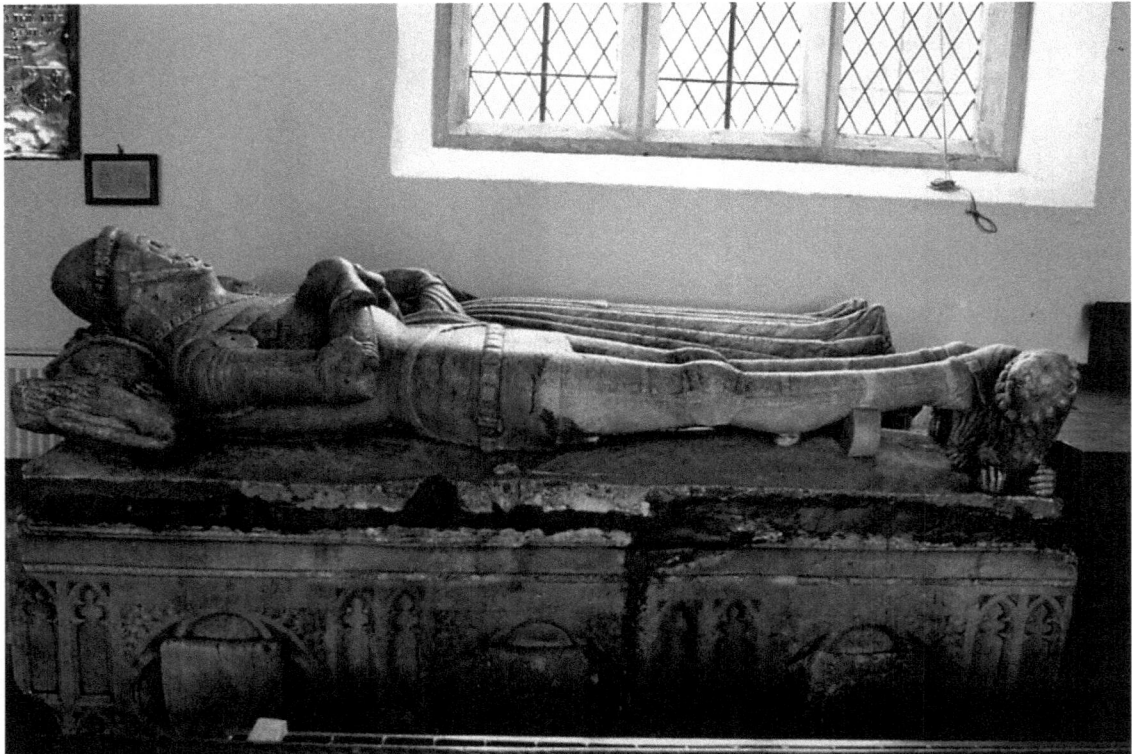

Fig. 133. Wellingore

Fig. 134. Rippingale (3)

wings, and are articulated to the upper and lower cannons by pairs of narrow lames. The hourglass gauntlets are decorated around the wrists by roped mouldings, flanked on each side by feathering. The breastplate is globular and has a skirt consisting of five transverse lames overlapping counter-tilewise. Projecting from below the skirt is the hem of the mail haubergeon.

The hip-belt consists of square pyramidal plaques and originally worn on the right was a dagger, only the suspension cord of which remains. Buckled diagonally from right to left across the waist is a sword-belt. The cuisses and greaves are without hinges or straps. The poleyns have a central longitudinal keel with the side-wings similar to those of the couters, each having two narrow and broad articulating lames above and below. The uppermost and lowest lames are attached to the cuisses and greaves by a turning-pin on their outer corners. The poleyns themselves, but not their wings, and the edges of the cuisse and greaves have applied borders; those on the poleyn itself are decorated with running scrolls of foliage and on the cuisses and greaves by a square flower motif. The sabatons consist of pointing lames. The arms of the spurs are strongly curved towards their terminals, with their straps decorated with a square floral motif and joined by a square buckle.

Length: 6ft 1½in.

Identification: Unknown. Holles recorded the tomb with three coats of arms; "*sable two lions passant argent crowned or* (Dymoke), *sable three bars argent* (no identification), *argent on a fess gules three fleurs-de-lis* (Disney). It is worth mentioning that a number of people are recorded from Wellingore, but none of the above families. An inquisition dated at Lincoln 23rd February 1406 records William de Blyton of Long Leadenham "held in his demesne as a fee Wellingore, the Lordship called 'Blytonfee', of the king of the duchy of Lancaster by knight service and a rent of 2s. for the guard of the castle of Bolingbroke, annual value of 13s. 4d. Robert his son and heir is aged 40 years and more".[556] In 1412 Randulphus de Middleton, Robert de Blyton and John Hamsterley held land for knight's service.[557] In 1430 John Boys is recorded of Wellingore, esquire to Robert Sutwelle and William Leventhorp.[558] The 1983 church guide identifies the effigies as Richard de Buslingthorpe and his wife Isabella; John Lord Monson, who recorded the effigies in 1833, remarks that they represent a Nevill,[559] but I have not been able to discover what connection, if any, the Nevill family had with Wellingore. Also it cannot represent Sir Richard de Buslingthorpe, as he was the last of the male line dying between 1361 and 1369, and is commemorated by a brass at Buslingthorpe.[560] The Disneys were sub-tenants of Wellingore from an early period and it was before his death in 1411 that William Disney married his eldest daughter and heir Elizabeth, to John Hamsterley, then a

widower. They had a son John, who inherited the Disney estates upon his father's death in 1415, and was killed fighting for the Lancastrians at the battle of Towton in 1461.[561] Because the Disney coat of arms was represented on the tomb-chest, as recorded by Holles, there is a strong case for the effigy to represent John Hamsterley, with the monument very likely being set up by his widow or son a number of years later.

Commentary: The effigy is the product of the well-known Prentys/Sutton workshop at Chellaston in Derbyshire,[562] of which related examples are at, Barmston[563] (Yorkshire East Riding) *c.*1420; Bottesford[564] (Leicestershire) *c.*1425; Bures[565] (Suffolk) *c.*1420; Kinver (Staffordshire) *c.*1445/50; Longford[566] *c.*1445/50 and Tideswell[567] *c*1430/40 (Derbyshire); Wadworth[568] (Yorkshire West Riding) *c.*1430; and Weobley (Herefordshire) *c.*1420. All these, like the effigy under discussion, although related in design, are of fine quality, carved when the workshop was at its productive and artistic peak.[569]

No.61: Rippingale (3) (St Andrew) *c.*1470/75

Fig. 135. Rippingale

Current position: In the middle of two females, each carved separately, on a high limestone tomb-chest at the east end of the south aisle. The south side of the tomb-chest is decorated with four standing figures holding frontal shields underneath crocketed gables. Each figure is divided from the next by an upright pinnacled shaft. On the north side are four hanging shields, of which one is held in the mouth of a bearded man and a second in the mouth of a lion. The third is suspended from the centre of a flower head and the fourth from a bird. The west end has two shields, each underneath trefoil-head arch. Positioned in the top left hand corner of the end is an owl. The east end has a large panel depicting a headpiece that

[556] *Cal. Inq. Hen. IV* 19, no. 18.
[557] *Feudal Aids* 6, pp. 481/2.
[558] *Cal. Close Rolls Hen. IV* 2, p. 65.
[559] Monson, p. 406.
[560] Blair, J. 1975-9, p. 268.

[561] Disney, pp. 101-110.
[562] See no.52 Stamford for a brief discussion on this workshop.
[563] Routh, Plate 3.
[564] Gardner 1940, Plate 175.
[565] Gardner 1940, Plate 164.
[566] Gardner 1940, Plate 86.
[567] Gardner 1940, Plate 169.
[568] Routh, Plate 78.
[569] In the opinion of the author the Prentys/Sutton workshop ceased production sometime in the 1450's, with the monument to Sir Richard Vernon, Tong (Shropshire) *c.*1450-1455. Downing 1999, fig. 20.

combines the features of a tilting helm with those of a great bacinet, the sight is formed by three rows of small holes, and its damaged animal crest surmounts a cap of maintenance. This is clearly a product of the sculptor's imagination. Below the helm is a shield with the upper and lower few inches inclined forwards and a bouched upper dexter corner.

Condition: Defaced and extremely mutilated (the arms, legs, footrest, sword and dagger are missing).

Heraldry: Tomb-chest: west end (right shield with very faint black paint, probably the ground coat), *impaled seven mascles* [for Quincy]. Holles[570] recorded the effigies together with heraldry on the tomb-chest, which apart from (1) have disappeared since he made a visit to the church, (1) impaled *gules seven mascles or* [Holles identification as Quincey], *gules bezantée, a canton ermine* [Zouch]; (2) impaled *gules seven mascles or* [Quincey], *Argent a lion rampant sable* [?]; (3) *gules bezantée, a canton ermine a crescent for difference* [Zouch].

Posture: Originally straight-legged with the hands joined in prayer and the head resting on a sallet, which has a central keel and large rivets encircling the scull.

Description: Limestone. The head is bare with the hair arranged in a bowl-crop. On the base of the slab is a buckled strap, which in reality would be utilised to secure the sallet underneath the chin. A standard of mail protects the neck, (mail realistically represented) and a chain with an SS collar, the letters on a narrow ribbon. The pauldrons consist of six lames. Upper and lower breastplates protect the torso, the lower extending upwards to a point on the chest and is hinged on the left side. Passing diagonally from right to left across the waist is a sword-belt, its buckle lying in the centre of the wearer, attached on the right are the remains of the dagger cord, the dagger fragment remaining on the base of the slab. The plate skirt is represented at the sides by upward-pointing chevrons, also a hinge remains on the left side.

Length: 3ft 6in.

Identification: Sir Nicholas Bowet. The revised edition of Pevsner's Lincolnshire states that the effigy represents Roger Quincey and his two wives.[571] A certain Roger de Quincey, who died before 1425, held land in Cambridgeshire, Huntingdonshire, Norfolk and Suffolk[572] but I have been unable to discover if he had any connection or held any land in Lincolnshire. The reason for an attribution to Roger Quincy probably lies with Holles, who gives the arms *gules seven mascles or* as Quincy; however, these were also the arms of Ferrers (the seventh Earl of Derby married Margaret, daughter and co-heir of Robert de Quincy, Earl of Winchester, and settled the manor of Groby on her second son, whereupon he assumed the arms of her family).[573] The effigy probably represents Sir Nicholas Bowet of Rippingale,

who married three times; Elizabeth Zouch,[574] Jane Berkeley, who died in 1471[575] and Anne. Nicholas was a knight to William Lord Ferrers of Groby, Leicestershire, and is it recorded that in 1437 he and Anne held the manor of Rippingale and two thirds of the advowson of the church, having been loaned money by William Ferrers.[576] I have been unable to discover if Anne was a daughter of William Ferrers, for if she was it would explain the *gules seven mascles or*. However it is also possible that given Nicholas was a knight of William Ferrers, the coat of arms may have been added on the tomb-chest to reflect kinship or brothers-in-arms. The earliest reference to Nicholas was in 1431, when he was a commissioner to raise a loan in Lincolnshire.[577] He was commissioner and justice of the peace many times from 1431 and 1473,[578] which is when he is last recorded, possibly dying shortly afterwards. He was also sheriff for the county in 1447 and 1451.[579] Holles recorded a stone tomb with an inscription to Jane; therefore we can assume that she had her own monument and that the two female effigies represent Anne and Elizabeth Zouch.

Commentary: Dating the effigy is problematic due to its mutilated condition and also we do not know if the monument was set up during Nicholas's lifetime. Given that the effigy is bareheaded, wearing a bowl-crop hairstyle and a plate skirt, it could date as early as *c.* 1440; however, should the effigy have originally been represented wearing large couters and tassets it would date from the 1470's. Considering that Nicholas died after 1473 the monument probably dates from the first half of the 1470's. The side panels on the east and west ends of the tomb-chest are different to those on the north and south. The large east end panel with the helm and shield is a very unusual composition and very likely not contemporary with the other sides. A drawing by Edward Blore, made probably between 1823-1855,[580] shows the north side of the tomb as having a high stone structure placed behind the head of the effigies. The side that is above the effigies (west) has two trefoil-headed arches and that on the north side in the top right corner is a bird, which is now fixed on the west end of the tomb-chest.

The monument is very likely from a Lincolnshire workshop, as at the time when it was carved most tombs were made in the Midlands from alabaster. The south aisle was used as a school when John William Monson visited the church in 1831 and the tomb was then covered in thick whitewash.[581]

No.62: Lincoln Cathedral (2) *c.*1470

Current position: Underneath a vaulted canopied recess, on a high limestone tomb-chest in the north wall of the retrochoir. The canopy, which is highly decorated,

[570] Holles, (n. 19), *op. cit.* p. 194.
[571] Pevsner and Harris, p. 612.
[572] *Cal. Inq. Hen. VI* 22, no. 472.
[573] Burke, p. 347.

[574] Maddison 4, p. 1198.
[575] Holles, p. 194.
[576] *Cal. Close Rolls Hen VI* 3, pp. 158-159.
[577] *Cal. Patent Rolls Hen. VI* 2, p. 126.
[578] *Cal. Patent Rolls Edward IV, Henry VI*, p. 620.
[579] *Cal. Fine Rolls* 18, pp. 81, 250.
[580] British Library Add. Ms. 42012, drawing no. 69.
[581] Monson, p. 303.

Fig. 136. Lincoln Cathedral (2)

consists of three cusped ogee-headed arches surmounted by tall pointed gables; each gable is decorated with foliage and divided from each other by upright shafts. The whole monument was conserved in 1994, and while under conservation it was discovered that the underside of the effigy has been hollowed out.[1]

Condition: Defaced and damaged (including the loss of parts of the hands, toes, dagger's pommel, grip and functional parts of the spurs).

Heraldry:[2] Crest: *a demi-lion rampant queue fourchée*. Above the tomb-chest is a triple-arched canopy, with heraldic shields along the upper edge, L-R; (1) *quarterly, 1, 4, semy of fleur de lys; 2, 3, 3 leopards* (England after 1340). (2) *quarterly, 1, 4, semy of fleur de lys; 2, 3, 3 leopards, a label of three points* (England with a label). (3) same as no.1. (4) same as no.1. (5) same as no.1. (6) *3 leopards, a label of three points* (Lancaster). The front of the tomb-chest is decorated with six cusped ogee-head arches, each divided from the next by pinnacled shafts, flanking either side of each gable are two shields with heraldry in relief (eleven in total, originally twelve). L-R; (1) *a cross between 4 lions rampant, tails forked* (Burghersh). (2) *a bend cotised between 6 lions, 3 molets of 6 points* (Bohun). (3) *quarterly, 1, 4, a maunch; 2, 3, barruly, an orle of martlets* (Hastings). (4) *a fess between 6 crosses crosslets* (Beauchamp). (5) *barry of six, on a chief two pales*

between 2 gyrons, on an escutcheon a lion (Mortimer). (6) missing since 1817 (originally *quarterly, in the first quarter a mullet* Vere). (7) *a chevron* (Stafford). (8) *a fess doubled cotised* (Badlesmere). (9) *fretty* (Verdun). (10) *3 water-bougets* (Ros). (11) *on a chevron, 3 estoiles* (Cobham). (12) *a saltire engrailed* (Tybotot). It would appear that figures originally stood underneath the arches on pedestals. Above the effigy's head is a carved panel decorated with two standing headless angels holding a shield with heraldry: *a lion rampant queue fourchée*.

Posture: Straight-legged with the hands raised in prayer and the feet supported by a lion looking towards the effigy's right. The head rests on a helm.

Description: The uncovered head has hair long at the back and short across the forehead. Around the neck is a standard of mail, the mail presumably once rendered in gesso. Pauldrons each of six lames, curving round the shoulder blades, and all-overlapping and on the third lame an arming point. The upper and lower cannons are closed with large couters, secured by an arming point (only the left remains). From what remains of the hands, they seem to have been bare. The breastplate has no straps or hinges; the skirt, consists of five hoops, over-lapping counter-tilewise, with a slight cusp in the centre of each. Attached to the fifth lame by straps and buckles are two broad, pointed shield-shape tassets; there are two additional tassets protecting the rump. Passing across the waist is a narrow sword-belt, decorated with square flowers; the rectangular buckle lies in the centre of the wearer with the loose end of the belt passing behind and through it, forming a knot. The sword on the left lies on the base of the slab, attached to the belt by two diagonal thongs; the pommel is onion-shape, with a grip tapering towards the straight quillons. On the right is a broken quillon dagger.

The cuisse and greaves are plain with no visible signs of straps, buckles or hinges. The poleyns are globular with turned over edges; their side wings large and lobed; articulated below is a cusped broad pointed-lame. Although the feet are damaged, sufficient remains on the right foot to denote that they were protected by sabatons, each lame cusped extending to a point. At the feet is a carved panel consisting of two angels holding a man in a napkin (depicting the soul being carried to heaven) and below the napkin are rabbits in burrows (representing the earth).

Length: 5ft 2in.

Commentary: The monument was the subject of an article by Lawrence Butler who discovered that originally there were iron railings across the front of the tomb; these were removed during the Civil War.[3] The tomb dates from c.1345 and the effigy from c.1470, but it is not known when the two were first associated with each other: it had already happened by the time William Dugdale recorded it for his *Book of Monuments* in 1641.[4] It is also not known where the effigy came from. It may have been in a former chantry in the cathedral or, as Lawrence Butler surmises, it could have been brought

---

[1] Butler, p. 119.
[2] For a discussion on the heraldry see Butler, pp. 135-139.

[3] Butler, p. 119.
[4] Butler, p. 130.

from another religious building in Lincoln or elsewhere after the Dissolution of the Monasteries.[5]

Identification: Unknown. The crest on the helm beneath the effigy's head, *a demi-lion rampant queue fourchée*, may be that of the Welles family, in which case there are three possible candidates; Lionel Lord Welles, his son Richard or grandson Robert, but all were buried elsewhere.[6] Lionel was buried at Methley (West Yorkshire), after the battle of Towton in 1461, and his alabaster effigy survives in the church.[7] Richard was buried at Stamford in 1470 after his execution and Robert also after his execution in the same year at the Carmelite friary, Doncaster. Lionel can obviously be discounted, but Richard or Robert may have had an effigy at their respective burial sites, which may have been transferred to Lincoln at the Dissolution of the Monasteries, but why such an effigy would not have gone to Towton is unclear. Traditionally the tomb is thought to commemorate Bartholomew Lord Burghersh (died 1355) or possibly his son, also of the same name who (died 1369), however both were buried elsewhere[8] and Butler argues that originally the tomb may never have had an effigy; rather it was a cenotaph and an Easter Sepulchre.[9]

---

[5] Butler, p. 130.
[6] Butler, p. 124, illus. 12.
[7] Gardner 1940, Plate 223.
[8] Butler, p. 119.
[9] Butler, p. 119.

Fig. 137. Lincoln Cathedral (2)

Fig. 138. Lincoln Cathedral (2)

The terminology I have employed in this glossary is English and contemporary while armour was still being regularly worn.

AKETON. A padded coat worn beneath the mail in the thirteenth and fourteenth centuries, and also often used as a defence in its own right.

AILETTES. Wing-like additions to the shoulders, normally rectangular, sometimes found laced to the mail in the later thirteenth and early fourteenth centuries. Thought once by many writers to have had a defensive purpose, but they were probably purely decorative and often serving heraldic significance, to display the wearer's arms. There use was almost wholly confined to England, France and Flanders.

ARMING POINTS. Cords furnished with tags and attached to the arming doublet, hose and shoes for tying on elements of armour, usually threaded through holes in the upper vambrace, couters, cuisses and sabatons.

AVENTAIL. A tippet of mail attached to staples (vervelles) along the edge of the face-opening of the bacinet to protect the throat and neck, and the top of the shoulders.

BACINET. The bacinet was originally a light helmet (the word means 'little basin' in French), but it was later applied to what is now called a great-bacinet, and eventually, in the sixteenth, the tilting-helm.

BESAGEW. The besagew was usually round or oval, and could be on the elbows, or even (horizontally) as a guard on the haft of an axe.

BEVOR. A defence for the lower part of the face.

BREASTPLATE. Protection of the chest, generally formed by one main plate of steel, but in the fifteenth century often of two plates, an upper and lower, the latter overlapping the former.

CAPE. A term used in this article to describe the lower part of a coif or aventail which covers the top of the shoulders and upper chest.

CANNON. One of the tubular plates protecting the upper and lower arms.

CHAPE. The metal terminal of a scabbard or a belt.

CIRCLET or CIRCLE. A narrow fillet around the brow of the head, worn over the coif. Sometimes circlets are decorated, at other times they are plain. In some case the plain examples may represent a strap, possibly securing a metal scull-cap under the coif.

COAT ARMOUR. See surcoat.

COAT-OF-PLATES. It consisted of metal plates attached by rivets to a textile cover or, more rarely, lining. It started to come into use from the first half of the thirteenth century. Surcoats lined with such plates, often only identifiable by the heads of the rivets holding them.

COIF. A hood. The mail coif fitted closely to the head and neck, and a flap crossed the chin and was fastened at the side, leaving only a portion of the face exposed. At first it was an extension of the hauberk, but about the middle of the thirteenth century it was made independent of it, falling to the shoulders.

COUTER. The defence for the elbow.

CREST. Heraldic device surmounting the helm, introduced in the second half of the twelfth century, but not common until the fourteenth century.

CUISSE. Armour for the thigh. Cuisses on effigies are often represented as mail, leather, metal and in some instances quilted.

CUSP. A curved projecting point in the ornamentation of architectural arches and armour decoration.

DAGGER. The dagger is first recorded as an accompaniment to the sword in the late thirteenth century. It first appears on English effigies in the early fourteenth century.

ENARME. A loop on the inner side of the shield grasped by the hand or through which the left arm was passed.

GAUNTLET. Defensive glove.

GORGET. Defence of the neck and throat, and upper part of the chest.

GREAVE. Plate armour for the leg between knee and ankle, introduced at first for the protection of the shin only and strapped over the mail in the second half of the thirteenth century. Closed-greaves consisting of a front and back plate, modelled to the calf and hinged together, came into use in the fourteenth century.

GRIP. That part of a weapon (e.g. of the hilt of a sword or dagger between the pommel and the guard) which is grasped in the hand.

GUSSETS. Mail patches sewn to the arming-doublet to cover parts not protected by plate: the armpits, elbows and fork.

HAUBERK. A shirt of mail.

HELM. The great helm, covering the entire head and face and reaching nearly to the shoulders, was introduced at the end of the twelfth century.

HOSE. Mail stockings.

LAMES. A thin plate, especially one of metal. Mobility was achieved by means of loose-fitting rivets and internal leathers.

LOCKET. Metal band encircling the scabbard, including that at the mouth of the sheath.

MAIL. Flexible armour made of iron or steel rings, each passing through its four neighbours.

MUFFLER. Muffler is the term for a mail mitten. A bag-like extension attached to the sleeve of a hauberk or gambeson with a separate stall for the thumb. The mail did not extend over the palm of the hand, which was covered by either fabric or leather, with a slit so that the hand could be released when fighting was not imminent.

ORLE. The orle was a roll worn around the skull of the bacinet. It was often represented as if decorated with precious stones and pearls.

PAULDRON. Plate defence for the shoulders, attaining its maximum development in the large Italian pauldrons of the fifteenth century, when it had large extensions covering the armpits before and behind.

POLEYN. Plate defence for the knee introduced to reinforce mail in the second half of the thirteenth century. It later had a fan-shaped wing on the outer side, and was articulated both to the cuisse and to the greave.

POMMEL. The spherical or other-shaped termination of the hilt of the sword or dagger on the end of the grip farther from the blade, acting as a counterpoise to the blade and giving support to the hand.

QUILLONS. A quillon is one of the two bars forming together the cross-guard of a sword.

SABATON. Armour for the foot, comprising a toe-cap and a series of overlapping lames crossing the instep. Introduced early in the fourteenth century.

SALLET. A light helmet shaped like a sou'wester, that in England, France and Germany during the second half of the fifteenth century virtually supplanted every other form for use in the field. The bacinet survived only for the tournament.

SCABBARD. The sheath of a sword or dagger.

SCHYNBALD. A plate defence for the lower leg, which was strapped over the hose.

SKIRT (of lames). A defensive skirt consisting of a series of hoop-like lames descending from the waist of the breastplate and overlapping upwards.

SKULL. That part of a helmet covering the cranium and occiput, sometimes referred to by old writers as the "basnet" or "bassinet-piece". Also used of a light steel cap.

SPAUDLER. The spaudler is the early term for the small version of what was to develop into the pauldron.

SPURS. Early spurs were of the prick variety, that is to say furnished with a simple goad or spike, often mounted on a ball, or cone. The rowel spur, with a wheel of five or more points, was introduced in the thirteenth century, but only became general in England from about 1330.

STANDARD OF MAIL. Upstanding collar of mail, frequently worn in the fifteenth century.

SURCOAT. A sleeveless garment worn over the mail in the thirteenth and early fourteenth centuries. It was gradually shortened, until in the second half of the fourteenth century it became brief and tight fitting (also known as a jupon).

SWORD. The medieval knightly sword was of simple cruciform structure with a straight, double-edged blade either with a central hollow, or sometimes of diamond section. Its component parts were the hilt and the blade with its tang, of which the former consists of the pommel, grip, and quillons.

TASSET. One of several shaped plates that normally hang from the front of the skirt, but also sometimes from the sides and rear (hind tassets).

VENTAIL. A flap of mail on the coif, drawn across the lower part of the face-opening and secured to the side of the temples.

VERVELLES. Staples along the edges of the bacinet. Over which a leather band with corresponding holes attached to the upper edge of the mail aventail was secured by means of a lace passed through them.

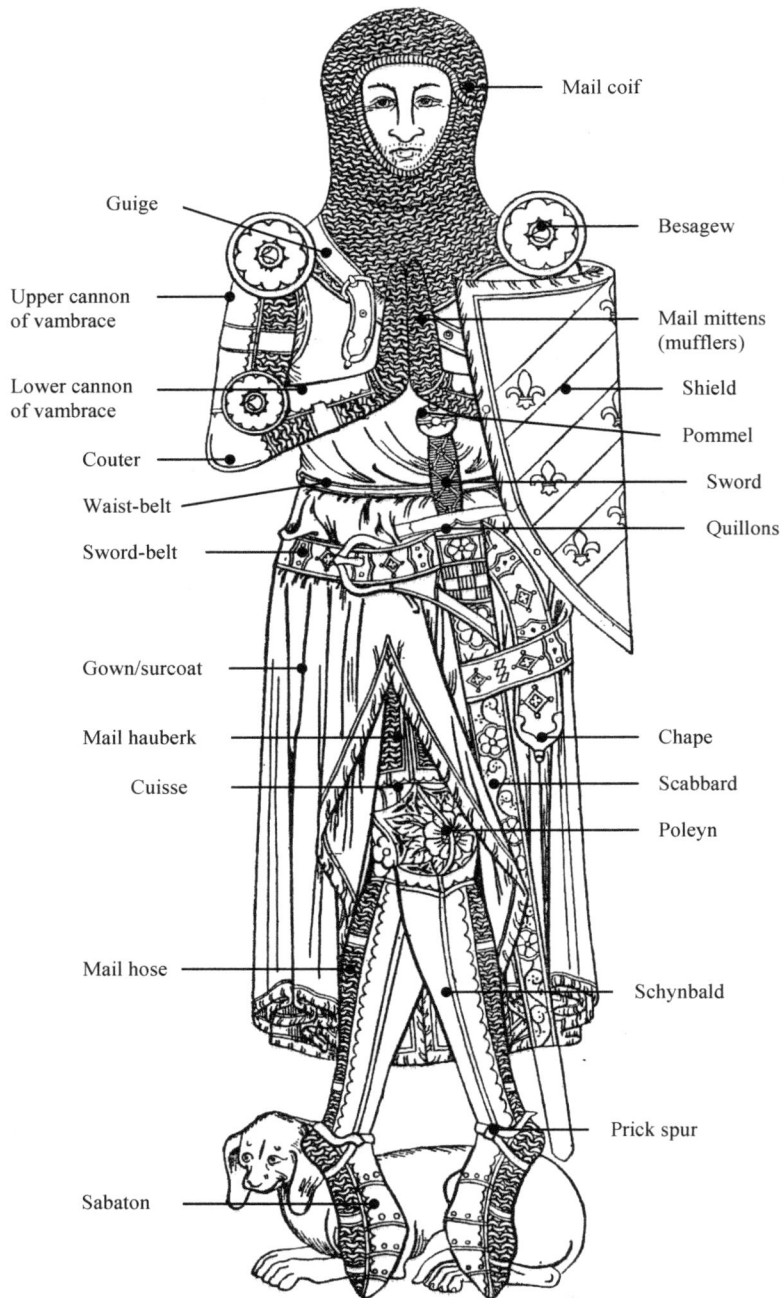

Guige

Upper cannon
of vambrace

Lower cannon
of vambrace

Couter

Waist-belt

Sword-belt

Gown/surcoat

Mail hauberk

Cuisse

Mail hose

Sabaton

Mail coif

Besagew

Mail mittens
(mufflers)

Shield

Pommel

Sword

Quillons

Chape

Scabbard

Poleyn

Schynbald

Prick spur

Fig. 139. Brass (c.1331-8) at Pebmarsh, Essex

Bacinet

Aventail

Spaudler

Upper cannon of vambrace

Plate gauntlets

Lower cannon of vambrace

Couter

Pommel

Jupon (worn over plate armour on the trunk)

Grip

Rondel dagger

Quillons

Hip belt

Locket

Cuisse

Lower edge of hauberk

Poleyn

Scabbard

Greave

Rowel spurs

Chape

Sabaton

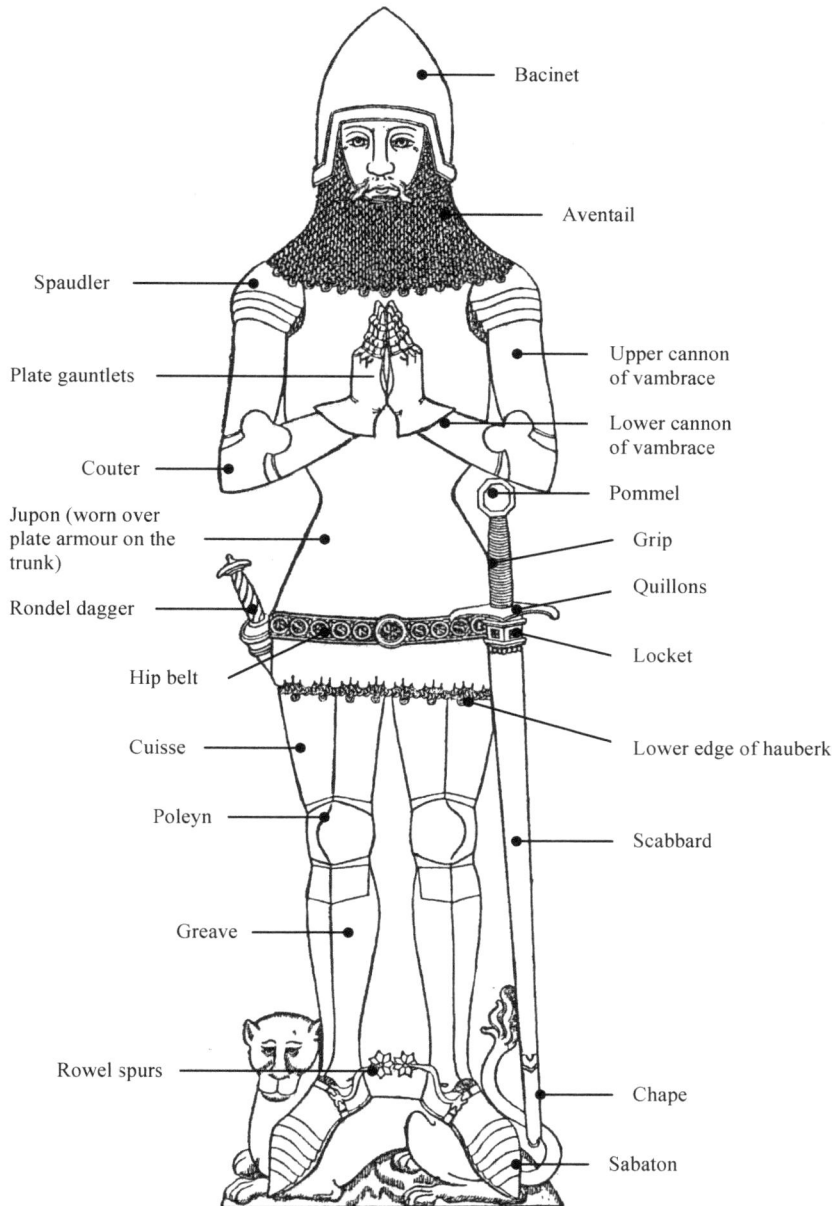

Fig. 140. Brass (1391) at Little Horkesley, Essex

Crest — Bacinet
Great helm
Gorget
Besagew
Spaudler
Breastplate
Plate gauntlets
Couter
Sword-belt
Plate-skirt
Rondel dagger
Cuisse
Poleyn
Greave
Rowel spurs
Upper cannon of vambrace
Lower cannon of vambrace
Pommel
Grip
Quillons
Locket
Scabbard
Chape
Sabaton

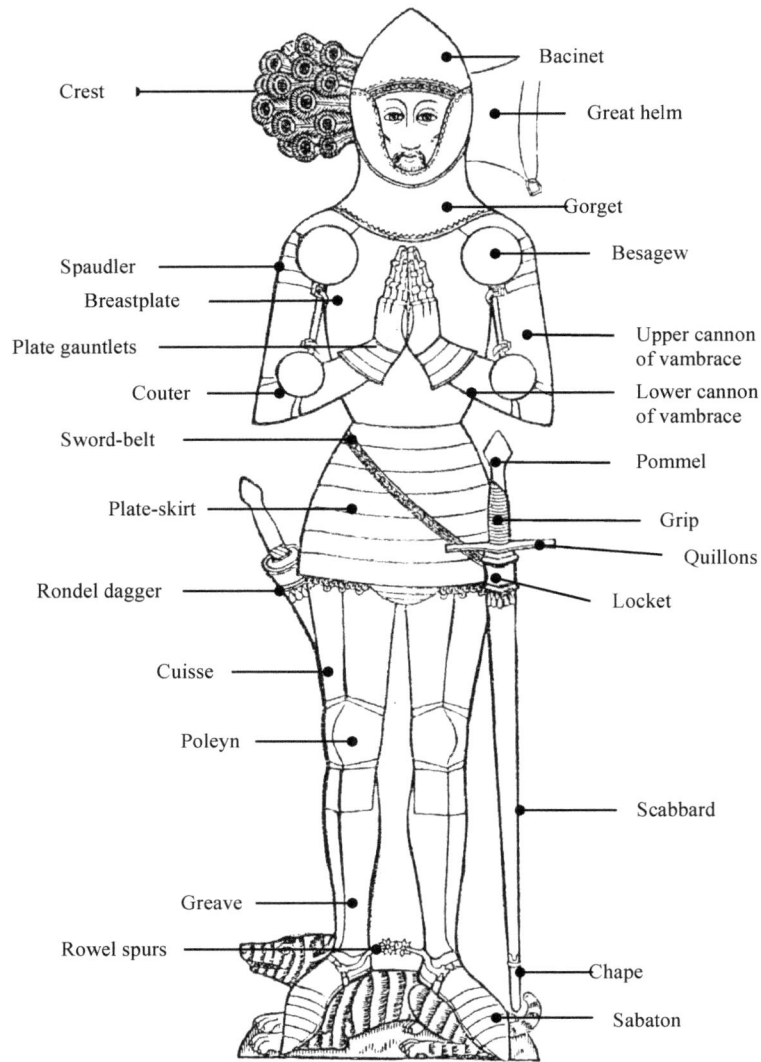

Fig. 141. Brass (1425) at Merevale, Warwickshire

Crest

Standard of mail

Lance rest

Upper cannon
of vambrace

Guard of vambrace
(secured to couter)

Rondel dagger

Plate skirt

tasset

Blade
(in scabbard)

Cuisse

Poleyn

Greave

Rowel spurs

Helm

Pauldron

Gardbrace
(over the Pauldron)

Lower cannon
of vambrace

Lower breastplate

Pommel

Grip

Quillons

Sword-belt

Lower edge of hauberk

Scabbard

Chape

Sabaton

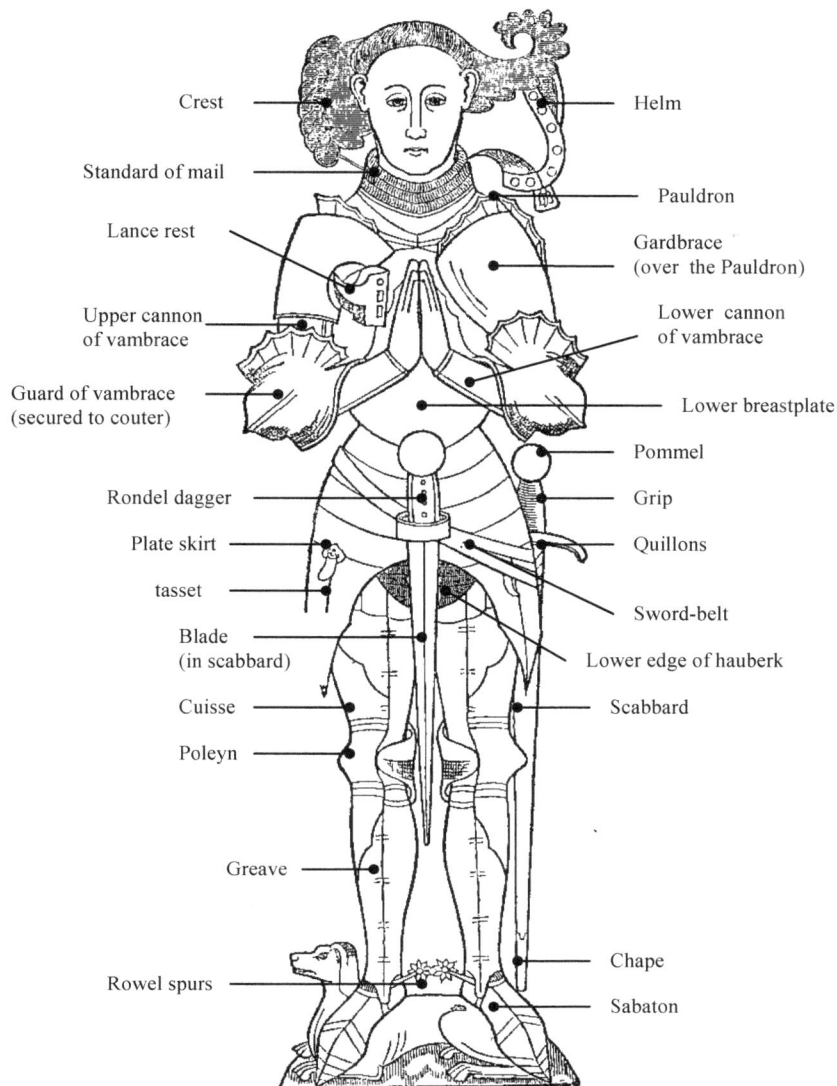

Fig. 142. Brass (1462) at Greens Norton, Northamptonshire

Fig. 143. Detail of the effigy of Sir John Leverick c.1345/50, Ash, Kent. Showing the coat-of-plates construction through the side opening of the coat armour

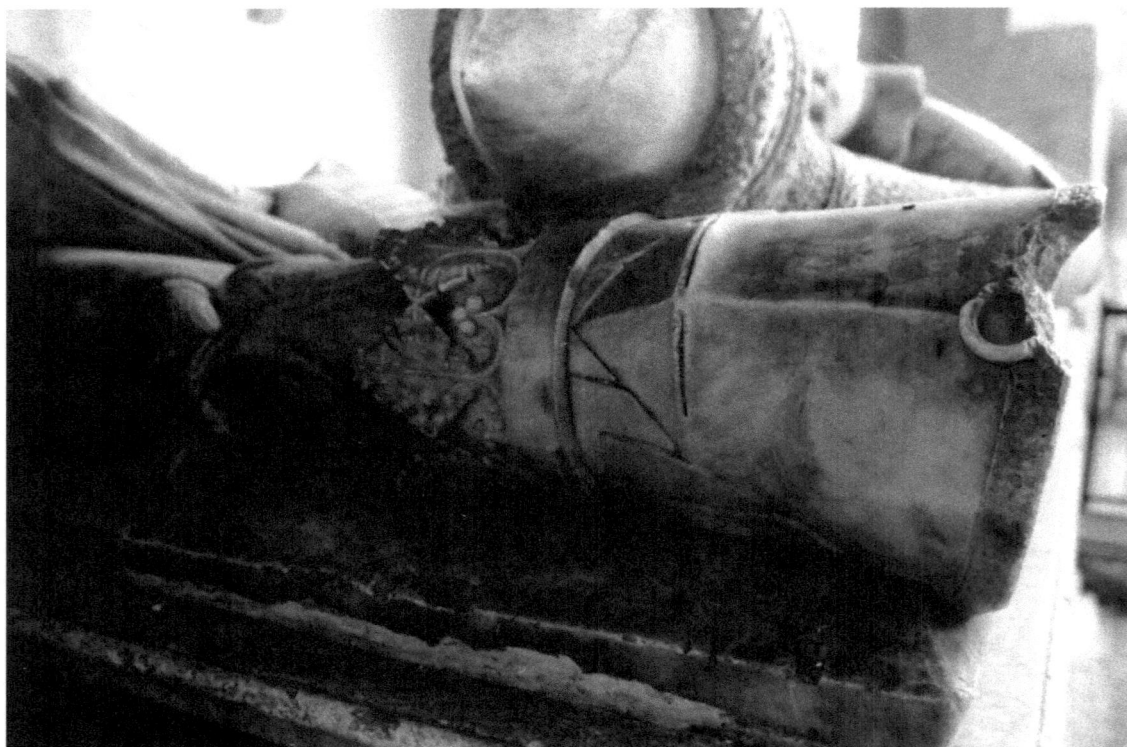

Fig. 144. Detail of great helm at Swine (4), Yorkshire, East Riding

BIBLIOGRAPHY

Primary Sources

Armitage-Smith, S., John of Gaunt's Register, *Camden Society* 3rd series Vol. 21, 1911.

Bodleian Library, Oxford, MS. Dugdale 11.

Bonney, H. K., *Bonney's Church Notes: being notes on the churches in the Archdeaconry of Lincoln 1845-1848*, edited by Reverend N. S. Harding, Lincoln, 1937.

Brault, G. J., *Rolls of Arms, Edward I (1272-1307)*, 2 Vols. London, 1997.

British Library Additional MS., 17462, *D. T. Powell's Collections*.

British Library Additional MS., 42012.

British Library Additional MS., 42013.

British Library Additional MS., 714, 74, *Sir William Dugdale's Book of Monuments, 1641*.

British Library Sloane, MS., 3836, Francis Thynne's Church Notes in Lincolnshire.

British Library Lansdowne MS., 99, *A Collection of Armorial Ensignis*.

Calendar of the Charter Rolls Preserved in the Public Record Office, 5 Vols, London: HMSO, 1903-1916. [*Cal. Charter Rolls*] Vol. 1, Henry III, 1226-1257 (1903); Vol. 2, Henry III-Edward I, 1257-1300 (1906); Vol. 3, Edward I-Edward III, 1300-1326 (1908); Vol. 4, 1-14 Edward III, 1327-1341 (1912); Vol. 5, 15 Edward III-5 Henry V, 1341-1417 (1916).

Calendar of the Close Rolls Preserved in the Public Record Office, 8 Vols, London: HMSO, 1895-1937. [*Cal. Close Rolls.*] Edward II: Vol. 3, 1318-1323 (1895); Vol. 4, 1323-1327 (1898). Edward III: Vol. 3, 1333-1337 (1898); Vol. 6, 1341-1343 (1902); Vol. 7, 1343-1346 (1904); Vol. 12, 1364-1368 (1910). Henry IV: Vol. 2, 1429-1435 (1933). Henry VI: Vol. 3, 1435-1441 (1937).

Calendar of the Fine Rolls Preserved in the Public Record Office, 11 Vols, London: HMSO, 1912-1939: Nendeln/Liechtenstein, 1971. [*Cal. Fine Rolls*] Edward II: Vol. 2, 1307-1319 (1912); Vol. 3, 1319-1327 (1912). Edward III: Vol. 4, 1327-1337 (1913); Vol. 5, 1337-1347 (1915); Vol. 6, 1347-56 (1921); Vol. 7, 1356-1369 (1923); Vol. 8, 1369-1377 (1924). Richard II: Vol. 9, 1377-1383 (1926); Vol. 10, 1383-1391 (1971). Henry VI: Vol. 17, 1437-1445; Vol. 18, 1445-1452 (1939).

Calendar of the Inquisitions Miscellaneous (Chancery) Preserved in the Public Record Office, 2 Vols, London: HMSO, 1916-1937. [*Cal. Inq. Misc.*]

Calendar of the Inquisitions Post Mortem and Other Analogous Documents Preserved in the Public Record Office, 16 Vols, London: HMSO, 1906-1995; Woodbridge, 2002-2004. [*Cal. Inq.*] Edward I: Vol. 2, (1906); Vol. 3, (1912); Vol. 4, (1913). Edward II: Vol. 5, (1908); Vol. 6, (1910). Edward III: Vol. 8, (1913); Vol. 9,

(1916); Vol. 10, (1921); Vol. 12, (1938); Vol. 13, (1954). Richard I: Vol. 17, (1988). Henry IV: Vol. 19, (1992). Henry V: Vol. 20, (1995); Vol. 21, (2002). Henry VI: Vol. 22, (2003); Vol. 23 (2004).

Calendar of the Patent Rolls Preserved in the Public Record Office, 20 Vols, London: HMSO, 1893-1914. [*Cal. Patent Rolls*] Edward I: Vol. 4, 1301-1307 (1898). Edward II: Vol. 1, 1307-1313 (1894); Vol. 2, 1313-1317 (1898); Vol. 3, 1317-1321 (1903). Edward III: Vol. 1 1327-1330 (1891); Vol. 2, 1330-1334 (1893); Vol. 3, 1334-1338 (1895); Vol. 5, 1340-1343 (1900); Vol. 6, 1343-1345 (1902); Vol. 7, 1345-1348 (1903); Vol. 8, 1348-1350 (1905); Vol. 9, 1350-1354 (1907); Vol. 12, 1361-1364 (1912); Vol. 15, 1370-1374 (1914). Richard II: Vol. 1, 1377-1381 (1895); Vol. 4, 1388-1392 (1902). Henry IV: Vol. 4, 1408-1413 (1909). Henry VI: Vol. 2, 1429-1436 (1907); Vol. 5, 1446-1452. Edward IV, Henry VI, 1467-1477 (1900).

Chesshyre, D. H. B., and Woodcock, T., (eds.), *Dictionary of British Arms, Medieval Ordinary*, Vol. 1, London, 1992.

College of Arms, *Visitation of Lincolnshire by Robert Cooke, Clarenceux, in 1592*, H. 11 C N.

College of Arms, *Lincolnshire Church Notes, 1634*, 2 C. 23.

Complete Peerage, by G. E. C., (V. Gibbs & H. Doubleday, eds), Vol. 3 London, 1913.

Complete Peerage, by G. E. C., (V. Gibbs & H. Doubleday, eds), Vol. 4 London, 1916.

Complete Peerage, by G. E. C., (V. Gibbs & H. Doubleday, eds), Vol. 5, London, 1926.

Complete Peerage, by G. E. C., (G. H. White, ed), Vol. 11, London, 1949.

Complete Peerage, by G. E. C., (revised by G. H. White), Vol. 12 pt. 2, London, 1959.

Dictionary of National Biography, L. Stephen (ed.), Vol. 8, London, 1886.

Gibbons, A., *Early Lincoln Wills 1280-1547*, Lincoln, 1888.

Holles, G., *Lincolnshire Church Notes by Gervase Holles, A. D. 1634 To A. D. 1642*, edited by R. G. Cole, Publication of the Lincoln Record Society, Vol. 1, Lincoln, 1911.

Inquisition and Assessments Relating to Feudal Aids, A. D. 1284-1431, Vol. 3, Kent-Norfolk, London, 1904; Vol. 4, York and Additions, London, 1920. [*Feudal Aids*]

Lawrence, H., *Heraldry from Military Monuments before 1350 in England and Wales*, Publications of the Harleian Society, 98, London, 1946.

Liber Feodorum. The Book of Fees, Commonly Called Testa de Nevill, 2 Vols, London: HMSO, 1920-1923. [*Book of Fees*]

Loyd, L. C., and Stenton, D. M., *Sir Christopher Hatton's Book of Seals*, Oxford, 1950.

Maddison, A. R., *Lincolnshire Pedigrees*, 4 Vols. Publications of the Harleian Society 50-55, London: Harleian Society 1902-1906.

Monson, W. J., *Lincolnshire Church Notes Made By William John Monson, F.S.A. 1828-1840*, edited by John Ninth Lord Monson, F.S.A., Publication of the Lincoln Record Society, vol. 31, Hereford, 1936.

Moor, C., *Knights of Edward I*, 5 Vols. Publications of the Harleian Society 80-84, London: Harleian Society 1929-1932.

Oxford Dictionary of National Biography, Vol. 46, Oxford, 2004.

Smith, L. T., (ed), *The Itinerary of John Leland*, 5 Vols. London, 1964.

Woodcock, T., Grant J., and Graham, I., (eds.), *Dictionary of British Arms, Medieval Ordinary*, Vol. 2, London, 1996.

Secondary Sources

Alexander, J. S., "Building Stone from the East Midlands Quarries: Sources, Transportation and Usage", *Medieval Archaeology*, Vol. 39, (1995), pp. 107-135.

Anon. *Descriptive & Historical Account of St Botolph's Church Boston*, Boston, 1842.

Meetings of the Associated Architectural Societies, Reports and Papers, Vol. 8, (1865), pp. 63-65; Vol. 30, (1909-10), p. 338.

Badham, S., "The Bacon Brass at Gorleston, Suffolk", *Transaction of the Monumental Brass Society*, Vol. 16, pt. 1, (1997), pp. 1-25.

Badham, S., "Beautiful Remains of Antiquity: The Medieval Monuments in the Former Trinitarian Priory Church of Ingham, Norfolk", *Church Monuments*, Vol. 22 (2007), pp. 7-42.

Badham, S. and Blacker, G., *Northern Rock: The use of Egglestone Marble for Monuments in Medieval England*, Oxford, 2009.

Bayley, T. D., "The Bourchier Shield in Halstead Church", *Essex Archaeological Society Transactions*, Vol. 25, New Series, pt. 1, (1955), pp. 78-100.

Bayliss, J., "An Indenture for Two Alabaster Effigies", *Church Monuments*, Vol. 16 (2001), pp. 22-29.

Bernard, F. P., "The Military Effigies at Maltby and Belleau, Lincolnshire", *Meetings of the Architectural Societies, Reports and Papers*, Vol. 30, (1909-10), pp. 367-78.

Bilson, J., "A French Purchase of English Alabaster in 1414", *Archaeological Journal*, Vol. 64, (1907), pp. 32-37.

Binski, P., "The Stylistic Sequence of London Figure Brasses" in J. Coales (ed.), *The Earliest English Brasses, Patronage, style and Workshop 1270-1350*, London, 1987.

Binski, P., *Westminster Abbey and The Plantagenets: Kingship and the Representation of Power 1200-1400*, Newhaven and London, 1995.

Blackley, F. D., "The Tomb of Isabella of France, Wife of Edward II of England", *International Society for the Study of Church Monuments*, Bulletin Vol. 8 (1983), pp. 161-164.

Blair, Claude, "The Date of the Early Alabaster Knight at Hanbury, Staffordshire", *Church Monuments*, Vol. 7 (1992), pp. 3-18.

Blair, Claude, "The de Vere Effigy at Hatfield Broad Oak", *Church Monuments*, Vol. 8 (1993), pp. 3-11.

Blair, Claude and Goodall, J., "An Effigy at Wilsthorpe, A Correction to Pevsner's Lincolnshire", *Church Monuments*, Vol. 17 (2002), pp. 37-48.

Blair, Claude, "An Identified Early 14[Th] Century Military Effigy at Little Shelford, Cambridgeshire", *Church Monuments Society Newsletter*, Vol. 11 No. 2, (1995/6), pp .36-38.

Blair, Claude, *European Armour, circa 1066 to circa 1700*, (reprinted) London, 1972.

Blair, C. H. Hunter, "Medieval Effigies in the County of Durham", *Archaeologia Aeliana*, 4 Series Vol. 6 (1929), pp. 1-51.

Blair, J., "The Buslingthorpes and their Monuments", *Transactions of the Monumental Brass Society*, Vol. 12 (1975-9), pp. 265-270.

Blair, J., "Henry Lakenham, Marbler of London, and a Tomb Contract of 1376", *The Antiquaries Journal*, Vol. 60, part 1 (1980), pp. 66-74.

Blair J., "Purbeck Marble" in Blair, J., and Ramsay N., (eds.), *English Medieval Industries: Craftsmen, Techniques, Products*, London & Rio Grande, 1991.

Boulter, S. J., *Victoria and Albert Museum Conservation Journal*, Vol. 8, (1993), pp. 4-7.

Boutell, C., *The Monumental Brasses of England*, London, 1849.

Brodrick, A., and J. Darrah, "The Fifteenth Century Polychromed Limestone Effigies of William Fitzalan, 9th Earl of Arundel, and his wife, Joan Nevill, in the Fitzalan Chapel, Arundel", *Church Monuments*, Vol. 1 pt. 2 (1986), pp. 65-94.

Burke, B., *The General Armory*, London, 1884.

Butcher, R., *The Survey and Antiquity of the Towns of Stamford in the County of Lincoln and Tottenham-High-Cross in Middlesex: together with the Turnament of Tottenham, or, The wooing, winning, and wedding of Tibbe the reeu's daughter there*, London, 1717-1718.

Butler, L. A. S., "The Tomb Attributed to Bartholomew Lord Burghersh in Lincoln Cathedral", *Archaeological Journal*, Vol. 159, (2002), pp. 109-141.

Byron, J., Notice of a Cross-legged Effigy in Goxhill Church, Lincolnshire, *Archaeological Journal*, Vol. 7 (1850) p. 37.

Chatwin, P. B., "Monumental Effigies in the County of Warwick, parts I & II. Knights, Laymen and Ladies of the 13th, 14th and 15th Century", *Transactions of the Birmingham Archaeological Society*, Vol. 47 (1921), pp. 35-88.

Clayton, M., *Victoria and Albert Museum, Catalogue of Rubbings of Brasses and Incised Slabs*, London, 1968.

Coss, P., *The Lady in Medieval England 1000-1500*, Stroud, 1998.

Coss, p., "Knighthood, Heraldry and Social Exclusion in

Edwardian England", in Peter Coss and Maurice Keen (eds), *Heraldry, Pageantry And Social Display In Medieval England*, Woodbridge, 2003.

Cragg, W. A., *The History of Threekingham with Stow in Lincolnshire*, Sleaford, 1913.

Crossley, F. H., *English Church Monuments A. D. 1150-1550*, London, 1921.

Deacon, R., and P. Lindley, *Image and Idol: Medieval Sculpture*, London, 2001.

Disney, H., *Disneys of Norton Disney 1150-1461*, Oxford, 2002.

Downing, M., *The Medieval Military Effigies Remaining in Shropshire*, Shrewsbury, 1999.

Downing, M., "Lions of the Middle Ages: A Preliminary Survey of Lions on Medieval Military Effigies", *Church Monuments*, Vol. 8, (1998), pp. 17-34.

Downing, M., "Medieval Military Effigies up To 1500 Remaining In Worcestershire", *Transactions of the Worcestershire Archaeological Society*, third series, Vol. 18, (2002), pp. 133-209.

Drury, G. Dru, "The Use of Purbeck Marble in Medieval Times", *Proceedings of the Dorset Natural History & Archaeological Society*, Vol. 70, (1948), pp. 74-97.

Dugdale, W., *Monasticon Anglicanum*, 7 Vols. London, 1846.

Fellows, G., *Arms, Armour, and Alabaster, Round Nottingham*, Nottingham, 1907.

Firmin, R., "A Geological Approach To The History Of English Alabaster", *Mercian Geologist*, Vol. 9, no. 3, (March 1984), pp. 161-178.

Firmin, R., "Early Midlands Alabaster: A Gypsum Prospector's Point of View", *Church Monuments Society Bulletin*, Vol. 9, no. 1, (1993), pp. 7-11.

Firman, R., "Purbeck Marble: Some East Midlands Examples of Mistaken Identity", *Church Monuments Society Newsletter*, Vol. 10 no. 2, winter (1994/5), pp. 30-34.

Fryer, A. C., *Wooden Monumental Effigies in England and Wales*, London, 1924. (A revised and enlarged edition of a paper read in 1908 and printed in *Archaeologia*, Vol. 61 (1910), pp. 487-552).

Fryer, A. C., "Monumental Effigies made by Bristol Craftsmen (1240-1550)", *Archaeologia*, Vol. 74 (1923-4), pp. 1-72.

Gardner, A., *Alabaster Tombs of the Pre-Reformation Period in England*, Cambridge, 1940.

Gardner, A., *English Medieval Sculpture*, Cambridge, 1951.

Gittos, B. and Gittos, M., "The Ingleby Arncliffe Group of Effigies", *Church Monuments*, Vol. 17 (2002), pp. 14-38.

Gittos, B. and Gittos, M., "Motivation and Choice: The Selection of Medieval Secular Effigies", in Peter Coss and Maurice Keen (Eds), *Heraldry, Pageantry and Social Display in Medieval England*, Woodbridge, 2003.

Gough, R., *Sepulchral Monuments in Great Britain*, 2 Vols., London, 1786.

Greenwood, J., *A Picturesque Tour to Thornton Monastery, with Notices of Goxhill, Nunney, Barrow, New Holland, and British Remains in the Neighbourhood*, Hull, 1825.

Greenwood, J. R., "Wills and Brasses: Some Conclusions from a Norfolk Study" in J. Bertram (ed.), *Monumental Brasses as Art and History*, 1996, pp. 82-102.

Hall, J. G., *Notice of Lincolnshire, Being an Historical and Topographical Account of some Villages in the Division of Lindsey*, Hull, 1890.

Hartshorne, A., *The Recumbent Monumental Effigies in Northamptonshire*, London, 1876.

Hartshorne, A., "On Kirkstead Abbey, Lincolnshire, Kirkstead Chapel, and a Remarkable Monumental Effigy there Preserved", *Archaeological Journal*, Vol. 40, (1883), pp. 296-302.

Harvey, A. S., "Notice on Two Heraldic Tombs", *Yorkshire Archaeological Journal*, Pt. 159, Vol. 40, (1961), pp. 462-477.

Harvey, J., *English Medieval Architects: A Biographical Dictionary Down To 1550*, 2nd edition, Gloucester, 1987.

Harvey, J., *Henry Yevele c.1320-1400: The Life of an English Architect*, London, 1944.

Hollis, George and Thomas, *Monumental Effigies of Great Britain*, London, 1839-1842.

Hope, W. St John, and Lethaby, W. R., "The Imagery and Sculptures on the West Front of Wells Cathedral Church". *Archaeologia*, Vol. 59 (1905), pp. 143-206.

Hope, W. St John, "On Early Workings of Alabaster in England", *Archaeological Journal*, Vol. 61, (1904), pp. 230-231.

Humphrey-Smith, C., *Anglo-Norman Armory Two*, Canterbury, 1984.

Hurting, J., *The Armored Gisant before 1400*, New York & London, 1979.

I'Anson, W. M., "The Medieval Military Effigies of Yorkshire", *Yorkshire Archaeological Journal*, Vol. 28, (1926), pp. 345-378.

I'Anson, W. M., "The Medieval Military Effigies of Yorkshire", *Yorkshire Archaeological Journal*, Vol. 29, (1927), pp. 1-67.

Jarvis, F.A., *The Parish of Burton Upon Stather with Flixborough*, Morecambe, 1922.

Jebb, G., *A Guide to the Church of S. Botolph*, Boston, 1821.

Kemp, B., "English Church Monuments during the Period of the Hundred Years War" in A. Curry and M. Hughes (eds.), *Arms, Armies and Fortifications in the Hundred Years War*, Woodbridge, 1994, pp. 203-204.

Lambert, M. R., and Walker, R., *Old Boston (England)*, Boston, 1930.

Lankester, P. J., "A Military Effigy in Dorchester Abbey, Oxon", *Oxoniensia*, Vol. 52 (1987), pp. 145-172.

Lankester, P. J., "Two Lost Effigial Monuments in Yorkshire and the evidence of Church Notes", *Church Monuments*, Vol. 8 (1993), pp. 25-44.

Lankester, P. J., "Drainage Holes in Effigial Grave-Covers", *Church Monuments Society Newsletter*, Vol. 11 no. 1, summer 1995, pp. 8-11.

Lankester, P. J., "Stothard's Drawing for The Monumental Effigies Of Great Britain", *Church Monuments Society Newsletter*, Vol. 20 No. 1, (2004), pp. 6-9.

Lawrence, H., "Military Effigies in Nottinghamshire before the Black Death", *Transaction of the Thoroton Society*, Vol. 28 (1924), pp. 125-126.

Lawrence H., and Routh, T. E., "Mediaeval Military Effigies in Derbyshire", *Journal of the Derbyshire and Natural History Society*, N.S. Vol. 1, (1924-25), pp. 92-107, 137-151. Pt. 1, 1198-1242 (1920); Pt. 2, 1242-1293 (1923).

Lindley, P., "Una Granda Opera al mio Re': Gilt-Bronze Effigies in England from the Middle Ages to the Renaissance", *Journal of the British Archaeological Association*, Vol. 143, (1990), pp. 112-130.

Lindley, P., *Gothic To Renaissance: Essays on Sculpture in England*, Stamford, 1995.

Lindley, P., and Galvin, C., "New Paradigms for the Aristocratic Funerary Monument Around 1300", *Church Monuments*, Vol. 21, (2006), pp. 58-93.

Lindley, P., *Tomb Destruction and Scholarship: Medieval Monuments in Early Modern England*, Donington, 2007.

Lord, J., "Repairing and Cleaning of the Said Burying Places", *Church Monuments*, Vol. 9, (1994), pp. 83-92.

Luxford, J. M., "The Tomb of Sir Humphrey de Littlebury at All Saints, Holbeach", in J. McNeill (ed.), *Medieval Art, Architecture and Archaeology in Kings Lynn and the Fens*, British Archaeological Association Conference Transaction for 2005, Leeds, (2008), pp. 151-172.

Meara, D., "The Lion and the Dragon", *Monumental Brass Society Bulletin*, Vol. 54, (June, 1990), p. 442.

Morganstern, A. M., *Gothic Tombs of Kinship, In France, The Low Counties, and England*, Pennsylvania, 2000.

Nash, S., (ed.), *Andrè Beauneveu. 'No equal in any land' – artist to the courts of France and Flanders*, London, 2007.

Norman, A. V. B., "Two Early Fourteenth Century Military Effigies", *Church Monuments*, Vol. 1 pt. 1, (1985), pp. 10-19.

Petch, D. F., "A Medieval Carved Stone", *Lincolnshire Architectural and Archaeological Society Reports and Papers*, Vol. 8, (1959-60), pp. 24-25.

Pevsner, N., and Harris, J., *The Buildings of England: Lincolnshire*, Harmondsworth, 1964.

Pevsner, N., and Harris, J., second edition revised by N. Antram, *The Buildings of England: Lincolnshire*, Harmondsworth, 2001.

Prior, E. S., and Gardner, A., *An Account of Medieval Figure Sculpture in England*, Cambridge, 1912.

Rogers, W. H. Hamilton, *The Antient Sepulchral Effigies and Monumental and Memorial Sculpture of Devon*, Exeter, 1877.

Roskell, J. S., *The Commons and their Speakers in English Parliaments 1376-1523*, Manchester, 1965.

Routh, P., *Medieval Effigial Alabaster Tombs in Yorkshire*, Ipswich, 1976.

Salmarsh, P., *Heraldry and Chartulary of the Hothams of Scarborough in the East Riding of Yorkshire 1100-1700*, York, 1914.

Scott, G. G., *Gleanings from Westminster Abbey*, Oxford and London, 1863.

Southwick, L., "The Armoured Effigy of Prince John of Eltham in Westminster Abbey and some Closely Related Military Monuments", *Church Monuments*, Vol. 2, (1987), pp. 7-21.

Stone, L., *Sculpture in Britain: The Middle Ages*, 2nd edition, 1972.

Stothard, C. A., *The Monumental Effigies of Great Britain*, London, 1817-1832.

The Topographer, Containing a Variety of Original Articles, Illustrative of the Local History, and Antiquities of the Kingdom, no. 22 for January, London, 1791.

Thordeman, B., *Armour from the Battle of Wisby 1361*, (New edition, two volumes in one) Chivalry Bookshelf, 2001.

Thompson, P., *The History and Antiquities of Boston*, Boston, 1856.

Trap, O. G., and Mann, J. G., *The Armoury of the Castle of Churburg*, London, 1929.

Tummers, H. A., *Early Secular Effigies in England, The Thirteenth Century*, Leiden, 1980.

Victoria County History, A History of the County of Oxfordshire, Vol. 5, London, 1957.

Victoria County History. A History of the County of York North Riding, Vol. 1, London, 1914.

Wagner, A., *Aspilogia II, Rolls of Arms: Henry III*, London, 1967.

Waller, J. G., "On the Monuments in Horley Church", *Surrey Archaeological Collections*, Vol. 7, (1880), pp. 184-191.

Weatherley, W. S. "A Description of the Tombs and Monuments having Sculptured Effigies up to the Close of the Seventeenth Century", in Alice Dryden (ed.), *Memorials of Old Leicestershire*, London, 1911.

Weever, J., *Ancient funeral monuments within the united monarchie of Great Britaine, Ireland and the islands adjacent, with the dissolved monasteries therein contained.* London, 1631.

Whittemore, P., "Sir William Dugdale's 'Book of Draughts'", *Church Monuments*, Vol. 18, (2003), pp. 23-52.

Willis, B., *A Survey of the Cathedrals*, Vol. 3, London, 1742.

Wilson, C., "The Medieval Monuments", in P. Collinson (ed.), *A History of Canterbury Cathedral*, 1995, pp. 451-510, pls. 87-129 (between pp. 352 & 353).

Internet sites

The soldier in later medieval England: An exciting new AHRC research project.
www.medievalsoldier.org

INDEX

Illustration references in **bold** type. Places are in Lincolnshire unless otherwise indicated.

www.ingramcontent.com/pod-product-compliance
Lightning Source LLC
Chambersburg PA
CBHW061001030426
42334CB00033B/3314